D1032982

Shrimp Highway

Shrimp Highway

*Savoring U.S. 17
and Its Iconic Dish*

JEFF JOHNSON

Foreword by DOCK HOOKS

McFarland & Company, Inc., Publishers

Jefferson, North Carolina

Photographs courtesy K. Jaeger.

LIBRARY OF CONGRESS CATALOGUING-IN-PUBLICATION DATA

Names: Johnson, Jeff, 1954 June 4–
Title: Shrimp highway : savoring U.S. 17 and its iconic dish / Jeff
 Johnson ; foreword by Dock Hooks.
Description: Jefferson, North Carolina : McFarland & Company, Inc.,
 Publishers, 2017. | Includes index.
Identifiers: LCCN 2017041334 | ISBN 9781476670744 (softcover : acid
 free paper) ∞
Subjects: LCSH: United States Highway 17—Description and travel. |
 South Atlantic States—Description and travel. | South Atlantic
 States—Social life and customs. | Restaurants—South Atlantic
 States—Guidebooks. | Cooking (Shrimp)—South Atlantic States. |
 Cooking, American—Southern style.
Classification: LCC F209 .J65 2017 | DDC 917.504—dc23
LC record available at https://lccn.loc.gov/2017041334

BRITISH LIBRARY CATALOGUING DATA ARE AVAILABLE

ISBN (print) 978-1-4766-7074-4
ISBN (ebook) 978-1-4766-3093-9

Front cover images: *left to right* pile of shrimp; Highway 17
sign; *background* the fleet behind Independent Seafood,
Georgetown, South Carolina (photographs by K. Jaeger)

Printed in the United States of America

McFarland & Company, Inc., Publishers
 Box 611, Jefferson, North Carolina 28640
 www.mcfarlandpub.com

For Gene Floersch
(1950–2009)
Artist. Guitarist. Surfer. Friend.

Acknowledgments

Thanks to K. Jaeger for images that really bring this trip to life.

Also to Dock Hooks, co-conspirator, over so many years, in so many misadventures.

Big thanks to my dad, who, at 91, still loves shrimp, and to my mom, an original "17-er."

Special thanks, as always, to Carla, for her support in yet another improbable project.

And finally, thanks to all the people who took the time to share with me what life is like eating shrimp off 17.

Table of Contents

Foreword
by Dock Hooks

I grew up traveling the world as the son of a military aviator. But our roots were in eastern North Carolina, where, on holidays and other special occasions, we often returned. The difference between that worldly exposure via my father's career—moving every two or three years between states, and sometimes countries—and returning to visit small-town eastern North Carolina was rather stark; the contrast left its mark in my memory, locking in the rustic bucolic calling of small towns, where everyone knows nearly everyone else, surrounded by time-preserved farms and forests situated along creeks and rivers feeding sounds and ultimately the never too distant Atlantic Ocean.

In the summer of 1970, before my senior year of high school, my father retired from the military and started a real estate company in North Carolina's small, rather provincial but undeniably charmingly quaint coastal colonial capital, New Bern, nestled within the angle formed by the confluence of the Neuse and Trent rivers, about forty miles from Bogue Banks, part of North Carolina's southern Outer Banks.

Of particular interest here, New Bern is both entered and exited, when traveling north or south, by U.S. 17. Also of particular interest here, New Bern is where I met my longtime surfing buddy and lasting friend, Jeff Johnson.

Dropping in and out of college was a sport for us back then, and during the particularly cold winter of 1972–73, Jeff had enough. He enrolled in a college near Cocoa Beach. I reckoned it was time for a break from academia and decided to roll down there with him to taste some warmer air and water and, of course, the then seemingly legendary surf spots along the coast between Second Light and Sebastian Inlet. So we strapped our boards to the top of Jeff's VW, threw in an extra pair of jeans and baggies, a couple of cans of tuna and jars of peanut butter, a case of beer, wished our parents a Happy New Year, and headed south—on U.S. 17.

As I remember it, somewhere near Charleston, South Carolina, it started to rain heavily, and the wind began to howl. Thrashing through the weather, we competed for road space, in Jeff's rather rough Bug, with a somewhat unusual and seemingly constant stream of tractor-trailer trucks. Later, as the downpour hardened, we learned, via the AM radio, that about a month earlier a fully-loaded freighter ship had slammed into the side of the Sidney-Lanier Bridge spanning the Brunswick River—U.S. 17—taking out more than four hundred feet of the mile-long bridge and rerouting traffic—an horrific event and one of only two recorded bridge collapses in Georgia's entire history. Not exactly prepared for all the detours, we somehow managed to weave our way through the storm on and off U.S. 17, navigating around the closed sections of the highway, until, as the rain finally broke, we hit the Sunshine State.

After days of good waves, securing our place in the lineup at both the popular surf spots and the local rock 'n' roll hot spots, Jeff settled into school, and I (having decided to re-engage in Chapel Hill) hopped a ride back north in the back of a van driven by a guy I knew from North Carolina who was on a surf holiday, and headed back up U.S. 17.

That's what it was like back then. You just knew people in the surf world rolling up and down the Coastal Highway between Florida and the Outer Banks, and you could always count on catching a ride, north or south—no problem.

On the particular January day that I headed back, it was eighty degrees in Cocoa Beach. I basically went straight out of the water from a morning surf session, tossed my board in the van, curled up in my wet baggies and fell asleep.

I didn't wake up until we had pulled over for gas, in Jacksonville, Florida, where the temperature had dramatically fallen into the 30s. Before long we were facing flurries, and, by the time we reached Charleston, we were encountering serious snow. Crossing the old Cooper River Bridge from Charleston to Mount Pleasant was both magnificent, offering a snow globe effect, and, in retrospect, a little crazy. Anyone who remembers that bridge will concur ... crossing it was hairy, no matter when, but at night, in a snowstorm ... it was surreal.

In any case, it was another adventurous night ride on U.S. 17. We made it to Wilmington, North Carolina, after another similarly hazardous bridge crossing tiptoeing across the Cape Fear River in the ridiculously icy weather, and on to Wrightsville Beach, which was uncharacteristically wearing about ten inches of snow. The next day, I worked my way back to New Bern and, eventually, on to Chapel Hill.

Jeff finished school in Florida and stayed in the area, becoming involved in the surf magazine business and working for various surfing companies before settling into a career as a college professor and writer. After Chapel Hill, I wound up living in Virginia Beach, where (but for running here and there operationally, vacations, etc.) I did the vast majority of my twenty-five-year career as a Naval Special Warfare officer. Through those years and more, my road home to New Bern, going south, was U.S. 17, as was Jeff's, going north.

Most people traveling north or south, through the states from Virginia to Florida, do so by blasting up or down I-95, the main interstate along the East Coast running parallel to U.S. 17 and the Atlantic Ocean. As one runs that course, at 80-plus miles per hour, amongst the relentless flow of tractor-trailer trucks and various other vehicles, the local landscape is often blurred in the breeze, as high-paced travelers set their sights on well-marked and advertised destinations like Virginia Beach, Wilmington, Charleston, Savannah, and Jacksonville. All of those places are well worth a stop and extensive exploration, each being rather brilliant in its own right. That written, there is almost always more than one way to get from point A to point B.

For those in the right frame of mind, willing or wanting to slow down a bit, U.S. 17, known to some as the Coastal Highway, to others as the Ocean Highway, and, to me, as simply "17," offers an abundantly more interesting alternative route.

U.S. 17 is, for the most part, closer to the coast, set between the ocean and the interstate. Slower, granted, than the rush of I-95, the Coastal Highway appeals to a different kind of aesthetic, to those who prefer to sample the indigenous culture, who appreciate the richly aromatic essence of the brackish, fecund flow of multiple waterways, both narrow and wide, where marinas are home to the local shrimping and fishing fleets situated along the picturesque waterfronts of small towns, quaint country stores, small family-style, character-rich restaurants (local to their core) occasionally contrasted against the sensory overload of spewing, often sprawling mills that have for years helped in fueling the economic base and livelihood of the local population generationally linked, perhaps locked, to the bounties of the water and the land.

This detail-rich route still gets you to Virginia Beach, Wilmington,

Charleston and Savannah, but also accesses the Great Dismal Swamp, Elizabeth City, Little Washington, Bridgeton, New Bern, Sneads Ferry, Bolivia, Oak Island, Murrell's Inlet, Georgetown, Beaufort, Darien, Brunswick, and a slew of other interesting places where you sip sweet iced tea and taste the shrimp, fish, and barbecue laced with tangy coleslaw, accompanied, of course, by cornmeal hushpuppies doused with hot-pepper vinegar, food that often more than anything else characterizes the region. It is in these special places, these capricious stops a traveler in a hurry might miss, where you really get to taste the soul of the South.

On U.S. 17, as opposed to the interstates, the pace and positioning is slower, more simplistic, regardless of your ride. But few people, perhaps, have experienced the highway as slowly and simplistically as I did during the winter of 2012, when I volunteered, as a fund-raiser, to complete a solo 1000-plus-mile cycling trip, from my beach house in Emerald Isle, North Carolina, to Key West. The uniquely distinguishing aspect of the ride was that I did it on a fat-tired Jamis Earth Cruiser bicycle—more generically known as a beach cruiser.

The Emerald Isle to Key West course, along U.S. 17 and on to Florida's A1A, was far from unknown to me. Through the years, I had made the trip numerous times by car, truck or Harley. Also, as a longtime distance cyclist and triathlete, I had experienced various segments of both U.S. 17 and A1A sprinting along on one of my lightweight titanium or carbon fiber hotrod bicycles aerodynamically pushing, head down and focused on the finish line, somewhat oblivious to the coastal grandeur slipping by to my left and right.

During those 600 or so miles I spent cycling U.S. 17, you could say that I gained a more unique perspective, slowly savoring the sweet and salty sensory sensations the highway offers any intimate traveler. But on a heavier, less aero, indeed slower Jamis Earth Cruiser, well … let's just say that I got to know the highway—and the region—up close and personal.

You travel a certain stretch of highway enough, you can't help but discover and revisit favorite venues. Most people who have made the run from Virginia to Florida on the Coastal Highway are familiar with the main cities—Wilmington, Myrtle Beach, Georgetown, Charleston, Savannah, even comparatively diminutive Darien—and they have probably slipped off the highway for side trips to places like Beaufort, South Carolina, or Fernandina Beach. Jeff smartly focuses on these small venues, out of the way spots, some hardly towns at all, just a trawler dock, surrounded by a few churches, some houses on stilts, a smattering of suspicious natives and, of course, a shrimp market selling the local catch.

Highlights of my U.S. 17 bicycle ride include three spots that I now rarely miss, even when I cruise in a more traditional (perhaps sane) fashion—on my Harley: the Sewee Outpost in Awendaw, South Carolina, a classic southern country store that just happens to make some amazing homemade smokehouse-aged ham biscuits and fresh shrimp salad sandwiches; Beth Ann Crane's Mediterranean-styled Muse Restaurant in Charleston, between Wentworth and Society streets, a romantic yet casual renovated Italianate Victorian structure, known for, among other things, fine wine, pickled shrimp and grilled calamari; and tiny but timeless Darien, Georgia, home of JoAnne Viera's Waterfront Inn, next door to the Waterfront Wine Bar, and the Waterfront Wine & Gourmet, all less than a hundred yards off 17 and featuring a superb view of the Darien River, the marina, and the local shrimp fleet, along with Skipper's Fish Camp, where the shrimp and collards are second to none.

Regardless of your ride, on U.S. 17 you'll likely be tempted to roll the windows down or put the top back, perchance catching the wistful but alluringly beguiling, seductive smell and lasting spell of confederate jasmine, or tea olive, or the fertile tidal estuaries, along which you might actually stop to watch various long-necked birds, in the still waters and sea grass, performing their artful dining, or others making amazing high-speed nosedives, snagging meals from just below the water's shimmering surface. U.S. 17 runs through a history of gnarly live oaks, colorful azaleas, sturdy dogwoods and redbuds spotting spooky ancient forests populated by deer, wild boar, and black bears. Crepe myrtles draped in Spanish moss line the entrances to antebellum plantations. U.S. 17 seductively steams with old-school coastal southern Atlantic culture and charm—some good, some bad; some gorgeous, some grotesque; but always strikingly visual and sensually intense.

Thinking back to that summer of 1970, in New Bern, when Jeff and I first met, partnering as foosball champs, shooting the breeze about Vietnam, racial tension, Woodstock, weed, rock, tomorrow's waves, and the proverbial "road ahead," it's hard to separate U.S. 17 from how we began our long friendship.

Since then, not all that much has changed. U.S. 17 still runs north and south—my route of choice. I can think of no one more thoroughly prepared to share the nuanced charm of life lived off 17 than an old-time "17-er" like Jeff.

Dock Hooks is a retired Navy SEAL, a second-career attorney, and a lifelong adventure sports enthusiast.

Preface

This book represents a love for two things: driving highway U.S. 17 and eating wild shrimp, especially fried shrimp.

It limits itself to restaurants close to U.S. 17 but not strictly to those alongside the road. In fact the original working title was *Eating Shrimp Off 17*—not meaning literally eating shrimp off the pavement, although on many a summer day the black asphalt south of Norfolk seems hot enough to fry a cornmeal breaded four-inch butterflied greentail to a golden crispy brown with just a dash of olive oil and cayenne, if you could find a stretch of highway with no traffic for half an hour, which, even on some of the most abandoned stretches of the old Ocean Highway, somewhere between, say, Scrubby Bluff and Billyville, would be tricky, as the Coastal Highway these days tends to be a bit too well traveled to try a stunt like that.

But the idea embodied by the phrase "off 17" is problematic: What does "off" imply? How far might one venture off U.S. 17 before entering an area no longer associated in any meaningful way to the highway? When does "off" become off the grid, out of the vicinity?

The remedy to this strategic dilemma, in the strictest sense, would be to stick to restaurants that directly front the highway, or that stand within sight of it, or lay within walking distance, or a stone's throw, or a mile or so, or … alas, the problem remains unsolved. Another thought was to limit the establishments under consideration to those situated east of U.S. 17, allowing the highway to form a sort of western barrier, corralling the restaurants into a zone between the Piedmont and the edge of the Atlantic. But that left a vast generic wasteland of strip malls and chain diners and local eateries sprawling seaward, an impossibly huge assortment of restaurants fanning out from the western reaches of U.S. 17 as it turns away from the coast and ribbons through the countryside, miles from the sea.

As for seeking out restaurants that could be considered "close" to U.S. 17, both physically and philosophically, the most sensible plan would be to include areas accessible only by turning off of and returning to U.S. 17, whose main routes in and out of town, for instance, are exclusively connected to the highway. Edisto, SC, is an easy example, as there is only one road in and out, SC Route 174, off U.S. 17, between Charleston and Savannah. Just south of Edisto and barely north of Hilton Head, Beaufort, SC, is a more complex but no less necessary example. Heading south on U.S. 17 out of Charleston, approaching from the north, you must take SC Route 21 to get to Beaufort, and then heading south out of town the only road back to civilization is SC Route 170, which leads back to U.S. 17, connecting just before the Talmadge Memorial Bridge crossing into Savannah. But the common factor, in both cases, is that U.S. 17 is the exclusive feeder artery to the coast.

Another factor was to exclude territory north of the Great Dismal Swamp, on the border of North Carolina and Virginia. Without admitting to a "southern" bias, this plan is legitimate and logical. Above Elizabeth City, the ruinous wasteland of Greater Norfolk and the tragic urban sprawl of Virginia Beach offers little in the way of a rural coastal adventure associated with the less salubrious sections of the Coastal Highway. And while north of Yorktown, as it skirts the Rappahannock River, the highway has its rustic moments, as it rolls toward the gentle mountains, but for much of the run near the coast the overspill from the Washington, D.C., metropolitan area, the several military bases, the proliferation of commercial businesses associated with the Chesapeake and Potomac rivers and the sheer population overload easily disqualify the area from this study. Highway 17 is a "southern" phenomenon, and within that context, at best, the region around U.S. 17 along the Rappahannock warrants a separate cultural demarcation distinct from the highway flowing south from Norfolk. The change in the climate—aesthetically, culturally and meteorologically—further fuels the notion that many people south of Virginia consider anything above Norfolk "the north."

But even the idea of a "shrimp culture" is discounted north of Pamlico Sound. The Chesapeake area is not primarily a shrimp harvesting ground. It is rightly famous for crabs, oysters, clams, scallops and flounder, actually in that order. But when it comes to commercial fishing, shrimping in the mid–Atlantic waters of Virginia does not rate.

Along the southeastern seaboard, the significant shrimping area runs from the near Atlantic waters off Mayport, FL, to Brunswick, GA, topography that includes Amelia Island, the Cumberland Island estuaries of St. Mary's River, Fancy Bluff Creek, and the Satilla River. Between Brunswick and Savannah, shrimping is concentrated around the Altamaha River and Sapelo Sound. Above Savannah lies the Lowcountry, encompassing the waters along the various arms of the Harbor River. From Charleston to Myrtle Beach, the richest grounds for harvest include the waters north of Cooper River, associated with the Cape Romain Wildlife Refuge and Winyah Bay. The coast from Georgetown to Wilmington, with direct ocean access and fewer inland waters, supports offshore shrimping. The string of barrier islands along the North Carolina seashore, known as the Outer Banks, creates on its western edge the Inner Banks, which allow inshore trawling in the Pamlico and Core sounds. These habitats represent the heart of Shrimp Country, off 17.

To get the picture from a shrimper's perspective, it's worth imagining the coast as seen from a trawler looking back toward land. Offshore, distances are different, the shoreline access points less diverse, the geographical distinctions not so pronounced as they might be along an overland coastal highway. Whereas a car might take hours to wind through the twisting route out to a loading dock, the lay-line distance from a trawler's position off the coast heading for Fernandina or McClellanville might not be so different. The seascape the trawlers ply erases boundaries and democratizes travel time. The ocean unifies the shrimpers, by their trade

The shrimp fleet in Mayport, as seen across the St. Johns River from Heckscher Drive. The fleet, though diminished, is still productive. The moniker "Mayport Shrimp" refers to shrimp harvested offshore between, roughly, St. Augustine, FL, and Brunswick, GA. "Mayport Shrimp" are famous throughout the region.

and by their view of the world to the west of their vessel. Offshore, the lay of the coast is different.

Also excluded from consideration are the stretches of U.S. 17 from Punta Gorda, FL, to Jacksonville, FL, a part of the highway inversely similar to the run from Elizabeth City, NC, to the Blue Ridge Mountains in Virginia. Omitting these areas makes sense both philosophically and demographically. First, the road through Florida is an inland highway, with nothing scenic or romantic to recommend it, offering little even remotely connected to the culinary fruit of an Ocean Highway. For a pleasurable tool along the Atlantic coast of Florida, state road A1A and U.S. 1 both run the length of the state through some of the most historic and aesthetically beautiful scenery—as well as the most congested traffic areas—the state has to offer. A1A hugs the coast so tight in many spots that nothing can be built on the east side of it, allowing direct oceanfront access to beach-seeking travelers, while the landscapes off U.S. 1 south of Miami to the Keys is remarkable, offering views unrivaled on a world class scale. U.S. 17 through a Bartow cow pasture, not so much.

So, the plan involved first limiting the geography, and second the selection of venues. To accomplish this strategy, the book is divided into several sections. The early sections set the tone, reviewing the nature of the highway and providing an overview of shrimp as edible food, glancing at a few common methods of harvesting and cooking them. The idea is to convey the magical sense of wanderlust that U.S. 17 created in the mind of an impressionable child longing to hit the road, finding in that highway the promise of a future quite different from the one that lay ahead were the highway not followed. And then to try to express the glory of the fried shrimp available along the coastal run of the Ocean Highway.

The narrative briefly traces the route U.S. 17 carves through the southeastern seaboard from Punta Gorda to the Rappahannock River, with summaries of the few large cities along the route, setting the context for a more detailed exploration of the funky shrimp eateries parked on the outskirts of those cities, where highway U.S. 17 always existed for me anyway, both literally and imaginatively, as a concrete reality and a mythological quest, just outside of town, at the edge of possibility. Avoiding the metropolitan areas of Jacksonville, Brunswick, Savannah, Charleston, the Grand Strand of the Myrtle Beach area, Wilmington and Greater Norfolk, stems from a basic necessary fact: the impossibility of reviewing even a select list of restaurants in those cities, all filled with innumerable franchises, chain cafeterias and fly-by-night startups, as well as established

and reputable—some famous—epicurean bistros. The number of restaurants in these cities, renowned and forgettable, is simply too extensive to
explore intimately.

What follows these initial sections is the meat of the book (as it were),
focusing on specific regions, restaurants and the characters—outside the
major metropolitan centers—associated with procuring, preparing and
serving shrimp. The strategy privileges towns along the route whose soul,
if not commerce, is essentially linked to shrimping, highlighting towns
that maintain and support a fleet, or that specialize in providing local
wild-caught shrimp. I tried to stick to the truly shrimp-rich areas of the
Coastal Highway, running from Mayport, FL, to Wanchese, NC. But even
this gauge needs tweaking. For instance, although Edisto has a history of
shrimping, no commercial industry has existed there for years. At one
point, a lone trawler supplied one restaurant, and though the commercial
fleet is still—to be polite—reconstituting its original charter, small boats
continue to offer day shrimping to tourists and fresh catches to their select
constituents. Most of the choices, places like Fernandina, Darien, Beaufort
(SC), McClellanville, the coastal communities just south and north of
Wilmington, and the spots along the Inner Banks of the Pamlico still have
operating fleets, which, most importantly, means fresh local shrimp are
plentiful in those areas.

As to which restaurants to include, and where to find them, I simply
used my "shrimp sense," an intuition developed after years of munching
through shrimp entrees—étouffées, fried baskets, peel and eat party boils,
cocktails and casseroles—ranging from the most elegant, white-table-
clothed gourmet brasserie to the raunchiest, lard-befogged, mosquito
infested, boondock biker dive.

In any case, this is not a technical book, about the shrimp industry
or the history of a highway. It is not intended to be. It's an impressionistic
glance out the window, or over the handlebars, of an enthusiast cruising
the open road in a restless vehicle, sharing the fun of a vintage historical
southern highway, seeking out the best fried wild local shrimp.

Introduction

My first memory of U.S. 17 is a night drive through a particularly desolate stretch just north of Wilmington, NC. I was around five years old, and I had just been diagnosed with spinal meningitis, which meant nothing to me, but Wilmington had the only hospital back then that could deal with the situation, and my parents were in a hurry to get me there. I wasn't exactly pre-conscious-young, but I was young enough to engage the world only impressionistically, without causality or continuity. In those days, the Coastal Highway was a dangerous two-lane, with few opportunities for clean passing and lots of impatient drivers. I remember lying across the backseat and watching the tops of the pine trees floating by, the headlights of oncoming traffic flashing off the headliner, the acceleration of my dad aggressively passing cars ... that sensation of swerving in darkness, my head splitting.

All I could focus on were Venus Flytraps. They were sold in ads in the back of *Creepy* magazine, of which, even at that age, I was an avid fan. But what intrigued me most was how they grew wild around Wilmington, in the damp forest floors of the Cape Fear basin, among all the waxy-leaved succulents, ferns and azaleas, pines, oaks and dogwoods.

So there I was. Traveling among Venus Flytraps. On U.S. 17. Dying of spinal meningitis. Too young to appreciate the metaphor.

But I also remember dreaming of fried shrimp. Like, somehow, the idea of a basketful of jumbo butterflied local fried fantails would erase the nightmare I was heading into.

I survived. So did U.S. 17. Both of us have been altered with age, and not necessarily improved. The shrimp industry survived too, and continues to offer, from the Inner Banks to the bottom end of the Lowcountry, fried varieties of wild local product as diverse and particular as the people that call the highway home.

I spent the first eighteen years of my life in New Bern, NC, a small coastal town nestled on the banks of two scenic rivers, the Neuse and Trent, at the western edge of the Pamlico Sound, once a pre-colonial hamlet settled and named by 17th century Swiss immigrants. After several attempts by early expeditions, these resilient Calvinists managed to tame the wilderness (and the local Tuscarora tribes) enough to form a lasting center of commerce, representing a century of progress, as earlier attempts to domesticate the region, best represented by the famous early settlement known as the Lost Colony, thirty miles to the northwest, ended in disasters.

Given its favorable locale, in a region known as the Inner Banks—to distinguish it from, at the time, the uninhabitable Outer Banks—New Bern later became the colonial capital of the Carolinas, an integral part of the Triangle Trade shipping scheme that connected the Caribbean with New England. New Bern is rich in pirate lore, rumored to be Blackbeard's playground—located, after all, a mere 60 miles west across the Pamlico Sound from where the marauder was killed by the British Navy, out near Ocracoke Island, now a popular, if semi-remote, vacation spot.

The confluence of U.S. 17 and U.S. 70, New Bern, looking east down the Neuse River toward Oriental and the Pamlico Sound. New Bern is an historic crossroads, where U.S. 17 crosses U.S. 70, and where the Trent River meets the Neuse, which flows out to Pamlico Sound and the Outer Banks.

The town center hosts a slew of antebellum houses, a revitalized town center, and a vibrant yachting community with first-class sailing from the western shores of the Neuse east to Oriental and the Intracoastal waterway, and further out across the expanse of the Pamlico Sound to the barrier islands below Hatteras. The outlying countryside was once a hunting and fishing paradise before the inevitable gentrification of the suburbs set in, but in and around the Croatan National Forest plenty of areas for hunting deer, bear and small game remain, with wetlands and waterways aplenty.

A colonial trading center, and a strategic coastal encampment during the Civil War, in the early twentieth century New Bern occupied the nexus of what became the most important crossroads in post-colonial America, the confluence of U.S. 70—once the main east-west route across the country, known as the "Broadway of America"—and U.S. 17, known as "The Coastal Highway," or "The Ocean Highway," running north-south from Virginia to Florida.

In the early days of modern coastal travel, road construction and mapping, U.S. 17 was part of a network of highways that ran the length of the eastern seaboard from Jacksonville, FL, to Norfolk, VA. In Norfolk, the Ocean Highway shifted to U.S. 13, a route that once crossed the Chesapeake Bay by ferry until the construction of the Chesapeake Bay Bridge Tunnel. The Ocean Highway continued up the Eastern Shore of Virginia, through Maryland and into Delaware, finally joining U.S. 40 across the Delaware River into New Jersey, becoming U.S. 130 and passing through Camden and Trenton before ending in North Brunswick. In the southern states, offshoots of the Ocean Highway ran east to various seaside locales like the Golden Isles of Georgia, and connected a host of beach communities along the South Carolina and North Carolina coasts.

In the 19th century, New Bern was probably exotic, like many small communities dotting the coastal regions along the Eastern Seaboard. New Bern's sea-lanes opened to the wild Atlantic, its east-west land routes directly linked the East Coast to the Western Territories, and its north-south routes connected the Lower Chesapeake to the Lowcountry south of Charleston. It was a nexus, a crossroads for some of the most important transportation roots on the southeastern coast of the young country.

But things change, and by the mid–20th century, for a resourceful child of the sixties, hungry for adventure, New Bern was just another small southern town, a parochial podunk from which escape seemed inevitable, if not ordained.

In my mind, going east held no hope. The Outer Banks were truly undeveloped in those days. Hatteras Island, a tortured windswept derelict series of dunes, offered little beyond fresh fish, good waves for surfing, and horseflies big enough to rut with a deer, flatfooted. A place to visit, briefly, not to live. Plus, the open vastness of the Atlantic Ocean was, ironically, a dead end, as escape by sea seemed practically impossible. To the west, another dead end: that world was land-locked and somehow beyond my imaginative scope. I was a surfer, a beach bum, and U.S. 70 was the road to the mountains, the Midwest, a desert, all the way to California, a land that, with my limited resources, seemed as impossible to navigate as the sea to the east. That left good old familiar U.S. 17—whether you called it the Coastal Highway or the Ocean Highway or just "17"—to feed, realistically, my fertile fever of romance on the road.

Highway U.S. 17 always held a mythological sway over me, mainly because it always seemed to exist just off the radar of my childish experience. In New Bern, U.S. 17 was a composite of throughways and generic store-lined streets. I could safely walk the boulevard it became as it cut through the commercial center, staring often in wonder at the semis and cars full of tourists. Fascinated with the parade of big rigs and the rainbow of license plates from states along the seaboard, I cultivated an early stirring wanderlust. But for the most part, U.S. 17, in town, felt secure, surrounded by familiar buildings, family and friendly faces.

Past the city limits, however, U.S. 17 existed at the dark border of my imagination. Outside of town, the Ocean Highway was a mysterious blacktop of forbidden possibilities, the id to the city's superego, a series of no-go zones fueled by rumors and vague threats. Saw mills and lumber yards seemed ominous and illicit. Logging roads disappeared into an unknowable wilderness. Old houses slumped in the middle of a cornfield, if not deserted, certainly haunted. Small creeks and "herring-runs" dissolved into an eerie landscape of open wetlands and stumpy, moss-congested swamps.

For a child not yet of driving age, the highway's identity outside the familiar neighborhoods came to me by word of mouth. Unverifiable, mystical events always occurred somewhere "out on 17." Epic wrecks filled with twisted metal and shattered glass and bodies hanging from trees like bloody laundry. Juke joints with blinking neon, loose women and fast cars. To the north, U.S. 17 crossed the Neuse River, linking New Bern to the weird, burb of Bridgetown. Like the river, U.S. 17 was unknowable, its origins disappearing, especially at night, into an impenetrable distant darkness.

But to the south, the route to Florida opened a totemic, irresistible vision of possibilities: U.S. 17 was the road to Florida!

As I grew older, the romance of U.S. 17 extended beyond its mythological draw. The highway began to produce real memories. Drag racing was a rite of passage. Hot classics—a '49 Ford with Edelbrock heads, a '55 Chevy coupe with a V-8 and straight pipes—and newer breeds, sixties' muscle cars—Malibus, GTOs, 'Vettes, and Chargers—flashed their polished chrome in the faint glow of neon lights illuminating the dirt lots of bars like Wooten's Drive-In, the exhausts arrogantly burbling in the line up, until one or the other exploded in an ear-aching revved-up challenge, followed by the obligatory positraction peel out, laying rubber along a section of U.S. 17 off limits even, somehow, to the highway patrol.

Fishing was another ritual, the highway connecting inland creeks filled with perch and brim to rivers teeming with rock, spot and puppy drum. Nights parked off 17 were spent in old sneakers, jeans rolled to my knees, brandishing a silver flashlight and a rusty spear, wading through the shallows of the Neuse, gigging flounder. Or gently rocking in a skiff tied to a buoy in another waterway off 17, practicing the craft of crabbing, meticulously drawing strings baited with fish heads up to the surface to net an unsuspecting Atlantic blue swimmer.

Nights, too, were enhanced off 17, for players new to the ritual of "parking," exploring the mysterious fumbling of high school sex … down dark, grooved dirt roads into woods infused with the scent of pines and the low smoke from smoldering summer fires, or in winter from fireplaces, turning the cold forest air into a tonic against the tension in the car.

It was magic, and it was all connected to that wild unknown stretch of blacktop running right through the middle of my life, U.S. 17. I knew that highway would be my escape route, both by choice and necessity, from the confines of the small world of New Bern, NC. U.S. 70 went inland, and I was a child of the coast. Sailing away beyond Pamlico Sound seemed too abstract. North led though the Dismal Swamp, and in my mind only to Virginia Beach, then the east coast surf capital of the mid–Atlantic, but, for me, in those days, the end of the line for surfing possibilities. The water was cold. The waves small. The boardwalk crowded beyond belief. Nothing above Norfolk seemed plausible. The map in my teenage brain regarded anything above Virginia Beach as New Jersey, and for the inexperienced ignorant southern redneck hipster I considered myself in those days, anything from the northeast was not just undesirable, it was philosophically anathema. And the Outer Banks—Kitty Hawk, Nags Head, Hatteras—were, back then, so relatively deserted that even the real surf and huge sand dunes and a mystifying vibe that basically canceled anything

Virginia Beach's boardwalk offered could not transform the Outer Banks from its empty reality, void of sustainable life outside a decent if desolate surfing experience.

When I was a kid, the world beyond a dark highway at night was still as alluring and cryptic as the night-black ocean, blinking headlights as cryptic as the lights of ships on the horizon. U.S. 17 was more than a highway; it was a promise, a state of mind, delivering me to the essence of all things cool ... if I followed U.S. 17 north, it was a temporary detour that led ultimately east, connecting with NC Route 264, which led through the Inner Banks to the Outer Banks and on to Hatteras, for surfing excursions along the deserted dunes, where the only structures back then were fishing camps and a few scattered cottages, and the loneliness seemed both palpable and transcendent. Mainly, though, U.S. 17 was a route south, an overnight 12 hour run, to catch the sun rising on the Welcome to Florida sign, where just below Jacksonville the route shifted east, over to A1A, to stay on the coast, providing access to numerous wide open surf spots between St. Augustine and Daytona, and, navigating occasionally over to U.S. 1 to circumvent the numerous inlets cutting into the coast, slipping south along A1A, reaching further down to the hot spots around Sebastian Inlet: Shark Pit. Spanish House. Wabasso....

So, U.S. 17, which began for me in New Bern, was more than an exotic highway. It was a fabled path connecting me to magical destinations, always near water, never far from the beach, or from the possibility of surf, no matter how "East Coast" and sloppy the waves.

And along this stretch of littoral southern states cut with that seacoast slither of highway, I fell in love with fried shrimp.

Part of the allure was because we never prepared shrimp at home.

Aside from what we considered "fake" shrimp—those bread-crumbed squishy bits of dull nubs—no one had heard of "farm-raised" shrimp, or "imported" shrimp for that matter. The corner fish market had shrimp strictly during season, and only when the monger had access to a trawler supplying his shop. The shrimp were usually fairly large, their dark eyes and shells glistening through the ice. Those shrimp usually ended up in a seafood casserole, or pickled and served in a punch bowl for special occasions. You didn't boil 'em or grill 'em or broil 'em.

But the best way to eat shrimp was fried, period.

Except deep-frying was not something we did at home. So eating fried shrimp was always associated with eating out.

In the hey-day of fast frozen seafood—ingesting wafers from the TV dinner Eucharist invented by Clarence Birdseye for the nuclear American family—the shrimp and fish that made up those meals were wild, locally caught off Labrador. (Odd side note: Mr. Birdseye began his career as a taxidermist, making his name weirdly eponymous and, in hindsight, his edible concoctions even more creepy.) The shift away from U.S. shrimp boats supplying the majority of the catch consumed in the country didn't shift until the late 1990s, when aqua-farming turned shrimp from a gourmet entrée to an all-you-can-eat buffet staple.

In the 1960s, foodstuff on the coast of North Carolina was still fairly regional. Meat was best if you knew a butcher. Chicken and eggs were best procured fresh from a farm. Even so, you could buy decent beef and poultry in the supermarket. And of course you could prepare meat loaf and pastas and casseroles easy enough in the kitchen, or chicken and steaks and hot dogs and hamburgers on a grill. If you wanted game, you shot fowl, deer, even squirrel. Or you knew someone who did. You want fish, you caught them. Or you knew someone who did. You netted crabs. You had a crab boil.

People did, of course, buy frozen breaded fish sticks or deviled crabs or popcorn shrimp. But nobody I knew that wasn't in a highchair wanted to eat that stuff, frozen breaded seafood, baked to a hot mush in the oven. If you wanted real shellfish like oysters and clams, or, most commonly, shrimp, for me at least, that meant going out to a seafood restaurant.

And best of all, when it came to eating out, were the places where you had to go.

The primo spots to eat "real" shrimp were rough raw bars usually set on pilings out over the water. Nothing fancy. Wooden tables or benches. Paper table cloths. Often served family style, platters were piled high with batter-fried scallops and shrimp and oysters and soft-shelled crabs served with hushpuppies and French fries. Often, the orders were delivered as "all you can eat." But it seems now in hindsight that these places were always on the water. Which made the places seem mysterious, magical. They transported you from an ordinary eating experience into an exotic episode that smacked of adventure. During the day, there were birds and aquatic creatures to marvel at. Boats cruising by. At night, the water always opened into darkness, the lights reflecting on the water faint and delicate. And the briny smell, combined with the sound of waves or gulls or wind and just all the natural action associated with the wild coastal Outer Banks or the marshy desolation of the Inner Banks, created an impression of simultaneous solitude and commotion, aloneness and community. And no matter how isolated the establishment, how lost on the edge of the continent, just off the Pamlico, along the shores of Bogue Sound, adjacent to the sport fishing docks, or in the middle of nowhere out along an estuary, to get there, you had to, at some point, turn off 17.

The magic of that highway, and the transcendence of eating those shrimp, shaped my life. I became a "17-er." One of the people who has never lived far from the highway. For whom the highway is a part of daily life. It has become a consciousness. A point of reference beyond maps. A road that, no matter how much time I spend in other parts of the world, working for extended periods in Europe, visiting various regions of the globe, traveling in disparate areas of the Americas, I can't escape, and seem always to return to. It is a defining geographical phenomenon—the Ocean Highway—carving out a very special section of the southern East Coast.

I wanted to rediscover that magic. To explore the essence of what it means to be a "17-er." To share the experience with fellow travelers, both outsiders curious to understand this funky chunk of Americana, and those residents who have either rediscovered the highway or never left it, whose being has been molded by 600 miles of road through a region known for its ugliness and beauty, its bigotry and generosity, its pettiness and grandeur.

And the best shrimp in the country.

⟫1⟪

The Highway

What makes a highway more than a highway? When does it become a signature? A metaphor? A poetic example of a specific wanderlust both lost and frozen in time? A promise? A reminder? Is it the scenery, the backdrop, the context? Is it the destination? Where the road goes? Where it takes you to? What it takes you from? What lies ahead? What behind? Is it the characters occupying the diners, the motels, the wayside inns and curious detours? Is it the length? The diversity? The fact that it is a mere ghost of what it was, the sightings of the actual artifact conjuring nostalgia, romance and adventure?

Years before Jack Kerouac hit the road in his barely fictionalized bromance with Neal Cassady, the cult of cars and the lore of the open highway in the collective imagination of America was well established. The mythical "road trip" is as American as apple pie, ice cream, the Marlboro Man, and gun violence. The Lincoln Highway, the first automobile road across America, ran from Times Square in New York City west to Lincoln Park in San Francisco and quickly evolved into a stage for heroic exploits, criminal mischief, and the deification of angelic hobos in early American legends. The Dixie Highway, more a network of interconnected routes than a continuous highway, consisted of a western branch joining Chicago and Miami, FL, and an eastern route joining Sault Ste. Marie, MI, with Miami. U.S. 1 travels the entire east coast, from Key West to Ft. Kent, ME. On the west coast, U.S. 101—offering some of the most spectacular scenery in the country—runs along the coast of California, Oregon, and Washington. FL A1A, immortalized on the cover of Jimmy Buffet's 1974 album, flows along Florida's Atlantic coast from Key West to Fernandina Beach. U.S. 61, "The Blues Highway," commemorated by Bob Dylan on his album *Highway 61 Revisited*, connects the Deep South to the far north, from New Orleans, LA, to Wyoming, MI.

Everybody's got a favorite, some popular cultural reference to a legendary highway figuring into the romance of youth. Tom Petty whining about cars "out on 441." Bruce Springsteen and his cryptic "highway nine." American roads in the collective imagination always lead to romance, to a past full of promise, to a recovery of self.

But of all the iconic highways in the country, U.S. 66, celebrated in song, cinema and literature, is the gold standard. The original itinerary rolled for 2,500 miles through Middle America, from Adams St. in Chicago to the Santa Monica Pier. Most Americans are familiar with the litany of towns along the way thanks to Bobby Troup's oft-covered rocker, with its catalog of cites, raucous chords, and that sing-along refrain of "get your kicks on route Sixty Six." Oldsters of today grew up watching the stylized insouciance of Herbert Leonard's *Route 66*, a television series from the Sixties that made hot convertible Corvettes cool, and promoted drifting from town to town, disconnected from middle-class contentment, as an antidote to the conventional American Dream. And in John Steinbeck's *The Grapes of Wrath*, it's U.S. 66 the Joad family follows, having piled their belongings into a converted Hudson jalopy, to push west from the dust bowl of Oklahoma to the nightmare of resettlement camps in the loamy dystopia of California's Central Valley. "Route 66" crosses a postcard landscape of cornfields and wheat fields, the Great Plains, the Rockies, the western deserts, all the way to the end of the line, the sun and surf of Malibu, the historical seedy glitz of Hollywood *noir*.

U.S. 17, half as long but more intact, may not be so glamorous, but it is no less iconic along the southeastern coastal landscape. Its reputation is complicated by the ordinariness of a road serving double-duty: a working highway feeding a tourism boom, and a commercial throughway serving the economy of the New South. Slicing through the Mid-Atlantic states, from the Appalachian Mountains to the prairies of south central Florida, through national parks, nature preserves, pine forests, marshes and lakes and rivers, cutting across the subtropical savannahs and oceanfront real estate along the Atlantic Seaboard, the route is complex: the scenery stunning and banal, the highway at once haunted and mundane, serene and congested, the coastal vistas, the towns and cities, all steeped in southern allure and history.

Yet the Ocean Highway could never claim the cultural cachet of Route 66. Sixty-Six had it all: intrigue; existential possibilities; dramatic natural scenery; eclectic, often bizarre architecture; quirky drive-ins and gas stations and roadside attractions. It was a transcultural, paved expanse that united a diversified nation.

But U.S. 17 has one thing Route 66 does not, never did and never will.

Shrimp. Local. Wild shrimp.

Problem is, running south to north, there's not much shrimping, or, for that matter, anything "coastal" about The Coastal Highway until it exits Florida above Jacksonville and begins snaking along the true coastline between the Florida/Georgia line toward Brunswick. It veers inland south of Savannah, moving further inland around the Hilton Head area before rejoining the coast north of Beaufort, SC. It continues to slither along the seaboard into North Carolina, looping inland again from Elizabeth City, NC, to Plymouth, VA, snapping back to the coastline north of Norfolk and running along the Rappahannock River until it turns away from the Chesapeake Bay region toward Fredericksburg, the Piedmont and Blue Ridge Mountains. Similar to the Florida stretch, there's not much local shrimping above Elizabeth City. That limits the prime shrimp zones off U.S. 17 to the coastal areas between the Pamlico Sound in North Carolina and Mayport, north of Jacksonville.

Since the completion of the southern stretch of Interstate 95, the character of U.S. 17 has become as eclectic as the landscape it traverses. In Florida, the highway is an afterthought, at best a novelty, often an inconvenience, at times a distraction. In Georgia, it's ignored, nearly abandoned in spots, before suddenly transforming into a congested thoroughfare connecting urban centers to malls, golf courses and the bedroom communities servicing urban sprawl and the influx of retirees flocking to southern climes, especially in the zone immediately west of Savannah. In South Carolina, the immediate stretch of highway is subsumed by I-95, but the road from the turnoff to Charleston all the way to Myrtle Beach is a major coastal highway. Into North Carolina and along the edge of the Inner Banks, U.S. 17 is still a main route connecting cities to coastal communities strung the Pamlico Sound and the beaches beyond. After being subsumed into the metropolis of Norfolk, it again emerges as the main road along the Rappahannock River until its terminus in the Appalachians.

Prairies, marshes, city centers, pine forests, rivers, beaches, horse country, farmland and strip malls, the vistas along U.S. 17 are as varied as the American character. But the route, in the end, is a southern phenomenon, representing not only a nostalgic era of American history—the advent of the modern highway system, signage and cartographic science—but also its racial divide. The highway bisects towns in which the phrase "wrong side of the tracks" still defines racial segregation. Most of the

Coastal Highway runs through Jim Crow territory, and even with the changing demographics, recent trends in gentrification, and the spate of new nest-building by snowbirds flocking down from the more progressive northeast, the highway continues to reflect a political landscape that for the most part remains reactionary, rooted in localism and minor xenophobia, steeped in a longing for a simple lifestyle and a return for a time when disaffected southern whites were an ascendant, dominant political force. The landscape is Red State red meat. It's in the blood. In the history.

It's not too much of an overstatement or gross simplification to point out the obvious: the prevailing political and cultural attitude along U.S. 17 is that the Civil War was a war of northern aggression. Confederate flags are prevalent. Racial tensions smolder beneath the social surface like a muck fire. The highway represents the eastern edge of the Southern Strategy, linking the southeastern states to their core constituents of the Deep South along the Gulf Coast: Alabama, Mississippi, Louisiana. The legacy of The Coastal Highway, its heritage, is indelible, as vivid as a turkey buzzard along the median, shredding road-kill. The landscape of U.S. 17 is firmly rooted in the harsh beauty of the American south.

Technically, in the south-to-north paradigm, the awful beauty that became U.S. Highway 17 begins on the Gulf Coast of Florida, in the center of Punta Gorda.

Yes, Punta Gorda. Which, back in the heady days of early highway construction, was little more than a mosquito-plagued, gator-and snake-infested, sink-hole riddled dead end with as much charm as any other muck camp on the edge of Bone Valley ... but, it was home to the largest phosphate deposits in the United States.

Nothing like rich, mineable deposits of toxic heavy metal to drive the economy of the Sunshine State.

But even with the phosphate connection, it would not be unreasonable to ask why, in the 1920s, would you run a highway across a deserted cow pasture full of displaced hillbillies and desperados to the edge of a swamp in the middle of nowhere?

Well, actually, even aside from the phosphate, there's no mystery here. The answer is Pure Foresight.

After all, the highway system, as designed by the Feds in the early 20th century, hoped to connect all the major sectors in the various states— in this case, Florida—with accessible, well-designed roads to promote tourism and commerce.

Still, spending money on such an ambitious highway system through this area in the 1920s must have seemed harebrained to even the most hesitant skeptic, because, let's face it, back then, Punta Gorda was little more than a honky-tonk, backwater, frontier port city.

Later, during the post–World War II boom, the city became known as a nice coastal retirement community with a reputation for sandy white beaches and sport fishing—famous for Tarpon, Snook and Redfish—popular with golfers, small craft enthusiasts and recreational fishermen. Even more typical are the city's efforts at revitalization, emblematic of so many "quaint" former ghost towns reinvigorated by waterfront developments— "Riverwalks," in common parlance, "Fisherman's Village" in Punta Gorda— full of chain restaurants and art malls selling trinkets and crafts and stuffed dolphins. The "historic district"—the name invariably given to the restored areas of these prefab hamlets—squats on the southeast corner of Gasparilla Sound, part of Charlotte Harbor, the bay just inside the cut south of Boca Grande, along the Gulf of Mexico, a picturesque waterscape of scarlet sunsets and promises of affordable romance sanctioned by the AARP.

But if these days Punta Gorda offers beautiful bay vistas and lush landscapes, in the late 19th century its claim to fame was being the center of a phosphate boom. In the early 1900s, it was the greatest phosphate shipping point in the world. And, at that time, as the southernmost stop of the Florida Southern Railroad, it was basically the last outpost on Florida's west coast before the wilds of the Everglades.

Punta Gorda was, literally, the end of the road.

What happened was, the designers of the nascent highway system envisioned a new section of U.S. 41, a major route connecting the west coast of south Florida with Michigan. Opened in 1921, the new route, named Tamiami Trail, runs across the Everglades and up the west coast of Florida, joining Tampa with Miami. To complete the crisscrossing pattern of new highways, U.S. 17, which, in 1926 terminated in Jacksonville, FL, was extended from Jacksonville through Orlando to Punta Gorda, traversing the heartland of the state and tying the northeast coast of Florida to the southwest coast and then over to Miami.

Until 2004, a sign in downtown Punta Gorda read "END 17." According to legend, it was blown away by Hurricane Charley.

Bleak is the world in east Punta Gorda, with its traffic and malls and chain restaurants and motels and bedroom communities and golf courses stacked along a once barren prairie and abandoned citrus groves.

Bleaker still is the stretch ahead, as U.S. 17 begins to wend its way north and east through south central Florida. This is a land-locked terrain of cattle grazing prairies and citrus groves, Sheriff's Boys Retreats and gun clubs, reminiscent of famous Florida business barons like Hale, Mixon, Griffon, Strickland, King and Collier. This section of the highway runs right up the spine of "cracker" Florida. (The term "cracker" originated with Florida cowboys.) The route threads backwater towns like Arcadia, famous, back in the zealous years of the Reagan Revolution, for burning down the house of two young boys who contracted AIDs from tainted blood transfusions. Zolfo Springs, Wauchula, Fort Meade, Bartow—this is cattle and citrus country, more famous for football, rodeos, steak and honey than fried shrimp, or any fresh seafood, for that matter.

As the highway approaches Winter Haven, once home of the now defunct Cypress Gardens and the Dick Poe, Jr., water-ski extravaganzas (now, Lego-Land), the scenery, no less land-locked, changes from cattle-and-grove flatlands to an urbanized environ teeming with lakes. Near Kissimmee, U.S. 17 skirts the resort-saturated Disney area tourist attractions, enters a maze of surface roads through Orlando, before slipping again into the sand and pine groves of north central Florida. Following the west bank of the St. John's River, the highway nears the east coast at Green Cove Springs, where the landscape changes again into a lush composition of Sweetbay and Swamp Tupelo lining the blackwater streams that feed the St. John's River, until the highway finally turns east toward Jacksonville.

The idea of eating fried shrimp on any part of U.S. 17 before Jacksonville seems counterintuitive, if not down right risky. Even so, nestled in fields of cow paddies sprouting psilocybin mushrooms, flush with wild pigs rooting among the shrub grass and palmettos, along the gauche prefab strip malls strung along the routes around Kissimmee, and lining the shores of various lakes and river alcoves, there are plenty of "seafood" establishments, independents and chains, offering patrons laminated menus chock-full with "fresh" seafood. Given the territory, the question is: Would these be "lake shrimp," a near cousin to the mythological "Rocky Mountain oyster"? More genuine are the wayside stands selling items indigenous to the area, like gator jerky and local honey, wild boar sausage and "authentic" Seminole moccasins, beads, and other assorted trinkets like Florida "wooden trunk" sculptures (clock frames, dolphins, birds, Tiki faces, etc.).

U.S. 17 finally approaches the coast at Jacksonville, about 20 miles west of the Atlantic Ocean. Just south of the city, right on the dunes, the famous Sawgrass Course in Ponte Vedra Beach hosts the P.G.A. Players Championship, the club itself indicative of the how Jacksonville has transformed itself in the 1980s from a mill-and-port, trucking-and-banking industrial zone into a world-class community of leisurely pursuits, retirement living and tourism. The largest city by area in the United States, Jacksonville is a sprawling suburban network, a mishmash of over 500 identified separate "neighborhoods," tract housing and condominium complexes surrounding a tightly packed downtown area hugging the St. John's River. Capitalizing on its strategic location, and with its mix of retirees and tourists, residents and transients, industry and leisure, the largest deep-water port in the southern United States, a Navy base, a Naval air station, rivers, beaches, sailing centers, sport and commercial fishing enterprises—Jacksonville has emerged in the twenty-first century as a bustling powerhouse of economic vitality and cultural diversity.

Conversely, Jacksonville has a reputation for being on the conservative edge of the New South, in contrast to the looser, more liberal coastal communities below the I-4 sector. If I-10 is the original Florida Bible Belt, Jacksonville is its buckle, securing the east end of the I-10 corridor. From its junction with I-95, the interstate heads west towards Pensacola through the Florida panhandle, via Tallahassee, stretching along the southern borders of Georgia and Alabama. It skirts the coast of the Redneck Riviera, and then continues its trans-continental run all the way to Los Angeles, CA. And it is the I-10 trek through the adjoining hardcore Red States that underscores Jacksonville's militant southern heritage, evident not only in its namesake—Andrew Jackson—but complemented by some of its favorite sons, including that once favorite right wing cultural rebel Pat Boone, famous for white shoes and Christian-themed ballads; iconic southern-fried rockers like Lynyrd Skynyrd and Molly Hatchet; and the exceptional Allman Brothers.

Beyond the Main Street Bridge (officially the John T. Alsop, Jr. Bridge), through the ruin of north downtown Jacksonville, U.S. 17 leaves the major chaos to I-95 and navigates away from the hectic and seriously snarled traffic of the city-center. On the north side of the river, 20 miles inland from the sea, any sense of ocean in The Ocean Highway still seems remote, especially for those who think anything west of A1A is "inland." But the landscape does begin to change gradually, and the industrial scabs of trucking businesses, derelict malls, bars with blackened windows, stranded diners with seafood themes all mixed in with desperate splotches of gentrification, walled-off gated communities and start-up electronics stores with cement facades ... all this urban wasteland thins out, and U.S. 17 soon morphs into a lonely isolated stretch of highway through the St. John's River Basin.

Midway to Yulee, south of the turn to Fernandina Beach, stands a reminder that, even though you are heading north on a major roadway in the first quarter of the twenty-first century, you are still in the deep south, where some things never change. On the left, at the edge of a swampy creek off the Nassau Sound, part of the St. John's flood plain, the illustrious Reni's Redneck Yacht Club proudly flies the Stars and Bars, Battle Flag of the Confederate States of America, drawing constituents from the surrounding area for sun-drenched mayhem, grilled steaks, pop and country rock music, and assorted biker bacchanalia. The motto is "No B.S." There's no shrimp either. Just beefcake, cheesecake and leather.

Entering the Shrimp Zone: the Main Street Bridge, Jacksonville, FL. The Shrimp Country stretch of U.S. 17 begins on the north side of the St. John's River in Jacksonville, as Main Street becomes the Coastal Highway. An alternate route south of the river leads to Mayport. On the north side, FL East 105 becomes Heckscher Drive, then FL A1A, on the way to Mayport. Outside of Jacksonville, U.S. 17 continues through the Timucuan Ecological and Historical Preserve to Yulee, and then across the St. Mary's River into Georgia, entering one of the most picturesque sections of the Coastal Highway, and some of the best shrimping grounds on the entire East Coast.

U.S. 17 continues its west/northwest direction, mainly due to the nature of the landscape below the Fall Line, filled with tidal basins and marshy spoils unsuitable for major highway construction. As the route curves north above Yulee, it crosses the St. Mary's River and enters the sand hills and pine forests that were once the ancient seacoast. The number of creeks, rivers and swamps the highway traverses gives an indication of why the area is known as the Lowcountry. After the North Fork of the Crooked River, the road crosses the Satilla River, White Oak Creek, and various flood zones and tidal basins, roughly parallels Interstate 95, veers sharply seaward, turns north across the Brunswick River as The Sidney Lanier Bridge—Georgia's tallest span—before stretching into Brunswick proper.

Statistically, Brunswick is the major economic center of the state's lower southeast, and the second-largest urban area on the Georgia coast after Savannah. But driving through the urban neglect of what's left of downtown Brunswick, you wouldn't know it. The main driving economic force—what draws tourists to the region—is the Golden Isles—St. Simon,

U.S. 17, Reni's Redneck Yacht Club, near Yulee, between Jacksonville and Fernandina. Realty along much of U.S. 17 thrives in the brutal machinations of Alt-Right Realpolitiks.

Jekyll and Sea Island, accessible via offshoots from U.S. 17 connecting the resort communities with the mainland.

The Golden Isles were once so popular that an old maxim goes like this: If you asked a Brunswick neighbor—"How ya' doing?"—the positive reply was, "Feels like I'm sitting on Jekyll." And while for lots of folks Jekyll still represents "the good life," downtown Brunswick seems tired and deserted. Rich in colonial and Civil War heritage, the area around Brunswick has become a retirement destination, although the environs lack the charm, wealth and sophistication of Savannah and Hilton Head just to the north, and the economic vitality of Jacksonville to the immediate south. Brunswick seems to occupy a middle ground between affluence and tackiness, kinetic possibilities and commercial lassitude. U.S. 17, ghosting along the waterfront as Glynn Avenue, reflects the enervated sense of a city left behind, backsliding into the twenty-first century.

The landscape improves again as U.S. 17 joins U.S. 25 and forms The Darien Highway, which slips quietly into serious shrimp country. Running past the edge of the Hofwyl-Broadfield Plantation, crossing Champney Island, Butler Island, Generals Island, the Champney River, the Butler River, several creeks, channels and various branches of the Altamaha River,

U.S. 17. Second Amendment and shrimp chauvinism.

The Sidney Lanier Bridge, U.S. 17, Brunswick, SC, looking south. The highway skirts the lowlands and marsh at the edge of Jekyll and St. Simons islands as it runs through Brunswick as Glynn Avenue.

the route enters the fishing village of Darien. As the highway works inland toward Midway, the landscape remains pocked with wetlands associated with the Sapelo River, Buck Hill Swamp, the South Newport River, and Porter Creek.

To give you a sense of the difficulty of navigating this landscape by car, much less building a highway capable of accommodating today's traffic, consider the road conditions before the modern section of U.S. 17 between Savannah and Brunswick was complete. The path—it would be overly charitable to call the it a road—passed through streams and creeks with no bridges, relying on fords in the waterway, passable only at low tide, and through bogs so muddy the intrepid trekkers often had to rely more on mules to pull them along in the muck. (Locals recall a popular quip at the time: "Takes more mule power than horse power.") Road maps, highway signs, filling stations, restaurants, hotels—such accommodations were futuristic fantasies. Tourists lucky enough to find a campsite or town center with any semblance of cooking facilities were usually limited to meals of fried mullet, cornbread and collards cooked around a fish camp. Natives still refer to the area around Midway, Georgia, as "Mullet Fish Alley."

Spanning the Ogeechee River into the sprawling suburban area of Richmond Hill, The Coastal Highway approaches the actual coast. Avoiding downtown Savannah via a bypass over the Eugene Tallmadge Memorial Bridge, U.S. 17 crosses over Bay Street and the main channel of the Savannah River and enters South Carolina. In the pre–I-95 days, when Savannah was a necessary transit point halfway between the mid–Atlantic college community and the Spring Break scenes of bacchanalia associated with Daytona and Cocoa Beach, downtown Savannah was a rough port city with little charm to recommend it. With the rise of "heritage tourism," coupled with the popularity of Southern Gothic literature—especially the best seller *In the Garden of Good and Evil*—along with the city's concentrated attempts at gentrification and the advent of Savannah College of Art and Design, the tenor of the city changed. Today Savannah is a must-visit city on the southern tour, heaving with tourists from around the U.S. and Europe. The restaurants, clustered around the waterfront, are mainly generic touristy digs, with some notable exceptions.

Love's, U.S. 17, Richmond Hill, GA. Situated on the east side of the Harvey Granger Bridge, where U.S. 17 crosses the Ogeechee River, Love's has been a landmark outside Savannah since opening in 1949. Several scenes for the film *Forrest Gump* were shot in and around the restaurant.

Whereas "Old" U.S. 17 can be exhausting as it runs through the densely trafficked Richmond Hill and the interior streets of inner city Savannah, as soon as it crosses the river into South Carolina the highway regains its authenticity and forlorn beauty, wending into the spooky desolate core of Lowcountry living.

At least, it was *once* spooky and desolate. Especially if you follow the original route that connects Hardeeville to Ridgeland and Coosawhatchie. But most travelers at this point either shift to I-95 or peel off U.S. 17 toward Hilton Head, an area newly civilized and teeming with retirement communities, gated housing developments, golf courses, marinas and country clubs. The original route U.S. 17 takes through this part of South Carolina is both convoluted and direct, as it tends to parallel and converge with I-95, sometimes maintaining its own identity and at other times masquerading as other routes. A careless driver, following the marked route, might well unintentionally merge off, on and around U.S. 17 without often being aware of exactly which road is which.

The necessity of the inland turn of the original route is evident in the landscape. Given the nature of the terrain, the highway had to skirt the Port Royal estuary, an interlaced system of waterways flowing east from the main branch of the Harbor River toward the various locales along the boggy, often inaccessible coastline. Some of the original shrimping communities east of U.S. 17 include Bluffton and Beaufort. U.S. 17 regains its identity as it heads through the ACE Basin (an acronym for Ashepoo, Combahee and Edisto rivers, part of a preservation project to protect the wetlands, hardwood forests and riverine systems between Beaufort and Charleston), before hitting the major congestion of the West Ashley neighborhood outside of Charleston. The bridge over the Ashley River, instead of skirting the center of town, as it does in Savannah by looping around and above the cityscape, empties U.S. 17 right into the heart of downtown Charleston. Entering near the City Marina, it passes directly through the urban center and exits onto the Arthur Ravenel, Jr. Bridge over the Cooper River, leveling out into the traffic rich stretch through Mount Pleasant and the tributaries leading east to the direct coastal communities of Isle of Palms and Sullivan's Island.

Charleston is, of course, one of the most celebrated cities in the South, if not in the nation. Infamous for its Black Belt slave trade and the slave markets during the antebellum era, and equally for the firing on Fort Sumter in 1861, initiating the Civil War, Charleston today is probably most notable for its culture and cuisine, a blend of French, West African and

U.S. 17, A.C.E. Basin. Between Beaufort and Charleston, the Coastal Highway crosses a prime, rural Lowcountry landscape. The road has been upgraded, but the scenery remains pristine and wild. In the warm seasons, gators can be spotted hunting the shallows right beside the highway.

Caribbean styles melded with Colonial and Federalist architecture. From that eclectic hodgepodge of international influences, Charleston has earned bragging rights for its culinary culture. Its various restaurants are prominently featured in travel guides, television specials, gourmet magazines and the style sections of major newspapers, at home and abroad.

But Charleston has its "other side" too, and U.S. 17 demarcates the split, bisecting the city, separating the generally fashionable historical district and French Quarter from the working class, residential, often dilapidated parts along other sections of the highway. While Charleston remains a working class city, divided by race, class and economics, the city does maintain a remarkably positive vibe. The contrast between the touristy, trendy, and crowded scene around Market Street, King Street and East Bay Street and the industrial areas around the docks, the Navy Yards and the pockets of poverty in much of Charleston is acute. Even so, the population seems preternaturally united in a spirit of shared purpose and upbeat conurbation.

The glaring contrast between the grimy and the glistening, in both the city and the suburbs, which is intense, in both theory and praxis, is somehow mitigated by its cultural ambiance: at least, to an outsider, even the urban blight seems charming. It's a fiction, certainly, but it's convincing. The city appears healthy, vibrant, thriving. And the locals take their farm-to-fork philosophy seriously. Even mediocre restaurants stress indigenous dishes. Especially fried shrimp. But, like the metropolises to the south—Jacksonville, Brunswick and Savannah—seafood restaurants saturate the area, and not even the locals can testify to the authenticity of the Lowcountry options.

The road from the Charleston metro area to Georgetown runs through the Francis Marion National Forest—named, as we learned in primary school, for the famous Swamp Fox, an America-born revolutionary officer famous for developing guerrilla warfare tactics against the British during the American War of Independence. Lined by a scrubby subtropical coniferous forest surrounding the rural communities of Awendaw and McClellanville, the route flows just to the west of the marshes associated with the Santee River system—creating some of the richest shrimp harvesting waters on the coast. Beyond the Santee, U.S. 17 runs through Georgetown, then exits heading east again, toward the ocean, crossing the Waccamaw/Pee Dee River system into a stretch of highway that literally abuts the Atlantic coast, connecting Pawleys Island, Litchfield, and Murrells Inlet, outposts of relative calm before the traffic and chaos of the Myrtle Beach nightmare. This part of U.S. 17, from Georgetown to Myrtle Beach, was part of the original Kings Highway, a road laid out on orders from Charles II in 1650 to connect Charleston to Boston. The area is developed beyond recognition from its fish camp days of just a few generations ago.

But the minor congestion of the run from the bridge outside Georgetown to the northern limits of Murrells Inlet cannot prepare a motorist for the madness to come. Here, U.S. 17 splits into a business route and a by-pass. The easternmost sprig spans the seaside resorts and the beach—a section known as the Grand Strand. The western branch skirts the outlet malls, performance arenas, theme parks, franchised insanity and tourist attractions that dominate the area. The whole scene, in recent years, projects a militant country western themed evangelical revivalist retreat for land-locked middle-America tourists starved for sun and modest abandonment. The smell of suntan oil and fried food, mixed with automobile exhaust and a faint spray of sea-scent permeates the environment.

As envisioned by one of the city fathers, Franklin Burroughs, as early as the 1880s, Myrtle Beach has been designed as a resort town. No one knows what Mr. Burroughs had in mind, but regardless of attempts to clean up the once renegade hangout and upgrade the culture, the Grand Strand retains an indelible mark of a Redneck Riviera. The vibe is more associated with the Panhandle of Florida—the beaches around Pensacola and Panama City—than, say, Charleston or Savannah or the beaches along the east coast of Florida that Mr. Burroughs hoped to compete with. The contemporary incarnation of his vision is based in a schizophrenia that pits the super-conservative adult political environment, affiliated with family friendly venues like the Carolina Opry and innocuous clubs like Hard Rock Café—American-flags, country-pop and NASCAR, and more churches per square mile than bars—against a milieu of teenagers and college-aged young adults demanding the right to spin out on beer and volley ball, sand, surf and other protean varieties of youthful debauchery.

This conflict between mawkish prudery and hedonistic revelry, if not hypocrisy, is best illustrated by the slew of beach shops and boutiques hawking skimpy outfits and surf paraphernalia, while the city council passes a "thong ordinance" disallowing bikinis in public that expose too much of a woman's bare buttocks. (Case in point: Myrtle Beach's famed bike week attracts its own particularly modest middleclass crowd more akin to Heck's Angels than the hard core Harley crowd that descends, like vultures to a carcass, on Daytona.)

But the Strand has its "dark side"—that is, a healthy reputation for partying—stretching back to when it served as a base in World War II. Perhaps its most famous contribution to decadence is still on display at nearby Ocean Drive (now North Myrtle Beach), home to the O.D. Pavilion and the Shaggers Hall of Fame. Shagging is a dance derived from the Jitterbug, also known as The Bop, best performed to "Beach Music," a style cultivated into an art form by bands like The Embers and Archie Bell and the Drells. The O.D. Pavilion continues to conjure images of more liberated days, unvarnished by the slick productions along the strip, where spring breakers and weekend coeds hungry for a sunburned-fueled beer bash, lots of skin and surf, can still find abandonment in the shadows of a sand dune or in the damp hidden alcove of a rented cottage.

A man-made island cut off from the mainland by the Intracoastal Waterway and zippered between U.S. 17 Business and its bypass, the Grand Strand represents one of the great "success" stories of the twenty-first century, illustrating the economic revitalization of coastal South Carolina, from an agrarian-based economy to a retirement-and-tourist-centered financial jackpot. It's also an example of the New South, which entails developers and real estate agents going wild in the name of capitalism and free enterprise and spoiling some of the most pristine coastline on the Eastern Seaboard. Why it happened on this stretch of coast is a mystery, but the wound caused by the traffic and housing developments from Litchfield to Little River aches like a stress fracture on the beloved Ocean Highway as it struggles, during the season, to handle the congestion, rendered nearly impassable by the crush of businesses, retirees, tourists and transplants repopulating Myrtle Beach.

The breakout from the madness of the Grand Strand is sudden and refreshing as U.S. 17 crosses into North Carolina, bending slightly around one of the original odd ducks of the seafood circuit: Calabash. The once tiny seaport—still no more than a pseudo-hamlet overrun by visitors and day-trippers—is not shy about its heritage, calling itself "The Seafood Capital of the World." Its actual claim to fame rests with the popularity of its style of corn meal battered and deep fried seafood, appropriately called "Calabash Style."

After the spoiled charms of Calabash, the route through the Tar Heel State continues rather inauspiciously, given the lack of attractive scenery. The road is lined with pop-up golf course communities surrounded by mobile homes, pre-fab swimming pool sales lots, strip-malls, used car dealers and auto repair shops, edging up against a smattering of repurposed tobacco crops and corn fields and cotton farms that dominate the area. Sweeping past the various beach communities—all almost identical in appearance, after the sudden boom of ocean front property sprouting cottages like mushrooms along the Intracoastal Waterway, and sleepy fishing towns, gentrified to affluence, clinging to some semblance of their simple past way of life—U.S. 17 bogs down again with traffic snarls as it nears the major port city of Wilmington. Crossing the Cape Fear, the highway offers a glimpse of the scenic waterfront shops lining the north shore of the river as it then eases into a pleasant if crowded stretch of road through a residential part of the city, although most of the through traffic is now diverted to a bypass connected to I-40.

Wilmington is a city that has managed to keep a small town feel to its center even as it copes with urban sprawl along the Cape Fear River and Wrightsville Beach, and a population that has increased exponentially since the 1990s. The popularity of the city stems from several factors, not least of which is the convenience of I-40 connecting the beach with the capital city of Raleigh. But also factoring in to the success of the city is the film industry, which set up camp in the 1980s. (Wilmington played a starring role in the David Lynch film *Blue Velvet*, but in an example of poetic license and metaphorical necessity, Wilmington in the film is called Lumberton, a different but actual town about 80 miles west of the city.) Also, the Wilmington extension campus of the University of North Carolina continues to be a major draw, expanding into a major university center since joining the UNC system in 1969. The city also maintains a sizeable port serving industries throughout the region.

But even with its burgeoning commercial development and lively waterfront scene, its rows of tree-lined yards surrounding some impressive houses, the annual Azalea Festival, the surfing and sailing, its role as beach playground for the Research Triangle, Wilmington somehow remains unremarkable. Even its history seems mundane, the city sharing common elements with most of the towns along the Kings Highway. However, there is one unusual historical fact that continues to provide an asterisk to the cultural context of the city—a remarkable bit of lore, and a reminder of the racism that continues to shadow U.S. 17. Wilmington can claim credit for the only successful coup d'état in the United States: the Wilmington Insurrection. During Reconstruction, in 1898, a band of 1500 white men (presumably Democrats, in those days, known as Waddell's Army) burned down the only black newspaper in town and ran the elected Republicans out of town, effectively disenfranchising the black community until the passage of the Civil Rights Act. The revitalized areas retain a "White City" vibe today, even as the restaurants and clubs along the riverfront draw an eclectic, progressive crowd.

The seafood restaurants scattered throughout the urban environs, including those along the roads out to the beach and along the shoreline, range from predictable franchises to Mom and Pop diners to haute French and Italian bistros. But, as in the other metropolis areas, the selections are too numerous for sampling.

After passing a series of manicured houses and a few shaded (and some shady) neighborhoods, U.S. 17 empties into a traffic-infested stretch of shopping malls and clusters of businesses, the road plagued with traffic lights. The congestion continues north, just west of the coastline, linking a series of bedroom communities and former fishing villages strung along the beach east of the highway, until reaching Jacksonville, NC—home of Camp Lejeune, a special forces training center—and then turning inland before entering the area of the Inner Banks on the western edge of Pamlico Sound.

Crossing the Trent and Neuse rivers at New Bern, U.S. 17 continues north and west to Washington (known to the locals as "Little Washington," to distinguish it, audaciously, from Washington, D.C.) The layout of U.S. 17 through this area offers an illustration of the watery nature of Eastern North Carolina on the west side of Pamlico Sound. At "Little" Washington, the highway crosses the Tar River, the Roanoke River, turns east and follows the north bank of Albemarle Sound, over the Cashie River, and the Chowan River, reaching Edenton at the scenic edge of the northern Inner Banks. Edenton, an historically significant town, home to the last screwpile base lighthouse, is more recently a reminder of the nature and character of the country that U.S. 17 traverses: this seemingly innocuous little town is the location of the notorious Little Rascals Day Care sexual abuse case, an egregious example of a modern witch hunt spawned from a toxic mix of religious zealotry and political hysteria prevalent in the area during the Reagan years.

Heading east, U.S. 17 leaves the deceptively sleepy town of Edenton behind, if not necessarily the hard right political philosophy that cast its pall the length of The Coastal Highway from Punta Gorda to the Blue Ridge Mountains—that southern-fried ideology barely tamed by gentrification and "Yankee" infiltration. The road continues along the northern edge of Albemarle Sound, crossing the Perquimans River and entering Elizabeth City, the furthest eastern point it hits before heading directly into Norfolk and turning away from the coast to run up the back side of Chesapeake Bay. Nestled along the Pasquotank River, Elizabeth City was historically a major outpost between the Great Dismal Swamp and the Outer Banks. Known as the "Harbor of Hospitality," the town acts as a crossroads linking the Inner Banks to the Outer Banks, Kitty Hawk to the mainland. Elizabeth City is also the northern-most limit of the major shrimp harvesting zones.

There is a U.S. 17 beyond the Inner Banks, although the historical U.S. highway 17, aka The Ocean Highway, or The Coastal Highway, immediately loses its identity, charm and character as it enters Virginia. After skimming the edge of the Great Dismal Swamp National Wildlife Refuge, the highway slides west of Norfolk before being swallowed by a puzzle of interconnected highways looping around and through Chesapeake and Portsmouth. Here U.S. 17 no longer associates in any meaningful way directly with the coast, the ocean, or any sense of beach life. Gone, above Elizabeth City, is any romantic charm the highway might evoke in the imagination of those living and traveling the 600 miles of coastline between Norfolk, VA, to Jacksonville, FL.

Across a branch of the Elizabeth River, it is possible to stick with the original highway, for the most part, over the Nansemond River, then Chuckatuck Creek, and the James River into Newport News. And beyond the York River, the highway briefly graces a scenic bit of the water's edge, spanning Gloucester Point and continuing through the Dragon Swamp area of the Piankatank River. But after sliding through Middlesex as Tidewater Trail, rolling along the western side of the Rappahannock River to Fredericksburg, where it leaves the coastal plain, U.S. 17 becomes a completely different highway, passing through the Piedmont into the Blue Ridge Mountains, terminating in the Shenandoah Valley.

⇛2⇚

The Shrimp

A quick Internet search reveals a surprising mix of hard scientific data, speculative historical trivia, and anecdotal ruminations indicating an unexpected interest in these critters commonly referred to as "shrimp." While exploring the number of RPMs a shrimp might produce on a treadmill makes for an intriguing afternoon read, snuggled into a comfy chair and your favorite cardigan, enjoying a glass of Pimms ... this isn't that kind of study. Even so, it doesn't take a lot of "research" to tickle up the etymology of "shrimp." The root of the term dates from Old English in the form of "scrimman," or to shrink. The Proto-Germanic "skrimp" is a word still in use today. In Old Norse, "skreppa" indicated a thin person. In Middle English, the term "shrimpe" means "pygmy"—all examples suggesting that, from the first time some hoary inquisitive Celt pondered the lowly, inelegant crustacean, the nature of shrimp was metaphorical, linked with being diminutive, but not, necessarily, insignificant. (Hence the oxymoron, "jumbo shrimp.")

Scholars of Latin point out that the Romans, more prosaic and less metaphorical, called shrimp "squilla" and enjoyed a variety of recipes featuring the mud-burrowing mantis. Evidence of shrimp being considered edible occurs throughout history, found on menus around the world, dating back several thousand years. According to *The Encyclopedia of Healing Foods*, Marco Polo recorded shrimp in his Asian travelogue. Reports indicate that the Chinese harvested shrimp as far back as the 7th century, 600 years before the intrepid Italian happened upon his first tiger prawn. Shrimp still hold symbolic meaning in Chinese, especially during the Chinese New Year celebration, when consuming shrimp brings happiness and good fortune. Jack and Anne Rudloe, in their *Shrimp: The Endless Quest for Pink Gold*, note that third century Greeks ate them fried in fig leaves, and that in Europe, evidence of trawling for shrimp dates back to the 14th century.

In the United States, shrimp harvesting was first recorded in the Louisiana bayou regions in the 17th century, where Cajuns used fine mesh nets imported from Europe to haul in the catch.

The consensus of zoologists who keep up with this sort of thing, determining the accurate taxonomic classification of shrimp quickly becomes confusing, and some mystery still surrounds both the familiar and scientific understanding of shrimp, possibly because over 3,000 species of "true shrimp"—infraorder *Caridea*—have been identified.

To keep it simple, all shrimp of commercial interest—that is, suitable for eating—belong to the Natantia, or decapod crustaceans.

Which is neither here nor there for the folks at Mudcat Charlie's, in Darien, GA, which sits right on the edge of U.S. 17, north of Brunswick, where shrimp are just called "shrimp." Of most concern to these discriminating diners is whether the shrimp are caught locally, or taken from other, relatively nearby southern waterways, or brought in from the Gulf Coast, or from Texas, or the Florida Panhandle, or down the west coast of Florida to the Keys, or from areas along the east coast between Miami and the Chesapeake. Because selling imported shrimp from another region, or from another country, especially from somewhere "foreign," like Asia or Indonesia—notoriously voracious industrial shrimping communities—would, at least in any "respectable" Lowcountry diner along the South Eastern Seaboard, be criminal.

Such an act of treason, quipped a restaurateur in Darien, would get him hanged.

(Or, as he put it, "Hung in a hurry in a public place.")

The punishment for serving farmed shrimp, he intimated, was even more grotesque and unsuitable for print.

So it seems prudent to dismiss farmed shrimp, the grey tasteless meat obviously unpopular with "real seafood" eaters (like that local from Darien), along with freshwater shrimp, closer in taste and habitat to crawfish and usually treated by saltwater shrimpers with the same disdain reserved for farmed shrimp. Also problematic is another funky cousin of "real" shrimp: the Rock shrimp, technically a shrimp but with a hard shell. Rock shrimp tastes more like lobster; in fact, they are usually prepared like lobster, broiled and served with hot dipping butter. Rock shrimp are not as common as standard varieties or local catch on menus along the southern Atlantic Seaboard, and when they do appear, they are often featured as an in-season novelty or special, not as a staple.

The most common shrimp—fresh or frozen—found along the Ocean Highway, discounting farmed shrimp and Rock shrimp, are called Brown shrimp or White shrimp. These are not color designations but types. And where they comingle, the rule of thumb for hobbyists and private netters is: brown shrimp are caught by night, white shrimp by day. Commercially, brown are harvested early in the season; whites, later. Most Brown shrimp are harvested from the Gulf of Mexico, but as a species they are common as far north as Massachusetts. Iodine rich, they have a strong flavor—and perhaps more sex appeal, due to all that iodine.

Good advice. Becks Restaurant, River Road, Calabash, NC.

(It turns out that, apparently, the iodine flavor is actually a by-product of bromine, found in sea worms—a detail perhaps best overlooked.)

Smaller and firmer than other shrimp varieties, they are ideal for gumbos and stews. White Shrimp are larger but milder; they tend to take on the flavor of the sauce in which they are cooked, which make them ideal for sautéing. Whites are also common to the Gulf and the east coast from Florida to Long Island, and they tend to be pulled from more shallow brackish water than the deep water Browns. More desirable are Pink Shrimp, the biggest and mildest of the common varieties. Although found throughout the usual areas from the Chesapeake to the Keys, Pinks prefer sandy bottoms and coral reef sea floors, so they are most prevalent in southwestern Florida and are often known as Key West Pinks. Sweeter, larger, and more tender than Browns and Whites, they don't require sauces or spices to add flavor, making them perfect for peel-and-eat dishes and grilling. Akin to the Pinks but in a class alone are Royal Reds, deep-water shrimp that thrive in the dark depths off the Continental Shelf. Sweet, delicate, buttery, their flavor is often compared to lobster, and these chunky morsels are best grilled and eaten without sauces or spices. Royal Reds are more difficult to harvest, so are harder to find, thus more expensive.

Key West Pinks and Royal Reds, needless to say, are not the first pick by any sane chef for a fried shrimp basket. Most fried shrimp along the Coastal Highway are Browns or Whites, and often it is impossible to tell the difference once the shrimp are cooked. While most of the wild shrimp served in restaurants up and down U.S. 17 come from the Gulf, especially Texas and Louisiana, and from Thai shrimp farms, in the traditional shrimping regions, the so-called Lowcountry, connoisseurs prefer the local product.

And they can tell the difference.

But finding a steady supply of locally caught shrimp for commercial purposes is difficult, to say the least. Part of the problem is the high cost of maintaining a trawler fleet. Other reasons for the decline of the industry along the southeastern coast include what many insiders feel is unfair competition from foreign markets.

Many experts, while not dismissing the unfair competition argument, point to more institutional problems. They say the main reason most of the wild shrimp consumed in the United States comes from the Gulf States—mainly Texas and Louisiana but including the panhandle of Florida—is because the infrastructure in those states is designed to support the quantity of the harvest, keeping processing and transportation costs competitive. The majority of commercial shrimping interests off U.S. 17 lack the savvy business sense to survive in such a cutthroat market. The disparate shrimping fleets scattered along the southern Atlantic coast, from Amelia Island, FL, to Engelhard, NC, are not integrated. Their business models are not coordinated. Many trawler fleets are small, family owned outfits. Others are strictly individual operations. Shrimpers along the Georgia coast and the Carolinas tend to supply local restaurants or individuals by selling their catch to small outlets and distributors or, if licensed, right off the back of the boat.

While acknowledging a lack of coordination and infrastructure for the absence of a viable shrimping industry on the southeastern Atlantic, many shrimpers attribute the decline of the industry—at least, the inability of the industry to become a profitable endeavor for seaside entrepreneurs—to the extreme individualism baked into the profession. The problem is the solitary nature of shrimping itself. Shrimpers along the U.S. 17 corridor through the Lowcountry and Carolinas prefer to go it alone, tending to their business as they see fit rather than joining any type of syndicate or combine that might restrict their freedom. No matter how tough the work or how difficult it is to actually make a living at their craft, shrimpers love their freedom. For many, the trawler is home; ashore, they're just visiting. There's just something inherently romantic in the shrimp culture.

In any case, finding local shrimp on the menu of even the most authentic seafood restaurants along The Coastal Highway is becoming rarer every day.

This state of affairs creates another paradox: The more rare the product, the more expensive. The more expensive, the less available. The less available, the more desirable. And if desire is a potent motivator, the desire for locally caught wild shrimp along Highway U.S. 17 is intense. And no longer taken for granted. The appeal is not just fashionable, part of the farm-to-table fad, or the slow cooking trend. And it's not rooted solely in the belief that unadulterated homegrown food is healthier than processed, farm grown shrimp. The bias is not necessarily regional; diners that prefer wild shrimp to farmed shrimp will not necessarily dismiss shrimp caught between Texas and Mexico and processed out of the area as "foreign." Nor is there a movement that rejects, out-of-hand, shrimp sold at supermarkets already shelled, de-veined, and frozen as a commodity pre-packaged into a five pound clear plastic bag.

A treasure trove of fresh South Carolina shrimp, right off the boat. Independent Seafood, Georgetown, SC.

For a connoisseur, it's all about taste, texture and the aesthetics of the experience.

"Right off the boat" represents an art, a signal living experience.

But not everyone is so enthusiastic. Lots of people in "the industry"—whether harvesting shrimp, cooking them or serving them—simply do not like to eat them.

Compared to lobster and other arthropods like crabs and barnacles, shrimp may actually be the authentic "sea roach." Still … the myth of a lobster being the cockroach of the sea persists deep in the murky collective cultural imagination—commonly referred to as urban legend. The origin of this defamation stems from the lobster's early status as food fit only for the underclass, including servants, the indigent and pets. Historically, eating lobster was a sign of poverty.

Lobsters and cockroaches do share taxonomic traits, like sporting a hard outer shell, a soft inside, laying eggs, navigating their surroundings by using antenna and scurrying when exposed, the visible likenesses between a cockroach and a lobster is a stretch. But a lobster simply doesn't resemble a roach.

Shrimp, on the other hand, look and behave a lot like their land-inhabiting cousins. Similar in size—the southern so-called Palmetto bug cockroach is often larger, and can fly—shrimp too have exoskeletons, segmented bodies, are hard on the outside, soft on the inside, dine on filth, lay eggs and hide among debris. They have crusty bodies, spindly legs and strands of antennae. They hide from light. They burrow in sediment to avoid enemies. For the undiscerning, these similarities mask the technical differences. Both are *Arthropoda*, but shrimp belong to *Crustacea*; cockroaches to *Hexapoda*. Their relationship is so close that many scientists believe that around 400 million years ago, shrimp stayed in the water while cockroaches migrated to land.

If this linkage is true, they are the same creature: one terrestrial, the other marine.

Of course, one final distinction separates the two utterly and finally: a shrimp has a unique flavor, simultaneously sweet and salty, with a firm whitefish aftertaste, whereas a toasted Madagascar Hissing Cockroach tastes, from what I've been told, vaguely like boiled chicken.

At some point, the reputation of shrimp was elevated by another widely circulated urban legend—accepted by most as gospel truth along The Coastal Highway: eating shrimp acts as a powerful aphrodisiac. A thoroughly plausible assumption, and not without scientific plausibility.

Turns out, these potent crustaceans are rich in iodine, a necessary component of proper metabolism and the production of thyroid hormones. That's code for kicking up the sex drive in the human body. One bumper sticker emerged that read: Eat Fish, Live Longer. Eat Shrimp, Love longer.

Retirees along the U.S. 17 corridor might be onto something, as the once desolate Lowcountry remakes itself into a retirement destination.

And if everyone agrees that the fresher the product, the more potent the ingredients, then local, wild shrimp found along the Coastal Highway provide a remarkably tasty natural source of natural Viagra.

But before World War II, while much of the world dined on crustaceans as delicacies, most Americans wanted shrimp only for bait. The problem was that most shrimp caught in warm southern waters had to be consumed basically on the spot or the catch would spoil. Canning solved the problem of shipping, but the processing was expensive, and canned shrimp did not retain the flavor normally associated with a fresh wild catch.

Two events changed this trend. The ability of seafood companies to quick freeze shrimp preserved the freshness, so the catch could be shipped out of the area, increasing the yield and profit. Some World War II veterans living along The Coastal Highway recall how, about the same time as Individual Quick Frozen (IQF) shrimp was initiated, the U.S. government began to provide fuel for fishing fleets along the East Coast to act as spotter patrols on the lookout for German combat vessels. This government subsidy not only encouraged trawling on a larger scale, but it also created a market for the abundant seafood harvested during the "patrols," including the new catch: shrimp. The palates of soldiers returning from far-flung regions of the world, where shrimp dishes were prevalent, became more adventurous. The south became a vacation destination, its seafood celebrated. Word spread. The industry responded. Innovators like Mr. Birdseye perfected frozen dinners. The rest is history.

In fact, shrimp are now the most-consumed seafood in the United States.

Still, some people find shrimp icky.

People familiar with Leviticus 11:12 know: if it lives in the sea but doesn't have fins, don't eat it. Of course, in our contemporary world, many Biblical prohibitions go unheeded. So ancient Hebrew customs do not explain people's aversion to shrimp. Like most phobias, the fear of shrimp is irrational. Then again …

Shrimp are weird. Their huge eyes bulge prominently but seem blind. Their tiny spastic legs look ill equipped for either swimming or crawling.

They are not cute, do not make good pets, and are very seldom seen in the wild. There are no "Swim with the Shrimp" resorts.

In fact, a shrimp is a very sophisticated biological phenomenon. Those alien bug-eyes have panoramic vision. Those ridiculous legs allow it to perch arrogantly on ledges. It has a beak for defense, eats with its hands—rather, its forward claws, the first two legs fetching food to its jaws. A shrimp grooms itself, broods eggs, and enjoys a healthy sex life. Its segmented body allows it to swim rapidly, propelling itself backwards through the water, utilizing the spooning action of its tail, a move called "lobstering." Basically, a shrimp lives a delicate life of high intensity sensory experiences.

Another reason people don't cotton to shrimp is that there are simply so many of them. It's hard to consider them individually. We don't consider them as having a unique singular life—except maybe as a garnish on a Bloody Mary, sharing a spear with an olive and a pickled onion, or when you order a fancy shrimp cocktail and you get, like, three for twenty dollars. You can order a Pompano whole. Red Snapper. Flounder. Blue crab. Soft shell crab. Lobster. These and similar samples are seafood ordered as a unit. You usually do not order a single shrimp. Shrimp come in bunches, in bulk, either scattered on a bed of ice in a fish market, or breaded and fried and tossed into a basket on top of French fries with a side of cole slaw, or arrayed on a grill, or boiled in a pot. Shrimp are anonymous, indistinguishable creatures.

Enjoying shrimp involves an obvious two-step process: catching them and cooking them.

Throughout history, and pre-history, for that matter, shrimp have been trapped, usually netted. But this rather primitive method of procurement was dramatically changed at the turn of the 19th century, concurrent with industrialization and the ability of shrimpers to wholesale the catch beyond their local ports. One legend propagated in Amelia Island (and generally accepted by the locals) is that a fisherman from Gloucester, MA (one Billy Corkum,), visiting the area in search of bluefish, invented the otter trawl net, replacing the cumbersome seine nets dragged between boats or along shore by people or tractors, and has been used by trawlers ever since.

The otter trawl consists of an open-jawed style device that drags the bottom of the seabed and a tickler mechanism to stir the shrimp from the sand in front of the net. The disturbed shrimp swim up from the sand and into the net. While the otter trawl increases the haul, the method also increases the destruction of various other fish and aquatic creatures. These days otter trawl nets are required to employee turtle excluder devices (TEDs), but other non-target species are invariably caught up in the net as by-catch, especially vulnerable finfish, and not much survives the trawl. This nifty invention, with all its pros and cons, along with more efficient diesel powered boats, mechanized haulers, offshore harvesting, huge processing plants and canneries, ushered in the modern shrimp industry, and has facilitated a domestic yield of hundreds of millions of pounds of shrimp a year.

While the otter trawl improved the ability to catch more shrimp, and turn a local industry into a multi-national, billion-pound mega-business, the efficiency of harvesting and the concomitant demand for shrimp has led, inevitably, to over-fishing. This over-fishing has led in turn to restrictions to help replenish stocks, which might be good news for conservationists (and shrimp lovers) along the southeastern stretch of U.S. 17, but this situation also has created a classic paradox. Overfishing drives the market price down, the shrimpers begin to lose money, and so they drop out of the industry, which leads to less fishing, allowing the population to rejuvenate but creating a lag in the ability to harvest the replenished stock.

In this shifting environment, between cycles of depletion and replenishment, several factors make it difficult to sustain the industry: the scarcity of the catch, a dearth of processing plants, a lack of coordination among the various fleets and lone wolf operators—all this, combined with the general expenses associated with operating a commercially viable seafood processing and delivery business, keep local shrimp rare, and therefore expensive.

Seldom do the prices of locally caught shrimp keep a fleet owner, much less a small trawling company, flush with cash.

The majority of trawlers hauling shrimp from the areas off 17 are individually owned. Threatened by imports, by farm-raised competition, by organized corporate industrialized fleets operated by huge Texas and Louisiana shrimp conglomerates, the local Coastal Highway shrimping industry remains at risk. Chefs that buy in bulk prefer to purchase shrimp already peeled and deveined, and they also prefer loads of shrimp that are relatively uniform in size—a rare processing capacity along the southeastern coast. Most shrimp in markets along route U.S. 17 are sold with the shells on. Peeling and deveining shrimp by hand is labor intensive. Add these drawbacks into the high cost of operating a shrimp trawler, and the outlook for sustaining local fleets looks bleak.

Medium-sized trawler, Engelhard, NC.

No doubt, the days of conglomerates staging fleets of trawlers along the southeastern seaboard are long gone.

But trawlers come in all shapes and sizes, from the day-fishing skiff with an outboard motor, wooden spar and hand-winched drag net to the modern steel-hulled mechanized hauler with 10,000 horsepower diesels and the capacity to stay at sea for weeks. A typical shrimp trawler prowling the southeastern seaboard adjacent to U.S. 17 is small to medium craft. The usual ship is a 60–80 foot-long vessel with a high prow, a forward pilothouse, and a low open deck to the rear. On each side hang nets attached to trawl arms that are lowered into position for dragging. An 80-foot shrimper, just for example, holds 7,000 gallons of fuel, 200 gallons of oil, 1,200 gallons of water, and fully loaded before its catch weighs 112 tons. A normal season starts in May, usually off the coast of South Carolina or north Georgia, where the shrimp begin to run in warmer water. When the water heats up, near the end of June, the North Carolina shrimpers leave Georgia and the north Florida zones and migrate back to their base in the local waters around Pamlico Sound. During a decent season, from May until October, a trawler in the 80-foot range can haul in approximately $150,000 worth of shrimp. Once the owner pays the crew—usually two men, clearing around $25,000 each—and pays for fuel—easily $50,000 for the season, based on 2016 price-per-gallon—and figuring in another $30,000 for maintenance, repairs and expenses, especially given the regulations, hassle, time away from friends and family and the raw conditions of life offshore, there's not a lot of profit in the game.

Still, these types of trawlers continue to provide most of the shrimp on the market, and offering wild caught local shrimp is a major selling point for many select popular restaurants. But where trawlers cannot supply the demand, many locals inhabiting the wetlands surrounding U.S. 17, tuned to the same wavelength as those determined to eat shrimp procured as close to their wild natural state as possible, prefer to catch their own.

But just as eating shrimp in its natural state—that is raw—is ultimately tricky, given the presence of bacterial and parasitic elements in the healthiest shrimp, and opting for ceviche style equally iffy (because no matter what "they" say, marinades do not kill those microscopic worms, which leaves drying, boiling, and grilling for the "purist")—the desire to "catch 'em yourself" is also fraught with peril. Setting nets in shallow water is a slog. You're prey to the elements. Lightning. Vicious thunderstorms. You're mingling with snakes, alligators, swarms of biting flies. You could slip in a trout hole and drown. Your boat might sink. But of all the hazards, the most dangerous are other shrimpers. Your neighbors. Dealing with Second Amendment remedies.

Nets are ripe for poachers, territorial disputes are common, and even non-commercial ventures spark intense competition and anger over trespassing.

But for many eco-minded citizens, besotted with a predisposition for self-sourcing, hell-bent on "living off-the-land," there is no substitute for harvesting their own shrimp. For some, it's economical. For others, it's philosophical. In both cases, it's a lifestyle choice. For gardening purists, buying vegetables at the grocery store, for instance, might constitute a sin, selling-out to Big-Agra, sucking up to the multi-nationals, serving food tainted not just with chemicals but also with the stench of profit margins, migrant labor, a lack of biodiversity, supporting faceless corporations that make a travesty of sustainable land management. Alas, it has come to pass that, among the pious determined to raise their own chickens, till backyard tomatoes, and tend communal collards, there are those just as determined to catch their own fish. And shrimp. For some, private harvesting is simply recreational, a fun outing with friends and family. Still others find the idea of staying up till wee hours of the morning, often between downpours, fighting clouds of mosquitoes, hostile reptiles, and hoards of aggressive fellow shrimpers, straining their backs hauling seine nets for a few pounds of shrimp, well, nostalgic.

One aficionado recalls living on the St. John's River south of Jacksonville in the early 1960s, just off a dirt road leading to Highway 17.

"My step father built a long dock on the river that went out 1,100 feet with a platform at the end. The river is three miles wide at that point. There is a sand bank that the dock went past, to be in position for shrimping. Once the shrimp started running, we would be out there every night to bait and net shrimp. My job was to pop the heads."

She muses and let's the memory settle, then concludes, with affection.

"We ate a lot of fried shrimp...."

In the briny rivers and marshland along U.S. 17, shrimp tend to "run" after a rainstorm, from the less salty inland water toward the saltier water near inlets to the ocean. Along with running for salt, shrimp also move offshore to spawn. Given the acres of wetlands and creeks surrounding the highway, lots of U.S. 17 locals have turned what might have once been a recreational pastime into a commercial venture. Savvy netters flock to a bridge or the end of a pier, and, illuminating the dark channel with a lantern, tease the shrimp up to net them as they cruise past.

It's not unusual for casual shrimpers to net a hundred pounds in a few hours. An industrious creek drag-netter, with a small boat and hand-cranked winch, could haul in better than 500 pounds a night.

One popular form of netting shrimp, illegal in some areas, involves hanging a lantern or some type of light over the side of a pier or bridge at night, and then using a long handled mesh net to dip for the shrimp as they swim up toward the light. Most bulk netters, however, use casting methods: a daytime cast net with sinkers that drop to the bottom of the deep-water harvest area, usually around 20 to 30 feet deep, yielding dozens of shrimp pulled right out of the sandy bed; or, for nighttime casting, shrimpers employ a shallow water net—effective in water depths of five feet or less—designed to nab the shrimp as they migrate from deep to shallow water, often aided by a light source and shrimp meal to draw them in.

Variations of these methods allow hardcore private netters to go for bulk. All they need to turn a pastime into an enterprise is a skiff, two nets from 40 to 60 feet in length, and a few traps made from mesh with a funnel opening. Having found a suitable site, the shrimper strings the nets, bobbing with floats, from the opposing shorelines to an anchored pylon on either side of the boat. He sets a few of the meshed rectangular traps at the end of the each net, and waits for dark. The shrimp, unable to pass through the netted water, swim along toward the edges of the net and right into the trap. The mesh wire allows the shrimp to stay alive until they are collected. They are immediately dumped into ice water, which kills them instantly, guaranteeing freshness.

For some netters, those blessed with a strong back, as well as others spindly as a willowy marsh reed but driven by an appreciation for the taste of a wild southeastern Georgia whites, going for shrimp with set nets is merely nostalgic. It's recreational, a back-to-nature hobby, with a heady gastronomical payoff. Other virtuous pilgrims are driven to mucking around in soft bog soil, reeking effluvium and coated in pluff mud, as a matter of necessity: they need the money, and the extra income earned off market prices for local shrimp can boost the income of any enterprising monger. Most enthusiasts, however, unwilling to settle for a plastic package of frozen imported farmed shrimp flush with the flavor of stale gum, tend to scrap the netting ritual altogether and simply buy fresh stock straight off the docks where the trawlers come in. And if netting is impractical, and visiting a remote dock at the end of blotchy, muddy, half-forgotten road outside the derelict end of a cove-side hamlet does not fit the evening's social agenda, pulling off the highway at a roadside vendor, if you happen to find one, and purchasing a bag of heads-on creek shrimp is another perfectly acceptable, if hygienically dicey, option.

Romance is well and good, and netting shrimp can be fun for some, but buying fresh off the boat, or from the old man with the cooler full of ice who beat you to the trawler, is probably a safer, and saner, alternative to self-harvesting.

In any case, once you have netted your prey, or scored a few pounds off the docks, or copped a baggie full of bliss from the crossroads shrimp stand, or, let's face it, like most of us, simply dropped by your favorite seafood store, you're ready to cook. Grill 'em. Boil 'em. Chop 'em into a salad. Suit yourself.

But for the cosmic confluence of flavor, texture, essence and pure transcendent gastronomic joy: deep-fry 'em.

Compared to the trouble of actually netting shrimp, cooking is the easy part. It's hard to mess up a shrimp dish. There's no accounting for taste, but when it comes to shrimp, as my father used to say, "You can't overcook 'em." People might disagree with that sentiment, but one thing about eating shrimp is true: less is more. The beautiful thing about cooking shrimp is that, basically, only the tools at hand and imagination limit preparation. At the primitive end, if you don't want them raw, all you need is a fire. At the other end of the spectrum, you can spend all morning meticulously concocting a fancy French shrimp soufflé. Boiling, grilling and a light sautéing seem to preserve the magic. But boiling tends to dull the nuanced character, and spicy dishes overwhelm the subtle flavor. Grilling is perhaps the one method that preserves the natural taste of a shrimp. Frying is genius.

Simplicity, however, isn't always considered a virtue. A quick browse through the cooking section of any of the trendy bookstores situated along the revitalized waterfront zones in the refurbished town centers off 17 offers evidence of what can be done to an unassuming shrimp beyond the basic campfire techniques. Specialized regional cookbooks offering "secret" or "family" recipes for shrimp are as plentiful along the southeastern seaboard as seagulls and dogfish. It seems that shrimp dishes, whether as hors d'oeuvres or entrées, have been a staple of cookbooks since their inception.

The 1965, 11th edition of *Fanny Farmer*, considered by many as the Bible of American cooking, first published in 1896, list shrimp recipes under "shellfish," lumped in with crab, lobster, oysters and other common crustaceans, which seems counter-intuitive but is not unusual in most cookbooks. Shellfish is a catchall term for mollusks, crustaceans, insects, squid, octopi, but most people separate, say, clams and oysters from calamari, shrimp from crabs, and snails from spiders. In any case, this venerable old standby sticks to the basics that rely on the strong rich flavor of unadulterated shrimp: boiling, deep-frying, sautéing.

But even *Fanny Farmer* can't help inventing ways to ruin the natural essence of shrimp, including such blasphemous spicy or creamy renditions that call for "canned shrimp," like Shrimp Newburg, Shrimp Louisiana, Jambalaya, and some strange concoctions like Shrimp Wiggle and Shrimp Mull, and the ungodly Shrimp Polonaise.

The more modern 1975 edition of *Joy of Cooking*, first published in 1931, lump shrimp with shellfish too, but differentiate—and prefer—"southern shrimp," called "crevette," from other varieties, and suggest butterflying them before cooking. Besides boiling and frying, other preparations include terrines served like shrimp Jello called "potted" or "molded," along with other standard styles like teriyaki, Newburg, casseroles and marinates.

A more contemporary book, offered by that WASP maven of cooking-as-lifestyle-statement, Martha Stewart, does not even mention deep-frying. She prefers sautéing and grilling, though she does manage to complicate a boiling recipe, and of course stresses that cliché du jour: shrimp and grits.

Exemplifying the eclectic array of shrimp cooking styles, Thomas Mario's *The Playboy Gourmet* offers recipes from that esteemed publication between 1954–1972. Mario provides the standard fare of marinated and fritter-fried entrees, but jazzes up the menu with soufflés, curries, chili and varieties of tempura—that fancy term for Japanese batter frying.

While the difficulty of harvesting wild Atlantic shrimp makes the catch a delicacy, the popularity of shrimp is indisputable, and the myriad recipes for preparing them tend to belie the disparity between the wild and farmed varieties. Simply put, the fancier the recipe, the less important the quality of the shrimp. Inversely, the more basic the preparation, the more the flavor of the shrimp is highlighted, underscoring the need for wild flavorful local catch. There also seems to be a correlation between the older, simpler approach to cooking shrimp, which relied on an abundance of a local supply, and the more contemporary, elaborate dishes, that don't seem to stress the source, and therefore the strong flavor of the product.

All the cookbooks present various styles of shrimp salads, dips, puffs, chowders ... shrimp can be pickled, skewered, broiled, baked, sliced, diced, or served raw rolled in rice and seaweed: The talent for spoiling the sweet, slightly salty, mystical flavor of shrimp is limited only by the ingenuity of the chef, dilettante or pro.

But anybody can light a fire or boil water. In the south, especially off 17, the culinary art of cooking shrimp is best expressed by deep-frying.

And the best method of frying shrimp involves a bit of magic, starting with a fresh, locally harvested catch, and then combining a coating, ranging from a light tempura coating to a thick cornmeal crust, concoctions designed to celebrate the adventurous varieties of fritter batter.

Fried shrimp are not, of course, unique to the maritime zones associated with the Coastal Highway. The ancient Egyptians developed deep-frying in the fifth century BCE. The early Greeks and Romans and other southern European cultures fried food in hot olive oil. Medieval traders brought the art of frying to Japan.

Turns out, French fries are literally as old as Methuselah.

If not fries, then certainly falafel.

But most experts on cooking history regard deep frying shrimp as a fairly modern phenomenon. Early shrimp recipes called for sun drying the catch. Later, more sophisticated recipes involved boiling, sautéing, grilling, stewing or baking shrimp into casseroles, gumbos or seafood pies. But the explosion in the shrimp industry in modern times is directly linked to the demand for fried shrimp. Deep frying breaded shrimp, and then flash-freezing them, allowed shrimp to be packaged and shipped globally with ease, making pre-cooked fried shrimp dinners available, affordable, plentiful and trendy—and especially appealing after World War II, when convenience became a virtue, and the fast-food market was geared toward a go-go lifestyle matched to a restless country on the move.

Too many casual consumers of fried shrimp are familiar with a nondescript batter encasing like a shell a chewy nugget of mushy white meat. That kind of preparation should be a crime, but when you are dealing with the kind of tasteless frozen farmed shrimp used by most chain outlets and fast food eateries, the batter at least gives the flaccid morsel some character.

In those parts of the coastal south that have resisted gentrification, fried shrimp are prepared with various modifications of a basic fritter batter composed of flour, baking soda, eggs, water—or beer—but also breadcrumbs or cornmeal, creating a thick coat that clings to the shrimp rather than merely encasing it. Southern fried shrimp batter is usually thicker, designed to complement shrimp that are deep-fried, not sautéed. Fritter batter should not be confused with tempura, the Japanese version, although most recipes imply that tempura is distinctively "lighter" or "thinner," more a coating than a jacket, mainly because the ingredients in true tempura, without much variation, consists of water, flour, eggs, and baking soda. No heavy meal, spices or beer.

Tempura may be an ancient style of cooking in Japanese culture, but it is considered relatively new to the American palate and carries a whiff of frou-frou trendiness with it. For instance, *Joy of Cooking* confirms that, although tempura and batter are synonymous, tempura is the lighter of the two, based on the water-based ingredients. In *The Martha Stewart Cookbook*, Stewart stresses the virtues of tempura over heavier batters, and suggests a theme party based on a tempura mix set out on an island-style kitchen counter arrayed with a deep fryer and assorted seafood and vegetables. For dramatic effect (in her eyes), guests should choose, and cook to taste, their own entrées.

The *Playboy* cookbook editor Mario concurs with Stewart, but he intensifies the party drama by suggesting the various dishes (including shrimp) be served by a geisha. One is safe to conclude that, in many of

Shrimp shoppers, Independent Seafood, Georgetown, SC.

the hard-core fried shrimp eateries along the Lowcountry strip of U.S. 17, describing battered shrimp as a "tempura" dish is not the cleverest idea, if such an entrée appears on the menu at all.

Privileging fried shrimp over other methods of preparation is evidence of a cultural and gastronomic bias, true. Many enthusiasts argue that the closer to the "natural" state of seafood—including shrimp—the better. Better flavor. Better nutrition. Better respect for the fruits of the sea.

In the case of fish, the raw catch is usually dried or smoked. Shrimp, in their early manifestation as eatable treats, were sun-dried too. But at some point the purists evolved, elevating tartare-style dishes like ceviche and sashimi into a spiritual experience, underscoring the phrase, "You are what you eat," ignoring the idea that many people following this logic would become parasites.

The original Cult of the Raw embraced the sushi trend, and legitimized eating all kinds of seafood raw, with rice. Anyone who even merely dabbles in culinary arts has encountered the Cult of the Raw. Perhaps the most famous and stringent example of raw devotion occurs at the altar of the oyster, creating a hierarchy of appreciation rivaled only by pretentious wine connoisseurs. Dismissing those who lack the *savoir faire* necessary for a religious palate, the Initiates of Raw, and the oyster bars they frequent, pride themselves on naming points of origin, types, sizes, depuration arcana and behavioral patterns of the sacred bivalves.

Okay. Eating raw seafood may be a healthy alternative to consuming over-processed food. It is definitely trendy. It may also be a spiritual complement to yoga and mysticism.

But raw shrimp? Not a good idea. Not even in sushi, although of course you can ... but even in ceviche, where the citrus marinade is designed to denature the ingredients, the shrimp (and other samples) are usually boiled. Peel-and-eat shrimp is another method preferred by purists, boiling a batch in water or beer, heads on to preserve the juices and flavor, then peeling them and munching away ... this style of cooking does capture the essence of the flesh, as does grilling, which perhaps offers even a better opportunity to seal in flavor, as boiling can be intense.

These methods, however, can dry out the shrimp. Less adventurous, and a step in preparation further away from the purity of taking that raw bite of unalloyed shrimp—not recommended by the health department or any responsible chef—is the option of broiling. In this method, the shrimp is usually part of a mixed seafood platter tossed in along with flounder and scallops or similar combinations.

But let's face it. Given all the styles—sushi, nigiri, ceviche, sun-dried, grilled, boiled, broiled, or roasted over a campfire on a sharpened stick—there is a reason why the Egyptians, 7,000 years ago, and the 5th century BCE Greeks, and the ancient Romans, and even the British with their shrimp and chip baskets, their cups of prawns on Whitby Pier, North Riding, Yorkshire, and the popularity of Mrs. Paul's prepackaged plates, Captain D's chew toy popcorn style, Red Lobster's pretentious abominations ... all through history, across the Seven Seas and the vast oceans of commerce, everyone knows that deep fried battered shrimp is the true path to culinary nirvana.

≈3≈

Fernandina Beach to Savannah

The coastal landscape north of Jacksonville gradually shifts from the hard sandy surf-pounded shores of typical central east coast Florida beaches to a more shallow water system of estuaries, especially just north of Fernandina. Estuaries are unique because they offer a protected waterway blend of fresh and salt water, creating a briny ecosystem perfectly suited to provide developing young aquatic species with food and protection until they reach maturity. Estuaries are considered the "cradle of the ocean," as most shellfish, fish and crustaceans thrive on the rich combination of sunlight, carbon monoxide, microbes of phytoplankton and other plant nutrients until, in the case of shrimp, they migrate offshore to spawn and begin their life cycle anew.

Coincidentally, the estuaries lining the northeastern sector of Florida above the St. Johns River Basin begin just as U.S. 17 hits the coast after masquerading as a land-locked trans-state runway traversing the maze of cow pastures, divots of lakes and turnip fields spanning central Florida from Punta Gorda to the edge of suburban Jacksonville. Nearly lost and quite unrecognizable, the Ocean Highway perseveres as it morphs through a tangle of intersections and mergers and alternate routes, from when it kisses the lower St. Johns at Green Cove Springs, to where it cuts into downtown Jacksonville, crossing the river as the Main Street Bridge before exiting the urban core on the north side. Immediately after passing the Trout River, U.S. 17 finally assumes its historical function as a major artery into prime Shrimp Country, an identity it will retain for the next 600 miles.

To initiate the actual coastal experience of the Ocean Highway between Jacksonville and Savannah, one approach would be to divide the route into two segments: before Brunswick and after Brunswick, as that oddly listless city serves as the nexus around which the major commercial shrimping industry in southern Georgia operates.

The "before" segment begins as U.S. 17 leaves Jacksonville, offering a detour on the south side of the St. John's River leading out to Mayport, a former fishing village not exactly appropriated by the military but surrounded and overshadowed by it, existing alongside the Naval Station Mayport. On the north side of the river, an eastern exit onto FL 105 meanders along as Heckscher Drive, eventually merging with FL A1A at the point where a ferry connects the northern and southern sections bifurcated here by the St. John's. FL A1A continues along the coast—much of it unspoiled, some pristine—winding through several state parks until finally arriving on Amelia Island, one branch following the beachfront to its termination in Fernandina Beach and another rejoining U.S. 17 at Yulee.

Across the river from Heckscher Drive, what's left of the village of Mayport, dwarfed by the sprawling naval base, squats like a miniature gnome in the garden of a gray ghostly behemoth. Mayport once rivaled Fernandina as the shrimp capital of northeastern Florida, but since the base was established, along with the Jacksonville Port Authority, the real estate has become less desirable, property values have plummeted, and many of the fleet of shrimpers that once called Mayport home have moved to other ports, even though the local economy of the village remains anchored in the seafood industry. The shrimp boats still operating out of Mayport moor along the docks behind Singleton's Restaurant and, further upriver, behind the Safe Harbor Seafood Market. Most of the trawlers are 100 footers; they cost around two to three million dollars apiece to build, burn diesel fuel by the tanker-load, and hold well over 100,000 pounds of shrimp. On ice.

There's not much to recommend the town, squeezed as it is between the busy waterfront and the military installation. The original settlement is older than St. Augustine, serving as a base during the 17th century for the French to launch raids against their Catholic rivals, the Spanish. As Jacksonville began to develop into a major city, Mayport became the natural beach town for the urban set to visit for fishing and partying.

Today, the action has moved across the river, to Heckscher Drive, with its upscale houses and easy access to both Jacksonville and points north, especially Amelia Island and the recreational parks along A1A north of the St. John's River. Along the way, before it becomes A1A, Heckscher Drive presents a mash-up of restaurants, fish camps, assorted RV parks, marinas and commercial docks, scattered in among luxurious riverside homes with pools and deep water docks ... but most importantly, Heckscher

Drive offers a selection of prime seafood outlets assuring customers off 17 access to certified local wild "Mayport Shrimp."

Of course, what "Mayport Shrimp" means is slippery. Basically, Mayport Shrimp are caught somewhere in the ocean waters from St. Augustine to Brunswick by boats that maintain a homeport near Mayport. If you visualize the coast as seen from offshore looking back toward land—a shrimper's perspective—the topology of the shrimping network seems more fluid, literally, less fixed, less specific. On terra firma, coastal towns and port locations are established by the landlocked logic of city limits and state lines, highways and incursive overland shipping routes. Accessing harbors by road is different from sailing into them off the open Atlantic. A trawler plying the waters around Jacksonville shares the same territory as a boat off Savannah. The waters are the same, and ports of delivery all along the coast much easier to access. Shrimpers unload at different docks for different reasons, some personal, some professional, but driving between Mayport and McClellanville is a different experience from arriving by boat.

The landscape of U.S. 17 looks entirely different from sea.

So, to claim a shrimp using land-logic ignores the vast impersonal expanse of the hunting zone along the southeastern coast, in an ocean that transcends "localism" and arbitrary lines of identity and ownership.

The point is, Mayport Shrimp are not imported and not farmed. They are wild, caught by men who live and work in the immediate vicinity.

One wholesaler, a legend on Heckscher Drive, is Miss Marilyn Louise, aka The Shrimp Lady.

In the lot of her riverside market, one early fall afternoon, it's ninety degrees Fahrenheit, with ninety-five percent humidity, and not a cloud in the sky. A light but steady wind ripples the steel blue water in the inlet under a relentless sun. Across the way, the cranes of the port of Jacksonville jab into the washed out blue sky; to the west, the 175 foot high Dames Point Bridge, a part of the I-295 bypass around Jacksonville, frames the distant downtown skyscrapers; and to the east, a short drive down Heckscher, toward the A1A Mayport Ferry, the profiles of naval warships seem like cutouts looming over the beach landscape.

The Shrimp Lady sells fresh frozen local shrimp from her shop, a modified, cut-down mobile home type shed set in a dirt lot surrounded by a wire mesh fence sparsely festooned with red, white and blue pennants. In back, a pier runs out to one of several ocean-going trawlers she owns that are part of a family business she inherited from her father and which she has been involved with all her life. She captained a trawler for twenty years, even while pregnant. Her children worked the boats, and her sons now operate their own trawlers. Shrimping defines her life.

The gentleman manning The Shrimp Lady's shop this morning wears Khakis held up by suspenders over a greasy white t-shirt, a pair of split-pea green Crocs and a beaked cap with "God's Army" emblazoned on the front. His skin looks like it's been sprayed a permanently glowing, nuclear tomato red, and it glistens with perspiration like a portable cooler defrosting in the heat of the room. He sports a perpetual look of vacancy that somehow seems feigned, unassuming but crafty. His face radiates in the dim light.

A few customers drop in to buy fresh frozen "Mayport Shrimp," heads on, 16 count to a pound. Cash.

"We love cash," the monger says. He speaks in a calm, measured cadence, expressing a deep, existential affection for local shrimp and the people who harvest them.

This part of Heckscher Drive is Trump country. The locals tend to buy into the myth of the self-reliant Marlboro Man. In this case, a solitary fisherman—maybe fashioned on the Gorton's of Gloucester frozen seafood mariner—profiled in a motorboat, tossing a throw-net with the silhouettes of naval warships as a backdrop, his government pension check safely deposited in the bank. So it didn't take long for the man at The Shrimp Lady's to blame the decline of the shrimping industry on Barack Obama and "big government."

"Trump will fix this," he says, explaining, in a colorful, cut-up narrative, that when George Bush was president, he set aside money "to help out the auto industry, but some of that money was supposed to go to us, too, 'cause we were another industry affected by the downturn in the economy"—by which he means, I assume without interjecting, the Bush-era recession—but "as soon as Obama got in," he goes on, as convinced as a lay preacher making his television debut, "he gave the money to Detroit and the banks, but he held back the funds for us … said we weren't part of the industry, so Obama spent most of those funds helping his friends, and the rest on foreign aid."

His contradictions are so rich, and so remote even from any comical sense of irony, that his inevitable rejoinder—"Trump will get us that money back"—echoes off the open freezer door. Melted ice puddles the floor.

As he slips into an easy, almost rehearsed mild diatribe against the Federal Government, particularly the Obama administration, my impulse, in order to process his perspective, is to identify with him, link to his core, to recognize a type ontologically more essential than his role as the Shrimp Lady Man. It's too easy to dismiss him as a student of life who skipped an opportunity for a formal education—you know, "book learning"—opting instead for the more immediate and in some ways more vital skills associated with living off the land as a commercial shrimper.

Clearly, this man's Wonder Bread Years were spent less on the humanistic impulse provided by a progressive syllabus at some liberal institution of higher education than on the rhythms of the natural world. His physical life, constrained by the dimensions of a trawler, the confines of a fish house, a local community a half-mile square, was informed solely by people he grew up with. The music of his spheres was tuned to the monotonous thrum of twin 800 horsepower diesels, the screech of seagulls trailing the nets, and the whistling of wind through the rigging. But then I imagine his reflective gaze turned toward the horizon, the unfathomable depth of possibilities out among the creatures of the sea, the seabirds, the vibrant abundant varietals of piscatorial visions....

I check the vision. My projections are, after all, a product of my own progressive syllabus. I am schooled in the condescending impulse to view the merely ordinary as profoundly tragic. The truth is, all complexity of the human experience aside, I know this man.

Shrimp?

"Fried.... But I do like shrimp and grits."

Impressions of U.S. 17?

You can see his mind slip back to his youth. "Highway 17," he says, effortlessly poetic, "runs through my life."

He recalls as a child driving The Ocean Highway up to visit family near St. Mary's, GA. He was fascinated back then with the highway bars and liquor stores than lined the route.

"You can still see the chimneys."

(Pronounced "chim-in-nees.")

"That's all that's left from where the revenuers burned the buildings down."

In his colorful memories, U.S. 17 was a road for "running liquor."

Even today, he notes, though he doesn't exactly live *on* the highway, referring to his home, "you couldn't get to it without it."

I revel in the moment, face-to-face with an authentic "17-er."

Seaside communities in Florida tend to romanticize A1A. That strip of coastal contradictions, a roadway fragile and overbuilt, countrified and urbanized and ultimately so diverse it defies easy classification ... except as the main conduit through the beach life of The Sunshine State.

And yet, off 17, along Hecksher Drive, the romance of A1A runs south, and the reality of The Shrimp Lady's vendor, who is not a surfer, or a beach bum, or a Speedo-clad volleyball playing, condo-dwelling, club-hopping, cabana boy, or any other stereotype associated with the leisure-class denizens of a typical stretch of Florida's "Scenic Byway"—no, he is defined by The Coastal Highway that winds its way north into the shrimp rich environment through Lowcountry Georgia.

I resist the impulse to stereotype him. After all, I recognize myself as a "17-er." I was born and raised off 17. Most of my life-shaping events occurred on or near that highway. My value system baked into my character like a heat mirage simmering off a summer blacktop. My own effervescence reflected in the steam after a summer rain misting off the road.

Still, to reduce a person to a categorical entity—jock, cheerleader, nerd—is a form of cheating, like creating a straw man in a debate. The process is reductive; it allows you to simplify the complexity, the subjective reality, of the human experience.

So, to humanize this man, I think back to the highway of my past, the U.S. 17 running metaphorically through my memory, as the actual Ocean Highway did literally through my neighborhood.

Truth is: I grew up with this guy, this "17-er." Had I not been satisfied with the narrow experience of simply living off 17, instead of following the escape route the highway provided me, and schooling myself in the life lessons travel inspires, I could have become him.

Wooten's Drive-In. Off old U.S. 17. A classic seaboard juke joint. Owner's quarters upstairs, tavern downstairs. Saloon-style bar, scattered tables, stools, jukebox, open wooden dance floor. Strictly local traffic now that the main north-south flow has been routed over to the new four-lane by-pass.

Night starts early in the late fall. The air is crisp with the promise of winter, mild as it is on the southern east coast. The parking lot is split between high school social factions. The students popular with school administrators and teachers on one side—known as "sochies"—dress in khakis, loafers, knit Lacoste shirts with the collars turned up. The kids on this side of the lot listen to beach music, occasionally cutting into a bop dance move, bantering about academic scholarships, class projects, flash cars. The gang on the other side of the lot, surfer types—the "heads"—favor jeans, faded t-shirts, chukka boots. They hang on the open doors of a Dodge van, meditatively dwelling on the intricacies of Hendrix, Cream, the Stones. When the principal passed a rule that a boy's hair could not cover his collar, they cut the collars off their shirts.

The Shrimp Lady's vendor would have straddled the two groups, trying to fit in with both, accepted by neither. At seventeen, he seems older than his years, his future fixed before he finished middle school. He works at a tire service center, a job he keeps after graduation. Keeps his girlfriend too, the one he's been with since he was a sophomore. She dated around before settling for him, but was shy, deferential, chaste. (I might have dated her.) He's not known as a ladies' man.

They are simple. "Good" in the way people are who are incapable of being "bad." He hunts, but isn't a particularly good shot. He can fish, but never catches anything remarkable. He drinks Schlitz beer, tries pot but doesn't like it. As a couple, they prefer movies to parties.

They marry. They buy a house. Just off 17. Have two children. Two cars. A fence. A dog. Their life together is tragically ordinary, although they would never recognize it as such. She hosts church events. He plays cards with his buddies, loses more than he wins. They eat fried shrimp on Friday night in a family style restaurant owned by a man who belongs to their congregation. They know the other diners by name. The waitress baby-sits their kids. They drink sweet iced tea.

They stay. They get by. They have roots. They are locals.

If you stick it out near U.S. 17, it's what you become. Part of a community proud of doing what's expected.

Place is character, choice destiny. The highway is in their blood.

They become their hometown.

In this part of the world, they are "17-ers."

The Shrimp Lady's Man jolts me back to the present. To the edge of the river. To shrimp.

"Thing is," he says, a little quieter, more serious, as if we are suddenly in conspiracy, "they won't let us shrimp the inland waters, which means the shrimp don't move, so they die off. If we could catch more shrimp, there would be more shrimp."

His logic seems surreal, but his confidence is unassailable. He's alluding to a proposal, already rejected by both state and federal officials, that would provide a marine sanctuary, mainly for whales and coral, by restricting commercial fishing from about 100 miles off the coast of Mayport to around 25 miles off Fort Pierce, a few hundred miles further down the Florida peninsula. This is the area where the bulk of "Mayport Shrimp"

Centre Street, Fernandina Beach, FL. A preserved Victorian town, Fernandina Beach features the oldest continuously serving bar in Florida, among other "oldest" buildings. Shrimp innovators in Fernandina Beach pioneered "otter trawl" outriggers, and until the mid–20th century, local boat builders were famous for their trawlers.

are harvested. Most commercial interests, including shipping, opposed the idea, and there was never any real chance it would be implemented. The Oculina Bank, a 90-mile strip of reefs that run offshore from Cape Canaveral to Fort Pierce, is already a protected area, closed to commercial shrimping, as are many areas of the water around the Florida Keys.

Though the proposal had been rejected, the idea that the Federal government might restrict access to an area rich in natural resources in order to protect those resources is anathema to the man in The Shrimp Lady's shop. But just the attempt to restrict open shrimping gives him a cause by which to define himself. In defiance. *Don't tread on me.* His militancy is reminiscent of the attitude of the Ammon Bundy gang and the standoffs they instigated with the federal government in Nevada and Oregon during several months between 2014–16, although The Shrimp Lady man cleverly couches his complaint in more naturalistic terms.

"It's a predator and prey situation," he explains. "The shrimp need something to keep 'em jittery, keep 'em moving, like when we're trawling the bottom, so there'll be more of them. Otherwise, they won't move, won't spawn, and they'll die. That's what needs to happen, just three miles off the coast. Speaking of which..."

He leans in closer, quieter. "You let the Chinese into our offshore waters, like all these trade deals want to do, and they won't abide by no rules. They'll be inside the three mile mark soon as they show up. With nets miles long. They don't care."

Somehow, he has a point. Then his narrative takes a decidedly more restrictive, nativist turn: He accuses Fernandina Beach of not only stealing the annual "blessing of the fleet" ceremony, but basically usurping the reputation Heckscher Drive has carefully nourished, as Mayport declined, as the real shrimp capital of North Florida.

"Mayport was the center before the military came in," he says. "They used to hold the event (blessing the fleet) in the USO building, but they moved it to Fernandina, where there's more tourists."

He looks wistfully out the door towards Mayport in the distance.

"They got a church in Fernandina," he says, "caters to homeless shrimpers."

Whether that church program still exits or ever did, the shrimping industry in Fernandina is definitely more of a nostalgic memory than anything resembling a reality. Fernandina Beach sits at the top end of Amelia Island, about 35 miles north of Jacksonville and 12 miles off U.S. 17. The strategic location of the town is immediately obvious, sporting the sort of landscape preferred by pirates, smugglers, and assorted frontier ne'er-do-wells. Situated along a confluence of waterways, including the St. Marys River, the Tiger River, Amelia River, Egan's Creek and the Intra-Coastal Waterway, the town has benefitted from its deep-water harbor since its establishment by French and Spanish expeditionary forces in the late 1500s. It has served as a haven for a rogue's gallery of explorers, privateers and entrepreneurs operating along the Spanish and British (later American) border. In the early 19th century, the fort provided the Spanish with their northernmost outpost intended to stop American imperialism. During its storied history, Amelia Island emerges as a mongrel state. It has been ruled not only under the flags of the major ruling empires of the time, but also under various rebel groups, including the United Provinces of New Granada and Venezuela, the Republic of Mexico and the Confederate States, eight in all, earning it, appropriately, the name "Isle of Eight Flags." Indicative of this pluralism, the town is named after King Ferdinand VII, while the island is named after Princess Amelia, King George II's daughter. The county bears the name of the Duchess of Nassau, from Germany.

Today the center of Fernandina Beach has retained its 19th century heritage, having preserved many of its antebellum brick buildings, Victorian homes, as well as the historic railroad depot anchoring the eastern terminus of the first cross-state rail line in Florida linking Fernandina to Florida's west coast at Cedar Key. The central tourist area begins at the intersection of A1A and FL 200. The main drag, Centre Street, running from A1A to the marina, is lined with typical novelty shops, a few bars and restaurants, many in restored 19th century buildings. The picturesque anchorage provides striking views of the savannahs north of the harbor and the expanse of the St. Mary's River to the east. A wooden pier forms a promenade along the edge of the boat slips from the ship's store and Waterway Café—built out over the water in the middle of the docks— to Atlantic Seafood, a red wood paneled bait and tackle shop. The town is home to the oldest bar in Florida, the oldest standing hotel in Florida, and an Old Town site listed on the U.S. National Register of Historic Places as the last Spanish city chartered in the Western Hemisphere. In its contemporary state, Fernandina offers a small-town feel with a gourmet touch, where the streets feel local even as they are swarming with tourists.

You could throw a rock (figuratively speaking) from the dock of Tiger Point Marina, located at the mouth of Egans Creek and have it splash across the Florida-Georgia state line. The point being, the Fernandina shrimping industry has more in common with the southern Georgia coast than the shoreline below the St. Johns River. The boat builders, the innovative net makers, the shrimping family dynasties have all faded into history, and although the shrimp are still there, the crusty shrimpers are not. The 20th century mystique associated with the shrimping industry in Fernandina has given way to the realities of market pressure. The Cook brothers, patriarchs of one of the original shrimping families, are gone, along with their fleet. The nets these days are made for sporting events. The custom trawlers that made the Tiliakos name famous from the Carolinas to Campeche are now an aging ghost flotilla, or scuttled. And everyone lays blame on the same scapegoat: cheap pond-raised (farmed) shrimp. Of course, the main culprit is the exorbitant costs—fuel, upkeep, salaries— of maintaining a shrimp trawling business.

But when customers are content to sacrifice quality and taste for an insipid cheaper product, harvesting local shrimp just isn't worth it.

Yet ... Fernandina clings to its reputation as the birthplace of modern shrimping, and each spring the city holds that elaborate Blessing of the Fleet ceremony to crank up the tourist industry, if not the shrimp business.

The fleet in Fernandina is clustered around docks along Front Street, just down from the public marina. The fleet is down to a handful—some sources suggest fewer than 20—a diminished, if still a productive number of trawlers supplying a few of the restaurants in the area with fresh wild shrimp. Most of the trawlers—those based in Fernandina and others from various ports-of-call along the coast—unload at Fernandina Seafood, at the opposite end of the river road from Atlantic Seafood. The facility is one of several major shrimp processing centers along the Georgia-Florida seaboard, sharing bulk shrimp deliveries with other centers from Darien to the north and Mayport to the south. These centers are major wholesalers that supply not just area restaurants but major chains and outlets that offer wild caught shrimp to its customers.

A block from Atlantic Seafood, which supplies lots of that shrimp, along with fresh fish and other fresh seafood, and just across the railroad tracks from the mooring site of the trawler fleet still operating out of Fernandina Beach, The Shrimp Museum is located in a lonely modern elevated building with a good view of the waterfront. The shop is filled with colorful brochures, photographs, whatnots and memorabilia. A video is available featuring a history of the local shrimping industry....

More informative, and livelier, is The Salty Pelican. In a town where the taste in restaurants runs from trendy fusion to fast-food take-away, from garden-to-table pretention to all-you-can-eat buffets, this establishment is a refreshing throwback to a traditional raw bar. A few years ago, a couple of enterprising buddies, T.J. Pelletier from the Ritz, and Al Waldis from the Omni Plantation, both staples of high-end Amelia Island resorts, decided to strike out on their own. They revitalized an old warehouse into their version of an old-fashioned seafood joint, and the result is classic no frills dining on the Fernandina waterfront.

The building stands alongside the railroad tracks, overlooking the harbor and marina. It's hot on the porch, with fans on high blowing the sweat into beady streaks beneath your shirt. The building shakes when the train rumbles past. The servers know where the food comes from, and like to brag that the shrimp are right off the boats moored within sight of the restaurant. Fat, firm and sweet, served with the fantails on, the shrimp are coated in a thick cornmeal and deep-fried to a nutty brown.

The meat is fresh and tasty enough to stand out even with the heavy batter. Rather than a distraction, the crust actually complements the heft of the shrimp.

The server looks healthy and happy, with a sunlit glow about her from, I assume, time outdoors enjoying nature. I ask her if she likes shrimp.

"I don't eat seafood," she tells me, matter-of-factly. "Don't like the texture. The whole idea of it."

What does she eat?

"Chicken and steak," she says.

Maybe her not liking seafood is a good thing, I suggest. So she's not tempted to munch out at work.

"I like Outback," she says, referring to the steak house restaurant chain. "I'd be big as a house if I worked there."

And U.S. 17?

"I don't use it. I live on Heckscher, so I take A1A. It's a whole lot better'n going through Yulee!"

Salty Pelican, Fernandina Beach, FL. A repurposed warehouse along the railroad tracks, the restaurant is based on the style of traditional raw bars. The building trembles when the train rolls by. The place to get authentic "Mayport Shrimp."

In her world, the idyllic isolation of Heckscher is Jacksonville. The fork-in-the-road town of Yulee, a traffic jam. U.S. 17, a road to avoid. She works and lives in one of the prime shrimping capitals of the East Coast, and she doesn't eat seafood.

I move on, searching for a shrimp eater.

Two other servers, one from North Dakota, the other from Las Vegas, prove to be as chatty as they are curious.

"Fernandina is an old folks town," the one from Las Vegas says. "You should talk to more old people."

The one from North Dakota chimes in: "They don't have boobs."

I can't fake not following this logic. I counter by asking if they like shrimp.

"I love shrimp," The one from North Dakota says. Her face is deliberately painted to look more clownish than whorish. She's having fun with it. A mask she wears to work reflecting (and deflecting) whatever character her customers need to project. She's a pro. A lifer. A professional server. Adept at slinging draft beers. Oysters on the half-shell. Baskets of fried shrimp. She cut her teeth waitressing in prairie breakfast diners.

"Sunday egg kind of places," she says. "Back there, I didn't know the difference between farmed shrimp and wild shrimp. Now..."

She winks through her make-up. I stare into her deep green eyes, sense the confidence of an initiate, a transient-local now versed in the mysterious scrumptiousness of wild Mayport shrimp.

"My eyes are blue," she says. "I'm wearing green contacts. Keeps you on your toes."

What does she think about U.S. 17?

"Renee's Redneck Yacht Club."

"I always feel out of my element there," says the girl from Las Vegas, edging into the conversation. And then adds, cryptically, "In a good way."

Her favorite shrimp?

"Fried."

Another server joins in. She's younger than the others, plump, healthy, freckles, light green eyes—"No contacts," she says. Pointedly. So the others can hear. She's from Ohio, same town, she says, as LeBron James.

"I used to serve him when I worked at Red Lobster. The shrimp does not compare."

She lives on the ocean now, and she can see the trawlers from her backyard.

"Our shrimp were swimming yesterday," she says. Her mood suddenly turns weirdly romantic. "The trawler lights are beautiful at night. Especially last week, during the Blood Moon."

She has lived in Fernandina long enough to have witnessed the shrimp industry dying. At its most productive, she claims, the town hosted 150 trawlers. Now it's down to 15.

Does she also agree Fernandina has become a town for old people?

"Yeah, but that's good for me," she says. I need to slow down."

And U.S. 17?

"It's a nice drive to Jacksonville, instead of the interstate. But for me, it's just a road."

"It'll kill you," says a another server, just coming on for her shift. A no-nonsense divorcee with hazel eyes and four kids.

"If I don't eat breakfast with 'em, I won't see 'em all day."

She moved from Valdosta to St. Mary's, GA, a small town just across the border, about 10 miles off U.S. 17, near the Kings Bay Nuclear Submarine Base. Home is a 45-minute drive. After several jobs working nine-to-five, she considers waitressing "retirement."

As for U.S. 17, she avoids it.

"The cops are bad," she explains. "But it's the deer that'll kill you."

She totaled three cars in one year hitting deer on her way home.

"Worst I got was bruises and a concussion. My friend's brother was killed. I quit driving it. I take I-95 now."

Besides the deer and cops, what does she think of U.S. 17?

"Middle of nowhere. Sticks. Nothing. Quiet."

She reflects on her comments, as if she's ashamed to be so negative. "I do like that little blue bridge."

She means the truss bridge crossing the St. Mary's River at the Florida-Georgia state line.

And shrimp?

"I don't eat a lot of fried food. I do like grilled shrimp."

She smiles. I bite into a fried Mayport beauty. Then it hits me like a blacktop bullet right between the eyes: I know her.

Not *her*, of course, but hypothetically ... these servers: They are all from somewhere else, different backgrounds, different realities. But they've turned up in place where so many do, and without denying them their individualism, their particular identities that make them unique subjective agents alone on the great spinning planet, they have become an aggregate, an effigy of truth. They have joined a sorority: Honorary "17-ers."

Once the highway gets into their blood, it's hard to shake. Moving here is easy. Moving away ...

Consider the girl from Wooten's Drive-In, off 17, circa 1966.

She slips a few coins into the jukebox and dances by herself. The Wurlitzer is loaded with Top 40 hits, country standards, a few odd nostalgic selections from the Rat Pack era. If no one plays it, the silence lasts no more than two minutes, which is the time it takes the proprietor to sidle around the side of the bar and drop a load of dimes into the machine, choosing a set of songs as eclectic as the string of husbands and lovers she has discarded during the decades she has operated the tavern.

But tonight, this girl has commandeered the jukebox. She is celebrating her claim to fame: Electric Shuffleboard champion of the bar. The table, set against the far wall, beneath the neon Pabst Blue Ribbon clock, is the most popular in town. To play, you slide a metal puck across a wooden bed sprinkled with sawdust, triggering metal tabs to score points. The girl dancing alone tonight has beaten all comers. A tomboy too young to purchase beer, she looks old enough to pass, even though everyone—including the proprietor—knows she's underage. But she's the proprietor's favorite. Tall, thin, she wears little make-up, just awkward enough to be more endearing than proficient with the complicated dance steps.

On another night, her junior year, she has a fight with her boyfriend in the parking lot. He fires up his SS 396, the twin exhausts spraying specks of oil across the freshly pressed khakis of his friends standing behind the car, and peels off into the late night darkness of Old 17. She shoots him an emphatic "bird" and stomps inside to play the shuffleboard game. Twenty minutes later, you can hear him, hear his exhaust, his V-8 wound up in low gear, coming hard. He misses the curve right in front of the bar and launches into the pine grove across the drainage ditch lining the highway.

Everyone in the bar that night attends his funeral. She moves away after graduation. Drifts into the service industry, works a string of bars along U.S. 17. Wilmington, Myrtle Beach, Georgetown, Savannah ...

She is a "17-er." She's worked the circuit from Norfolk to Jacksonville. Fishing pier restaurants. All you can eat buffets. Truck stop diners. Each beach town off 17 always the same: strange and familiar. New people, same types.

One constant beyond the human community: the smell of deep-fryer oil. Peanut, canola, sunflower, coconut palm, beef tallow, lard ... a rancid smoky kitchen odor permeates her skin, her hair. It's a smell she can't wash off. Laundering can't eradicate.

It becomes her oxidized soul. Fried seafood conjures memories of what-if nights gone in an irrecoverable past. Up the coast, down the coast: She's measured out her life in fried seafood platters, draft beers in plastic cups. Cole slaw, French fries, hushpuppies.

A shuffleboard champ.

Now in Fernandina.

She'll always be from somewhere else, no matter where she lands. I've seen her in four bars in three states in two years. She's a ghost. Haunting The Coastal Highway.

It's just too easy, and so natural, to swim in the current of the southern stream off 17. The highway seems so comfortable here. It suits a type. And like the people who inhabit the environs through which U.S. 17 runs, the highway itself changes character, as most roads do, with the landscape, like the weather in seasons.

Another constant along the Ocean Highway: the weird feeling of desolation that is both real and artificial, contrasting with the urban sprawl and gentrification spilling out of the city centers and creeping occasionally off I-95. No matter how isolated some of the towns and communities seem in the backwater sections of U.S. 17, the "civilized" crash of coastal development is always only a few miles away. While the resorts and the seaside cottages provide excitement and possibilities for those who can afford the real estate, the locals populating the insalubrious areas seem hemmed in by the creeks and marshes, their small lawns demarcating the edge of property, of home, hearth and family. The quarter-acre clearings represent little chance for opportunity, sparse hope for the mobility that, ironically, the highway, like an unfulfilled promise, cannot provide.

Through this region, I-95 shadows The Coastal Highway like a turkey buzzard hovering over fresh road kill, melds distinctions into green and white exit signs, identical signifiers and numerical demarcations. In contrast, traveling U.S. 17 creates a real sense of actually going somewhere, of moving from one place to another, connecting places that retain distinct identities.

And yet, from one end to the other, U.S. 17 seems to lead back to itself....

After all, what does it mean to "be" from Kingsland, GA, a few miles north of St. Mary's River? Near Catfish Creek? Below Crooked River? To meet at Steffen's Restaurant, a self-described "old-school diner serving comfort food since 1948"? Or Woodbine, a town with one stop light, its major draw the Satilla River? To name your business The Krusty Krab—

Above: **The Krusty Krab, Woodbine, GA. U.S. 17 turns inland at Yulee as it rolls toward Brunswick, but on the Coastal Highway, you're never far from an "ocean" motif.**

with no qualms as to what it means for a crab to be crusty, or why the K's add to the charm. To boost "event" traffic by peddling a Crawfish Festival?

In U.S. culture, identity is rooted in landscape. Terms relating place to character abound. Salt-of-the-earth. City boy. Country girl. Homegrown. Heartland. Down-Easter, Mid-Westerner. Southerner. Northerner, Hayseed. Tree-Hugger. Chowder-Head.

Left: **Secondhand store, Woodbine, GA. The residents along U.S. 17 through southern Georgia tend not to mince their words.**

If location equals destiny, where is the future for the children of the present-day "17-er"? A dead end or open road? The adults, in pick-ups dressed out with dog boxes and raised "deer stands" in the bed of the pick-ups, park twelve deep mid-morning at the local liquor lounge on the edge of the city limits, or vie for a spot in the queue at the boat launch to spend the afternoon bobbing a cork or casting flies for mudfish ... a gross simplification, because, yes, there are jobs—at the Hot Cars auto repair garage, the supermarket, the local school, sundry shops, the paper mill in Riceboro—but, really, what do the children dream of, frolicking in yards sectioned off in a field of rusty trailers—(im)mobile homes—behind a huge wooden sign shouting at passers-by the letters TRUMP, adorned with a huge *huge* American flag?

The highway markers along U.S. 17—from Eulonia through Midway to the spoils of Richmond Hill—plea for significance: "Historical Liberty Trail."

But the history here is one of poverty and illiteracy. Hope is transcendental, vested in the predominance of churches throughout the area.

The network of creeks, rivers and marshes that make up the coast of Georgia provide approximately 350,000 acres of briny wetlands with an average six to nine foot tide, a perfect environment for nursing shrimp from their early stages in life to maturity. Having spawned offshore, the post-larval shrimp migrate into the estuaries to feed, riding the high tide in, burrowing into the muddy bottoms on the ebb, molting and maturing every season into the delicacy—millions of pounds worth—that ends up on your plate.

The sodden mix of scrubby pines and reedy savannahs along the A1A loop from Heckscher Drive to Fernandina Beach and back to U.S. 17 is a fitting introduction to the reputation historically enjoyed by this southeastern section of The Coastal Highway. This motif continues up the immediate coast, as does the eerie desolation that once defined the rural sections of the highway, evident as soon as you cross the "through truss" bridge over the St. Marys River at the Florida-Georgia state line. The traffic here is decidedly sparse and local.

Entering and exiting Brunswick proper, bypassing the cross-causeway links to the Golden Isles, is easier than it would seem, as what's left of Brunswick has moved away from the downtown area of U.S. 17 out to the beaches and into the bedroom communities and retirement properties that line the inland coast. Some rehabilitation has been attempted around the Mary Ross Waterfront Park, next to the Brunswick Landing Marina, west of U.S. 17, near the intersection of Gloucester Street and Newcastle Street, where a few restaurants and shops try to reclaim "charm" in the abandoned city. But even during rush hours, the stretch of U.S. 17 known locally as Glynn Avenue can be navigated with surprising ease and only minor traffic distractions.

The after-Brunswick section of U.S. 17 traversing coastal Georgia begins in Darien, a town in which "shrimp life" is a given. Everyone knows somebody involved in the industry, everyone is familiar with "the life," everyone living along the Darien River has probably forgotten more about shrimp and the shrimp business than most people who don't live in that area ever knew ... as common knowledge. These are the facts of life: that wild Georgia shrimp are the best in the world, Darien is the center of the Georgia shrimp universe, and no one in the area would ever be caught dead eating any other kind of shrimp.

Death, taxes ... the scrumptious essence of wild Georgia shrimp.

But the weird thing: a question about shrimp tends to prompt locals to open up, not about the shrimp industry, but about themselves. Ask about shrimp, and they might identify someone else you should be talking to, or someone you should know, absolutely need to know, if you really want to learn about the local shrimping business. But then, after a moment of reflection, as if the mention of shrimp triggers some deep primal mnemonic response, they begin to relay, to a complete stranger, intimate details of their lives.

I drop into Mudcat Charlie's, Monday late lunch, mid–August. The restaurant, on the edge of the Altamaha River and just on the southern outskirts of Darien, about 15 miles north of Brunswick, sits immediately off U.S. 17 in the yard of Lee's Marine Services. The heat in the parking lot is intense, the way only heat emanating off a patch of pavement set in the middle of a swamp can feel, with no whisper of a breeze, no shade, oppressive humidity and blazingly clear sky.

The a-rhythmical thump of a detuned tractor pulling a boat across the marina work area smothers the screams of seagulls as I step into the frigid air-conditioned main dining room and head for the bar. Outside, over the water, travelers having strayed off I-95 sit at wooden benches and tables and bask in what shade there is, finishing lunch and admiring the assorted watercraft listlessly tugging at their moorings as the tide ebbs. The freshly exposed pluff mud flats are just beginning to glisten in the relentless sun. Inside, a half-dozen people occupy most of the tables by the windows overlooking the docks—older couples off pricy yachts, retirees from the Brunswick suburbs. Two co-eds sit at a center table, bleached-blond but authentically tan, their summer break nearly over, out for lunch on a lark before heading back to college.

I take a stool at the bar.

When the waitress comes over, mustering all the southern charm she can to impress a stranger, I ask, "You serve local shrimp, right?" I know the answer, but ask anyway, cynically, to check her reaction.

"I think so," she said, surprising me. She's in her late thirties but her bangs, hairclips, her overall style seems right out of high school. She absently wipes the counter in front of me.

"*Think* so?"

Her training kicks in, I suppose. As if by rote, she says, "All our seafood is locally caught." No trace of pique, sarcasm or cheekiness. She's dead honest, and takes no offense.

"Nobody around here ever asks."

She looks suddenly authentic, her charm less affected.

I feel guilty.

"Mostly it comes from Darien," she says. "I guess."

"Then it must be fresh," I say, trying to recover my own credibility.

A young man behind the bar steps up. He looks too young to be a bartender. Not a day out of high school. Short cropped hair, clear honest eyes. I ask if he has any imports.

"No," he says, not disappointed. "We keep it pretty basic around here."

I wonder if he's being contemptuous, toying with an outsider, but with all the diners obviously passing through, I reconsider his prickliness, interpret his attitude as posturing, or maybe naivety.

"Bud. Miller. Pabst. Yuengling," he says. "Heineken..."

Naivety. I order a Heineken and an appetizer portion of fried shrimp.

A guy beside me chimes in.

"I should've ordered that."

Meaning the fried shrimp. Not the Heineken. He's lean and tan, around 35, hard, like a construction worker. His arms are tatted in sleeves. He's finishing a pork sandwich, leaving his French fries untouched.

"I come in here every day," he says, "and I never try the shrimp." Pause. "Lived here all my life and hardly ever eat seafood."

"The local shrimp are famous," I say. The waitress, now in my confidence (I think), nods.

"Long as they ain't from the Savannah River," the guy says. "Or the Ogeechee. They are the dirtiest rivers in Georgia."

He turns away from me and continues his former conversation with a couple sitting across from us at the bar. He's been talking with them for a while, interrupting himself, suddenly, to mull my order. It's obvious he's been narrating a story, intensely, and that no one's listening. The couple nod absently and check their phones. I worry now that I've opened a channel. But he resumes his thread with the couple. His story involves being a farm team player that got moved up to the majors for a few games, fifteen years ago. Played for the Red Sox. Hates Cleveland. Hates Detroit.

"The ruination of that city was not the state's fault," he says. "Not the union's neither." He knocks a cigarette out of a pack of Marlboro Lights, indicates he's "going for a smoke" and heads out, calling back over his shoulder with an enviable certainty, "It all come down to the incompetence of the mayor and city council."

The waitress rolls her eyes. "He's in here every day," she says. "Same stories, different audience."

The couple stare at their phones.

I exploit the gap. Ask: Local girl?

"Born and raised."

Graduate high school?

"I did."

How long has she worked here?

"Thirteen years. I left for a while. Up the coast. I just got back."

It's a feature of true "17-ers": They come back. No matter how far they roam to escape the homeland of the highway, they return....

I feel a mix of appreciation, complicity, camaraderie, and, somehow ... despondence, disappointment. U.S. 17 is in her, but as a curse or a blessing? Does she love it, or is she trapped?

She graduates from a high school that sits off 17. One of those towns bisected by the highway, that the highway essentially puts on the map, that helps define the community, channeling a flow of travelers, local and foreign. It's her road into town, out of town, to work, to home. The route that frames the best years of her life....

Do she like shrimp?

"I love shrimp."

I wonder if she gets tired of seafood, like a baker that hates donuts.

"I have a Grouper sandwich everyday."

When the guy comes back after his cigarette break, he asks why I'm in town.

"Shrimp," I say.

The guy snorts.

"You catch a shrimp in the Savannah River, it's likely to look like a lobster. Or Godzilla."

The bartender brings out my order. The shrimp are plump and firm, *al dente*. The batter is light, barely a dusting, but it clings evenly to the meat. Sweet and crunchy.

After a few bites, the waitress checks in. I suggest it's the batter that makes Mudcat's shrimp so distinct. She just smiles. I ask if the chef will share his secret.

The waitress shakes her head. "That wouldn't be fair," she says, enigmatically.

As I munch away, the guy tells me, if I want to know about shrimp, I should talk to a man named Rusty Brown.

"I was told," I said, "to talk to some people at Skipper's Fish Camp."

"Just go down to the docks, other side of the bridge. Ask anybody. They'll tell you all you want to know about shrimp."

The couple across the bar briefly confers, and then hunch back into their cell phones.

"Shrimp," the guy says. The way he says it makes the word sounds somehow derisive. "Reminds me of my ex-wife. She loved shrimp. Now she gets half my pension, child support. The judge, he liked shrimp too...."

I get his story between bites. At some point it occurs to me that it's pushing three o'clock on a weekday afternoon, and no one—except the restaurant staff—seems concerned about jobs or working. The guy is complaining about alimony. The couple remains silent, intrigued with their phones. The coeds whisper over iced tea. The lunch crowd is leaving. I flow with them ...

The guy calls after me: "Don't go to Skipper's. Just walk the docks. Ask for Rusty."

The waitress waves. Like we share a secret.

I head for Skipper's, just below the Darien Waterfront Inn, off Screven Street, Darien.

The bridge across the Darien River leading into town offers a picturesque view of the region's soul. Just below Cathead Creek, a mile north of Mudcat's, where the marsh fans out east toward the coast, trawlers, often three deep, loll aside the city docks in a tangle of mesh and nets and outriggers. Beyond the waterfront, the town is fairly generic, with a smattering of modern brick, glass and steel buildings, businesses and homes common to the post-war, depressed areas along the southern path of the highway.

The completion of I-95 a few miles west moved the bulk of traffic away from U.S. 17, allowing the town to resume its charming life as a heritage tourism gem for history buffs, a launching point for bird watchers and kayakers eager to explore the waterways surrounding the town—gateway to Sapelo Island, a haven for fisherman and outdoorsmen—and, yes, as home to its famous shrimping fleet.

But shrimping as an industry came late to Darien. The settlement was established in 1736 as a shipping center for lumber brought in from the inland forests on barges. Darien remained an important port on the eastern seaboard throughout the 1800s. Severely damaged in the Civil War—in a notorious action, Union Forces indiscriminately bombed, looted and burned the defenseless town in 1863—Darien was restored during Reconstruction, and soon it resumed its importance as a timber industry shipping center, becoming, at the turn of the 19th century, one of the world's leading exporters of pine timber.

The city went into decline after World War II, when interest in the area moved toward the beaches and developments around Brunswick and the Golden Isles. The few blocks that comprise the waterfront, however, retain a rustic attraction, nurturing a fishing-village appeal, especially

U.S. 17 crossing the Darien River, Darien, GA. The shrimp fleet lies to the east. This tiny town just north of Brunswick enjoys an outsized reputation in the world of shrimping. Local shrimper Sinkey Boone invented the prototype Turtle Exclusion Device (TED), designed to reduce bycatch, which is now required equipment for all U.S. shrimpers.

along the wooden promenade and pier from Skipper's Fish Camp to the working docks and the shrimp boats moored around the bridge. The boardwalk runs past an old warehouse made of seashells, and on the bluff overlooking the riverfront, the Darien Waterfront Inn anchors the historic town-square, surrounded by a wine and cheese deli, assorted small shops and antique vendors. Off the water, around Vernon Square, several historical homes share space with St. Andrew's Episcopal Church. Further east along the creek lies the Fort King George Historic Site. The church, rebuilt in late 1870s—after being burned in that Union raid—is a good example of American Gothic. The fort is a reconstruction of the original design constructed in 1721, and served as the southernmost defensive position of the British Empire in the Americas.

But even with all its nostalgia, history and lore, dramatic scenery and wildlife, the town takes shrimping seriously enough to host a Blessing of the Fleet in April, highlighted by fireworks and a Shrimp Boat Marine Parade.

After all, shrimping these days is the reason for Darien.

Perhaps the most famous local shrimper in Darien is Sinkey Boone, who, in collaboration with the University of Georgia Marine Extension Service, pioneered the first turtle excluder device (TED), designed to release turtles and other air-breathing sea creatures from trawler nets without losing the primary catch—in this case, shrimp. Boone originally invented the "Georgia Jumper" to keep jellyfish from fouling his nets, but he soon discovered the design not only effectively reduced the number of turtles that inadvertently drowned in the nets but also allowed other unwanted by-catch like sharks, rays and dolphin to escape. While reducing the environmental damage caused by the needless killing of various ecologically sensitive species, the device actually improved the volume of shrimp caught and increased the efficiency of trawling. After his TED design was granted federal certification, laws requiring the commercial use of TEDs soon followed, and now all commercial shrimpers in the U.S. must use turtle excluder devices in trawl nets.

(A slew of variations on the original design followed, each attempting to improve the efficacy of the device but all sharing the same intent: cutting down on needless killing of unwanted by-catch.)

Because Darien sits at the center of the shrimping industry in Georgia, a sizeable chunk of the town's economy is affected by the fluky nature of the industry. The impact is not as acute as it was a few years ago, thanks to the shifting demographics of the area. But even though the economy

has diversified, taking advantage of the town becoming a tourist destination, a target for retirement communities, and profiting from being a part
of the draw associated with the Golden Isles of Brunswick, the instability
of the shrimp industry still plays heavily into the local economy. During
crisis periods—due to extremely cold winters, or droughts, or over-
shrimping, or the notorious black gill disease, or an influx of fresh water
in the briny estuaries after too much rain—when the shrimp stock is seriously depleted—shrimpers tend to head south, to warmer waters, usually
off Key West.

Most idle crews find work off the boats. Some go fishing. Some go
into construction. Many give up and move on.

In Darien, the ones that stay resort to "jellyballing."

"Jellyballing" refers to trawling for jellyfish, a fairly new enterprise
along the Georgia coast. In an inspiring effort to keep their boats employed
through moratoriums, extended off-seasons, or when there simply isn't
enough shrimp to be found, industrious shrimpers turn to harvesting Can-
nonball Jellyfish, or *Stomolophus meleagris*, the very same round, gelati-
nous sea-pests Sinkey Boone wanted to combat with his original TED
device. The catch is highly prized in China, where it's considered a delicacy, and thanks to local processing plants capable of drying and packaging
the catch, exclusive along the east coast, the profits keep local shrimpers
in the black.

But catching shrimp is one thing. Jellyfish another.

And while "jellyballing" hardly conjures up the poetic image of an
intrepid sea captain nobly battling natural elements, fighting through cold
lonely nights and stiff arthritic joints to bring home that rare esteemed
catch of wild white shrimp that keeps Georgia at the top of the food chain
along the Atlantic Seaboard, trawling for jellyfish, easier than shrimping,
insures a decent profit for desperate shrimpers who might otherwise be idle.

"Jellyballs" are not on the menu at Skipper's Fish Camp.

Overlooking the estuaries of the Altamaha River, where antebellum
rice plantations once lined the shores, there is nothing "camp" about Skipper's, neither in the sense of being rustic or ironic. The restaurant features
two modern buildings, one an elevated sports bar with an open porch-
like dining area, and the other an air-conditioned room with traditional
table seating, large windows and a small bar. The sports bar exudes an
aroma of smoky barbeque and features wine, draft beers, brilliant views
of the marsh along the creek, live music some nights, and, at times, vicious
mosquitoes.

Interior, Skipper's Fish Camp, Darien, GA. The owner of Skipper's warns that, in this area, serving anything but local shrimp is a hanging offense. Or worse.

"It sits in the middle of a marsh," explains the bartender, helpfully. He's a good-looking, athletic young man, with dark, neatly trimmed hair, blue eyes. He'd worked here most of his short adult life: five years. (He's barely twenty-one.) He started as a "shucker," knifing open oysters in the kitchen. He now attends college, hopes to be an elementary school teacher and coach. He stresses the fact that he doesn't live in Darien, but about fifteen minutes away, in north Brunswick.

The difference between living in Brunswick and Darien seems to reflect some essential quality, something existential. I shift to the elemental virtues of shrimp.

At Skipper's, a thicker batter sleeves the shrimp instead of sticking to it, like the flakey crust on the shrimp at Mudcat's. The jacket makes the shrimp crunchier, but the thickness detracts from the natural texture and sweetness of the flesh.

I mention the heavy batter to the bartender, noting the contrast with Mudcat's.

"Yeah," he says. "Chef here likes more breading. But we get 'em from the same place. All the restaurants around here do."

Is that the main difference? The batter?

"Well, you might notice, we're more ... what's the word? Fancier..."

A dishwasher idly watching the muted TV offers, "Upscale."

I look around at the sports bar/hunting camp ambience. The mounted animal heads on the walls. The huge stuffed alligator. The rustic wood and saloon style dining room.

The guy picks up on my skepticism.

"Well the downstairs is anyway. Mudcat's uses paper plates, plastic forks and knives. No glassware, no plates. They don't even have a dishwasher."

The dishwasher nods.

"The other places, like B and J's, in the center of town, they're famous for buffets. Same as The Fish Dock, over to Pelican Point. All you can eat."

More in confidence, he adds, "These country people like that shit. Buffets. All you can eat."

I see an opening and pull the trigger: "You like shrimp?"

He shrugs. I might as well have asked if a catfish has whiskers. But then the weird thing happens, the ... well, confession. The question about shrimp seems to spark a deep need to explain something intimate in his life.

"Most of my friends dropped out of school to work on the boats," he says. They're free to travel, so they can move from boat to boat during the season. From Brunswick to the Keys. Alabama."

He unlocks his cell phone.

"Check this out."

Photos of an eighteen-year-old girl. A posed headshot, her even smile disarmingly honest, her bright eyes untroubled by the mayhem of the world beyond Camden County, GA. Another shot of her in a bikini, lying back in a chaise-long on a sandy beach, mugging for the camera with friends, her demeanor carefree and young. A shot of her in a short shift at a picnic with her parents. Another in a high school graduation hat and gown. He slides through the collection.

"Does she look pregnant?"

She decidedly did not.

"I didn't think so either. Neither did she."

Then he shows me a photo of her in a hospital bed with a newborn baby.

"That was three months ago."

He goes through a series of before and after. She looks the same in every shot. Thin but shapely, effervescent, optimistic, fresh ...

"She didn't even know she was pregnant. Only clue was when my family and I went out to lunch after church where she's a waitress. My dad noticed her ankles looked swollen, but I figured she might just've been on her feet a lot, being a waitress and all. I knew she'd been eating more than usual. Hungry all the time. Turns out she was eating for two."

I guess I look incredulous.

"I know," he continues, any discussion of shrimp batter, competitive buffet pricing, jellyballing, itinerant shrimping fleets or disputes among local distributors subsumed in the steady reconstruction of his girlfriend's Cryptic Pregnancy.

Turns out, according to him, his girlfriend had what he called "an inverted uterus," or in more precise medical terminology, a "retroverted uterus," in which the uterus is tilted backwards. Instead of having a uterus pointing up and down or tilted slightly forward, hers tipped essentially backward toward the spine.

He tells me that, throughout the pregnancy, she continued to have scanty, irregular periods up until the day she delivered. It seems women with this condition are much less likely to show their pregnancies, and she tended to have irregular periods anyway, so ... the baby, to say the least, was a surprise.

"One night out of nowhere," he continued, "she just started bleeding. A lot. Her parents took her to the emergency room. Once they got her in there, the nurses said it must be a premature birth. They thought she must be about four months along, but without really showing. They called a specialist in from somewhere and a helicopter to fly her to a facility that could handle super-early babies."

He looks at the other bartender, for both affirmation and sympathy. The dishwasher shakes his head.

"Next thing you know, she's having the baby. Right there in the emergency room, like it was nothing. Surprised everybody. The nurses. The doctor. Her parents. Mostly her. And me."

I was thinking of the season. Was it the right time for white shrimp, or brown.

He flips through his phone, finds photos of his son, three months old.

"She's living with her parents, until she gets used to the situation. I'm still living at home too, saving money. I need to finish college ... then we'll see."

I feel ashamed, like I'd peeked through a window of his life and saw something I wasn't supposed to see, but I remind myself that he volunteered this story, which was, after all, not a tragedy, just another misadventure in the real world along the Ocean Highway, in southeastern Georgia. But the bar is dead quiet. The dishwasher changes the TV channel. The bartender stares at his cell phone.

I ask him what he remembers most about growing up "off 17."

"Jekyll Island," he says, almost dreamily. "The wildlife in there. So many deer."

A mosquito buzzes in my ear. I think of Zika Virus.

"And rabbits," he adds, as if remembering something important, that would explain everything, the pregnancy, his situation, the shrimp industry in Darien. "There's millions of rabbits out there."

I consider a shrimp. I consider dipping it into cocktail sauce. I think of rabbits. Mosquitoes. The social life of America's youth. I hesitate, as if the planets were aligned, awaiting my next move....

Beyond Darien, another loop road off U.S. 17—GA 99—tracks east of The Coastal Highway, along the spoils of Blackbeard Creek, a system of waterways spanning the Georgia coast from north of Brunswick to

U.S. 17, Eulonia, GA. The Coastal Highway through Georgia remains authentic and basically unchanged since it was first paved.

The fleet at Belleville Point, Crescent, GA. Given the price of waterfront property, shrimpers seek out isolated areas unsuitable for gentrification. Otherwise, the land values would price them out of business. Access to open water is essential, but so is shelter from rough weather. The creeks, canals and estuaries along U.S. 17 on the Georgia coast are ideal, offering cheap real estate, protected harbors, and navigable channels out to the Atlantic.

Savannah. Outside Eulonia, just before Bubba's Quick Stop, officially located in Crescent, GA, on the south side of the Sapelo River, an access road runs through a square plot of rooted mobile homes, makes a turn leading past creek-front properties and cottages on the water, a boat yard and a seafood supply warehouse, before it literally dead ends at The Fish Dock Restaurant at Pelican Point, home of the Seafood Buffet, with nowhere to go once you're there but back.

The Fish Dock occupies a faux dilapidated building with an oddly sterile, generic interior, a deck, a "widow's walk," and benches overlooking the water. A huge fake Great White shark graces the exterior top of the entrance alcove. The shark seems somehow appropriate. Not that the creek would feature any man-eating creature like the one haunting the collective imagination of galeophobic cinephiles ever since Spielberg's classic made the fish famous, but because the place seems like the perfect set for a Shark Week style horror film, with a cast of characters that might have escaped from a Dadaesque *Deliverance* type film and wound up at a window seat for the all-you-can-eat buffet.

A shark leaps from the scum and flies through the plate glass window, shearing off the bearded head of a diner at the shoulders, leaving an Alaskan king crab leg hanging midair.

The neighborhood exudes authenticity. Shrimp trawlers line the creek, along with seafood wholesalers, an operating boat yard. People here fish for a living, as well as for love of the sport. The area is not so much isolated as it is insular. How people find this place from I-95—or why they risk it—remains a mystery. But for all its spookiness, the place is harmless.

Still, the locals don't ignore you. They stare.

Along the river's edge, a series of small warehouses and oversized tool sheds front a line of shrimp trawlers moored against wood plank docks. Contemporary split-level homes, ranch-style villas and a smattering of vacation cottages spruce up a rather ordinary neighborhood supporting the seafood business surrounding it. The work-buildings contain scales, equipment, nets, miscellaneous detritus in various states of repair ... and disrepair. The trawlers are in for routine maintenance. The docks are quiet but busy. A few animated families restock the fleet. On a separate dock, two men splice a three-inch cable. In the parking lot outside Skinner's Seafood, a bumper sticker on one of the cars sports an upside down American flag over the quote: "Our Government is Out of Control."

I turn back to admire the shark. A lady on a nearby pier—a youthful octogenarian—tosses a weighted shrimp net into the murky water, hauling in a mess of shrimp out of the ebbing current. I wave. She makes a quick movement with her free right hand. I don't wait around for her to complete it, flashing on *Second Amendment remedies.*

Too early for the buffet anyway.

Highway GA 99 rejoins The Ocean Highway and continues north until, less than five miles up U.S. 17, another easterly turnoff leads to Pine Harbor Marina, straight across from Pelican Point, off to the southeast. The road makes a T at Fairhope, a trail that runs south and then west back to U.S. 17, while Belle Hammock Road slips north along the river to Shellman Bluff. The waterfront is a patchwork of dirt pathways lined by small rustic cottages, a few well-heeled estates, some with pools, most with long docks running out into navigable water, clearly a mix of scrappy local fishermen dependent on natural resources and wealthy Savannah suburbanites enjoying a backwoods playground.

The Pine Harbor Marina consists of a two-story wooden building overlooking a planked dock where a few small commercial boats, few over 19 feet, creak in their berths. The manager and his brother tend to business from their perch on the porch, the one a huge, taciturn idler, prone to employing a bench for peeling oranges, the other a thin, garrulous set-net shrimper, stingy with his remaining teeth, amused by a new app on his cell phone.

Do they like shrimp?

The one tosses an orange peel at a dog in the yard, a Chihuahua and Jack Russell mix. The mongrel lifts its head to sniff the rind, and then resumes a sort of vigilance, one eye on me, one on the man with the knife.

"Yeah. Fried," says the thin one, suddenly ready to talk. His boat, an 18 footer docked along the pier, is set up for inshore drag-netting.

"No set-nets allowed in Georgia. Not for shrimping. Not legally, any-ways," he says and looks at his brother. His brother scowls. "Right out there's all I need to catch."

He indicates the Sapelo River, which Google identifies as Blackbeard Creek.

"The whole coast from Brunswick to Savannah is Blackbeard Creek to them," he says. He squints at the horizon. "They need to upgrade their maps."

Looking across the savannahs at Belleville Point, seen from Pine Harbor Marina, Pine Harbor, GA.

Pine Harbor Marina, Pine Harbor, GA. *Top:* The main marina building, on the banks of the Sapelo River. *Bottom:* Small trawler.

He then launches into a familiar diatribe, as if every shrimper along the coast was reading from the same script. The industry is shrinking. The villains: Asians. Big government. Regulations. Obama. He points across the water toward Pelican Point.

"Used to be trawlers in there—big ones—six to eight boats deep. Now..." He shrugs. "They can't compete with farmed shrimp, with imports."

He notes how many shrimpers were selling shrimp along the highway, off the back of their trucks, or right off the docks the boats operated out of.

"Ain't no money in wholesaling."

What about Highway 17?

The sweet scent of orange fills the breeze as his brother cuts into another fresh orange from his basket. He laughs and throws another scrap at the dog. This time the cur seems to resent the gesture and slinks away into the shade of the building.

"Scenic," says the thin man, putting his phone away. "One thing they need to do though to really improve that road...."

The big man pauses mid-slice. The dog looks up. Tension, as if, around here, the next utterance will pass for actual news.

"Bike lane," the thin man says.

His brother bites into a thick juicy wedge. The dog relaxes.

"Ain't nothing more precious than human life."

Belle Hammock Road winds north along the waterfront until it connects with Shellman Bluff Road, which then leads out to the community of Shellman Bluff. Aside from the new inland developments off the water, and the golf course shoe-horned in around Southerland Bluff, the neighborhood looks lost in time, somewhere around 1930. With its leafy yards, bungalows on stilts, a maze of tidy cottages, it looks like a place Bonnie and Clyde might hide out in. It sits at the northern arm of a Y in one of the Blackbeard Creek forks. Pelican Point occupies the southern arm. The stem of the Y joins just east of those promontories with the deep water of Sapelo Sound leading out into the Atlantic. In essence, this is beachfront property, Lowcountry style. The original village, bunched around Shellman's Fishing Camp and Hunter's Café, remains a throwback to a rural, homespun version of picturesque America that lovers of Norman Rockwell commemorative calendars would appreciate.

The Fish Camp sits at the junction of Club Street and River Road. At the water's edge, a sign reads "Downtown Shellman Bluff." There's a working lift, along with fuel pumps and docks for small craft. The camp is a one room wooden structure, with a small porch. Inside, the store offers miscellaneous fishing gear, souvenirs and sundries, cold drinks and snacks. An American flag flutters above the roof, alongside a short wave radio tower.

Two men who look to be in their mid-sixties hold down the only table in the room, sharing the space with a woman of the same age playing solitaire. Mounted on the wall, a huge deer head with a full set of antlers stares at visitors.

The silence when I enter is startling.

The lady flips a card. It snaps the emptiness. I ask if they like shrimp.

One of the men smiles.

"Looks like they found us," he says. Meaning, I gather, "New Yorkers," who, to the locals, means anybody from north of Savannah. The non sequitur seems perfectly logical, from where I stood, staring back at the deer.

U.S. 17? The Coastal Highway?

"We live on Bluff Time," says the other man.

"Like Italians," the lady explains.

Their laughter is not reassuring.

I had decided to avoid downtown Savannah. Too much variety. Too much concentration. But The Pink House deserves mention. Officially named Ye Olde Pink House, the restaurant is composed of three main components: the formal dining area, the street level bar, and the cellar piano bar. The cellar bar is open only at night, the street café lunch and dinner, the piano tavern after five pm.

In its current iteration, the stucco exterior is definitely a pastel pink. Construction of the original Georgian manor began in 1771 as the private home of James Habersham, Jr., and was completed in 1789. Having survived the great Savannah fire of 1796, the building went through several reincarnations, including as a bank and, During the Civil War, the headquarters of a Union general. The building was restored to its current state as a pricy, crowded, destination restaurant, and a popular stop for Savannah ghost tours. (Supposedly, Habersham hanged himself in what is now the tavern area.) The first floor dining rooms are small and cozy, with a few tables in the desirable front room situated by windows overlooking Reynolds Square, some near the fireplace, others romantically secluded. The upstairs room is open and spacious. The staircase is an architectural novelty.

Shellman Bluff, GA. *Top:* Just up the river from Pine Harbor and Belleville Point, "Downtown" Shellman Bluff is the center of social life at the edge of Blackbeard Island National Wildlife Refuge. Golf course culture is encroaching on the original fish camp style of the area, but resistance to gentrification is stiff. *Bottom:* View from Shellman Bluff. Increasing numbers of leisure craft are changing the nature of the community.

U.S. 17, Savannah, GA. Signs of old and new, classic and funky. *Top:* The Olde Pink House, on Reynolds Square, dates from 1771. The tavern downstairs is a hot spot for locals and tourists alike. *Bottom:* Thunderbird Motel, where the original U.S. 17 enters Savannah from the north. Once a seedy introduction to the less salubrious side of the city, the renovated motel is now ranked as one of the nation's top retro "hip" motels.

In the sidewalk café, which shares its kitchen with the tavern as well as the other main dining areas, I meet a chef that has worked at Pink House for more than seven years. He readily confesses with little prompting that he prefers sautéed shrimp to grilled, mainly because grilling dries out the meat; plus, sautéing allows him more control of the heat.

He admits, "Most people in the south prefer shrimp fried." He then adds, "Of course, they'll fry anything down here."

Spoken like a true ... well, northerner, but, actually he's a local, from Savannah ... has no formal training, worked his way up from apprenticeships to his current position.

And he recalls when U.S. 17 was "just a road through Savannah with a few gas stations and sad developments."

But now, according to the chef—and one of the servers who happens by—these new developments along the highway have blossomed into what some consider a second city between Savannah and Richmond Hill. The server explains that, as the price of downtown living rose, people that work in the city—many of them professionals, as well as pros in the service industry—cannot afford to live there. So they move to the suburbs, serviced by U.S. 17. In that sense the highway improves their quality of living—if "quality" is synonymous with convenience and access to the variety of services available ... a tricky assessment, since in this case "improved" means taking on the character of other generic communities strung along The Coastal Highway: lots of apartments, condos, restaurants—especially chains—and affordable recreational pursuits.

What is lost is a sense of place, identity, and uniqueness. But whatever soul is sacrificed in the suburbs is recovered in the Pink House kitchen.

Although partial to shrimp and grits (naturally), when it comes to fried shrimp the chef prefers the 21–25 count, basically medium sized, and, it goes without saying, wild shrimp caught off the Georgia-Carolina coast. Smaller or larger shrimp lose flavor. Frozen, peeled and deveined imposters, or farmed Asian imports, lack the crispness and character necessary for quality dishes. The secret for frying shrimp, in his view, is the batter—no surprise. He likes to blend all-purpose flour with corn meal. Keep the seasoning basic, balance the salt and pepper, let the corn meal prevent the batter from getting soggy, and you've got the key, the secret to preparing fried food—oysters, fish ... and, of course, shrimp.

"The corn meal keeps the crunch," he says, emphatically.

After five pm, the cellar tavern opens. It's more spacious, busier than the curbside bar upstairs. The original room, which dates back to 1771, is rich in brick and dark wood. Fireplaces at either end of the room frame the polished wood bar, a few tables line the perimeter, a couch beside the piano.

A bartender from Miami, having worked at The Pink House for three years, wasn't familiar with U.S. 17, and admitted that, before moving to Savannah on a lark, was never acquainted with the city.

A passing server overhears us, and volunteers that she likes her shrimp "spicy, blackened, grilled."

Not an auspicious opening to the evening. A guy from Miami who can't tell The Coastal Highway from Biscayne Boulevard. A server who prefers shrimp spicy and blackened ... as if shrimp were merely a handy vehicle for infusing spices.

But then another bartender appears, a local. He's talkative, stocky, bristly, with short-cropped hair and whiskers, greying but animated. He sparks to life when U.S. 17 comes up, and doesn't hesitate to offer an unqualified affirmation of the treasure that the Ocean Highway, at least the run from Savannah to Darien, offers those attuned to its naturalist vector.

He remembers when U.S. 17 was "the most depressing street in Savannah. Nothing out there but the Thunderbird Motel."

He's referring to a motel off the highway that, he recalls, in days of yore, was a shabby dive servicing local prostitutes.

"But," he says—and sounds disappointed—"it's all cleaned up now."

(In fact, The Thunderbird Inn, restored and upgraded in 2016, bills itself as the "hippest hotel in Savannah" and claims to be ranked by *USA Today* as "one of the top ten best retro hotels" in the country.)

"There's quality restaurants all over the highway now," he says.

He then reels off names that sound to him as familiar as family friends. Finishing with a flourish: "Love's."

Dropping the name of Love's signifies, to the initiated, instant street cred. One of the early legendary Savannah restaurants still operating on its original site (est. 1949), the diner is perched on the banks by the bridge where U.S. 17 crosses the Ogeechee River, across from Kings Ferry Park. Along with its longevity, partly attributed to its location—those bloody (Mary) sunsets, louche river views, the funky wildlife, an occasional gator—plus its numerous awards, its uncompromising use of fresh local products and seafood—especially local shrimp—perhaps Love's most impressive claim to fame is, alas, its connection to *Forrest Gump*.

I let the Gump connection go.

The bartender nods, resigned to the Hollywood hype. But as if to rescue Love's reputation—and his own—he acknowledges that any establishment that wants to maintain a loyal customer base in the Savannah area must serve wild caught Georgia and Carolina shrimp.

"The local places couldn't stay in business if they didn't. The people that live around here, they know."

For him, U.S. 17 is more than a platform for his favorite seafood restaurants—too plentiful to catalog. His local knowledge of The Coastal Highway borders on encyclopedic. He is a true aficionado. It connects him to the quintessence of life. An avid outdoorsman, hunting and fishing for him are ontological extensions. His sense of the road complements his essence. An authentic "17-er," he uses the highway as a conduit into fields of play, for sport. He brags about his last weekend shooting wood ducks off 17 with his Benelli automatic, launching his Boston Whaler at Kilkenny Marina. Or shoving off from Shellman Bluff, navigating out to St. Catherine's, one of the few privately owned islands off the Georgia Coast, for an extended fishing expedition.

"When you see the yellow butterflies," he says. "It's time to go."

(Apparently, mild weather indicated by the butterflies is a good sign that the Red Fish are biting.)

"Nothing like sitting on the beach with a Bloody Mary, surf-casting for Red Fish."

Indeed.

U.S. 17, the Ocean Highway, intersects with U.S. 80, known as The Dixie Overland, in downtown Savannah. When it was designed, U.S. 80, improbably, stretched from Tybee Island, the barrier island immediately east of Savannah, all the way across the country to San Diego, CA. Today, its route is interrupted outside of Dallas, TX, but The Dixie Overland persists as a major highway through the Old South, the way U.S. 17 runs the coast. The terminus of U.S. 80 is located at the tip of Tybee, on the edge of the Atlantic Ocean.

Tybee Island, like most of the pre-colonial islands along the southwest Atlantic territory, was inhabited by indigenous tribes—in this case, the Euchee—and were under constant threat from the Spanish. Once the English prevailed, the island quickly cultivated its natural resources, especially the seafood industry, and existed quietly as an adjunct beach community for Savannah. During the Civil War, the island served as a siege battery site for the conquering Union Army, and because of its location at the mouth of the Savannah River, Tybee's lighthouse was among the most important on the coast; the original, built in 1736, was the highest structure in the Americas at the time of its construction.

To accommodate the 19th century craze for "salt air cures," Tybee, like many of the barrier islands, drew wealthy industrialists and their minions in droves, turning Tybee into a vacation destination. Renamed for a while "Savannah Beach," to reflect its reality as the seaside resort of choice for inland city dwellers, Tybee became famous for its Pavilion (since destroyed by fire), and the first hotel of the Days Inn chain.

In its modern state, despite being a bit shabby (Paula Dean bought a house here) and shamelessly appealing to a low-budget tourist aesthetic, the area is lovely, and the shrimp superb.

I was not planning on a visit. Tybee lies 18 miles off U.S. 17, although there is no way to get there without at least crossing The Coastal Highway, so it fit my self-imposed (and perforce very flexible) paradigm. Also, the server who said she liked spicy shrimp leaned into me as I sat at the Pink House bar and, unsolicited, whispered, mischievously, "If you're hankering for shrimp, check out Crab Shack."

Above and opposite: **The Crab Shack, Tybee Island, GA.** *Above:* **A few miles off U.S. 17, on U.S. 80, the Crab Shack is an unabashed, classic tourist trap, but one of a kind in the usually quiet Tybee Island vibe.**

Among the more curious gimmicks at the Crab Shack, a pond with live, domesticated alligators sunning for eager photographers.

Her eyes were full of promise. "A landmark," she assured me.

Well, landmark it is. But I should've known better.

I immediately sense something is off ... pick up a weird vibe as soon as I pull into the lot and encounter, on one hand, colorful carved tiki poles loitering around the parking lot, leering like displaced refugees from Pedro's South of the Border, and on the other, a row of shotgun shacks occupied by actual people, some of whom, I find out later, work at the restaurant.

Hordes of domestic cats haunt the grounds.

The compound includes several buildings, an inside bar and dining area, an outside bar and dining area, a "party lodge" with seating for 300, integrated into a puzzle of sheds and shops and piers and walkways. Strings of lights, brightly painted screens and scrims and bamboo and wood, flags and lanterns and plaques galore add to the calculated clutter and madness. The eclectic hodgepodge is breathless.

But it gets weirder. Scattered throughout the property and carefully orchestrated detritus, a collection of colorful, decorated signs, carnivalesque posters, circus-like billboards, odd plaques scrawled with quips, statuettes of sharks and fish, a giant crab archway and ... alligators, fake and real, the huge facsimiles leading to the main draw of the compound: a pond full of live baby gators, at least 20 of the critters, huddled together, one chilly day, mid–December, under a fountain. They look disgruntled—cold, miserable, pissed-off at being reduced to a prop for busloads of tourists seeking photo souvenirs.

One of the cleverly hand-painted signs by the gator pond reads: "Gator Treats Sold in Gift Shop," which, I figure, explains the creatures' belligerence, but soon I realize that the treats are made for, not from, the gators, delivered to them on the end of a stick, prompting the surly amphibians out of their natural stupor to snap at the bait.

The Crab Shack's motto is: "Where the Elite Eat in Their Bare Feet." The rhyme is as cheesy as it is effortless, which perfectly surmises the, well, ethos of the owners of this once and future "fish camp." Emphasis on "camp." Surely, I thought, camp would be the operative term, but on consideration, camp implies irony, often an in-joke shared with a wink by conspirators against a third, naive party. The problem with the irony at the Crab Shack is that one wonders which party is naïve. The owners? Hardly. The staff? Maybe. The tourists? One can only hope ...

The Chinese tourists exit the bus, decked out incongruously in their best J. Crew (bought on a spree at the outlet mall), and head straight for the gator pond, cameras snapping, selfie-sticks held aloft like spears in the hands of ancient conquerors, marveling at the comic book version of America they had heard about but never imagined true....

The more straightforward aspects of the Crab Shack—the honest bit?—are based on the marina area, designed to accommodate customers with small boats, including a working hoist for maintenance. Adding to the authenticity of, at least, the setting, a small trawler across the creek idles at the end of a floating dock, nets still wet.

But any sense of local charm fostered by the work area is immediately undercut by an eight-foot statue of a gator-cum-supply-shelf guarding the entrance to a gift shop beside the boat lift festooned with more oversized sculptures of sharks and manned by a woman peddling t-shirts, hats and various Crab Shack gear. There's even a "Bird Room" showcasing non-indigenous parrots that, I guess, complement the equally non-indigenous gators inhabiting the pond.

A small working trawler across the creek from the Crab Shack docks lends a sense of authenticity to the surreal cartoon world of the compound.

I waylay a bustling "underling"—everyone's busy, but there's nothing happening—and ask her for a menu.

"It's all on the website," she says, and proffers a colorful brochure featuring Tybee Island restaurants.

"Maybe this'll help." She hustles off, unhelpful.

"You do," I manage to ask, calling out before she disappears into a screened porch, "serve fried shrimp?"

She stops, door ajar. A parrot screeches. The gators remain dead calm. For the first time, she actually sees me.

"All our food is boiled," she says.

I'm not sure I heard her right. "Boiled?"

She looks at me like I'd suddenly sprung an antler from my forehead.

"Boiled," she says, slowly, humoring her dim-witted pupil. "As in, you know, a Lowcountry boil?"

She exits. The door slams behind her, dramatically.

I consider the gators. The birds. The cats. The parking lot full of cartoons. Potential Chinese tourists.

And feel cheated.

I take it up with the woman behind the bar at Sundae Café, a small eatery tucked into a non-descript strip-mall along the main road onto the island, just inside the city limits. I would never have found Sundae Café, much less visited, were it not for a tip from the bartender at The Pink House—the "17-er," not the server who liked her shrimp spicy and grilled (the one who sent me to the Crab Shack).

"It's a tourist trap," the bartender says, matter-of-fact. "They don't even serve local shrimp. They import 'em. Farmed, frozen, bulk. I'm not supposed to say that, so you didn't hear it from me."

She tilts her head to hold the phone while writing an order, looking pleased with her espionage.

"Of course, given their volume, they have to."

I flash on the sign at the entrance to the Crab Shack directing busses into a special parking lot. Think of the disgruntled gators. The birds ruminating in their cages. The cauldrons of shrimp bubbling in brown suds among bits of sausage, okra, potatoes and rice....

"The place might be a joke," she adds. "But he turns seven million a year."

Dollars, I gather. Not shrimp.

Sundae Café occupies a slot in a non-descript mini strip-mall on Tybee Island and offers some of the best shrimp on the coast, fresh off *The Agnes Marie*, Lazaretto Creek. The incongruous name was held over from the previous incarnation of the business as an ice cream parlor.

She should know. She confesses to having worked there for over eight years. But after five years at Sundae Café, she seems to have reconnected with what she loves about the industry: serving authentic, local seafood.

Her new gig could not be more opposite from The Crab Shack. Low key to the point of boring. The name Sundae Café was retained from the site's former life as an ice cream deli. The restaurant is flanked by a liquor store ("Beverage Shop") and a BP convenience store with a gas pump island in the parking lot.

The small room and bar space fills up quickly with a local lunch crowd, the kind of clientele that knows each other by name—construction workers, suits, small business owners, other restaurateurs (including, once a week, the owners of The Crab Shack)—while the bartender, a healthy, happy, no-nonsense brunette, takes reservations for dinner non-stop and rings up to-go lunch orders one after the other.

"Kinda' slow, today," she says.

Established by two schoolmates, Keven Carpenter and A. J. Baker, Sundae Café has thrived since 2002. After working through their youth in various service industry jobs, the two entrepreneurs attended Johnson and Wales College of Culinary Arts in Charleston. After Carpenter died suddenly in 2015, Baker decided to continue what the two friends started.

"The thing is," the bartender volunteers between prepping take-aways. "His name is Baker, but he doesn't like to bake, doesn't like baked goods. Which is good for us"—she means the staff—"because we get to taste all the deserts."

The memory pleases her.

"Quality control," she says, raising her eyebrows.

The local lunch crowd at the Sundae Café expects the fried pork chop special, the meatloaf platter, fried chicken—even specifying white or dark meat. But the actual menu is standard, limited "gourmet," including southern standbys like shrimp and grits but also unusual items like shrimp and porkbelly egg rolls. The key, of course, is fresh seafood—especially wild shrimp. Split, plump, moist, meaty, cooked tails-on, lightly breaded, tender, firm and buttery.

The bartender points to a huge, sectional photograph on the wall: a trawler at sea, The Agnes Marie.

"That's the boat we get our shrimp from," she says. "Captain J. B. Riffle."

On the menu, the fried shrimp entrée is marked: Wild Georgia Shrimp.

"He comes in here at lunch." She considers the photo, and then glances over as the door opens and swings shut. "Mainly to pick up his check for the shrimp."

Does she like shrimp?

"Not really," she says, with only a modest hint of shame. A third generation Tybee Island girl, "born and raised," she spent her youth "catching, heading, and deveining" shrimp with her father. His weapon of choice is a cast net, tossed from his 14-foot Key Largo.

"Or else," she says, "right off the dock at the house."

When her brother pops in to pick up a to-go, I ask if he likes shrimp. "Any way you cook 'em," he says. But he prefers them boiled.

Shades of the Crab Shack ...

I ask him about his sister's aversion to shrimp. She answers for him. "I'm a weirdo."

He and I share a look.

"Good luck," he says and leaves with his lunch.

She smiles, enjoying her status. Almost anticipating the next question.

The Coastal Highway?

"I leave the island more than most," she says. "Vacations and stuff. But 'town' to me is Southside Savannah, not Highway 17."

She leans in, as if in confidence, and tells me Captain Riffle's trawler is docked at CoCo's Sunset Grille, a restaurant beside the bridge leading off Tybee toward downtown Savannah.

Worth a visit, she assures me.

A small sign on the entrance deck reads: "Our Shrimp Comes from These Docks Every Day." Sure enough, Captain Riffle's *Agnes Marie* sits out back, rocking in the steady northerly.

The interior is rough but clean, and authentic. The bait shop décor and *diner moderne* is tempered with a hint of nautical truck stop. High ceilings. Exposed heat and air-conditioning ducts and piping. Open floor plan. Booths and tables, some with waterside windows overlooking Lazaretto Creek, the trawler docks and the marsh rolling into the distance. Typical L-shaped bar. Kenny Chesney on Pandora.

"I love me some Kenny Chesney," the bartender says. She is mannish and prim, hair trimmed short. Her southern accent is too mild to place exactly. She's belting samples of tequila from a visiting liquor rep, pausing in spots to sing along with Pandora. Between shots, she explains the intricacies of purchasing locally caught shrimp "right off the boat."

"We can't buy 'em 'right off the boat.' You need a special license for that. Captain Royce (Woodard) used to bring in loads, but since (Hurricane) Matthew wiped him out, most of the restaurants serve wild shrimp only when they can get 'em. Right now, the boats still operating can't meet the demand, so lots of the restaurants rely on Ambos."

Ambos is an institution in the Lowcountry. Operating as a seafood dealer for over 150 years, but having branched out into other food groups like chicken, meats and even pasta, the company's emphasis remains, and its reputation has been built on, supplying local and wild domestic shrimp.

Among its other notable achievements, as early as the late 1940s the company was the first business in the country to innovate the frozen seafood industry, advancing the distribution of ready-to-fry fan-tailed shrimp to parts of the country that had never previously considered serving shrimp for dinner. The headquarters is located in Thunderbolt, GA, a small community at the edge of Savannah, on the Intracoastal Waterway just off Tybee Island, where U.S. 80 crosses the Wilmington River. Thunderbolt evolved from the main dockage and processing center for the local shrimp industry to an area known for full service yacht construction and

Captain Riffle's *Agnes Marie*, behind CoCo's Sunset Grille, Lazaretto Creek, GA. Riffle supplies the real thing for shrimp lovers.

repair. But for local restaurant owners around the Savannah area, Ambos is the go-to supplier when the small outfits simply cannot satisfy the demand.

"We're still rebuilding," the bartender says. "The docks were destroyed. Lost the Las Niñas (Captain Royce's shrimper)."

She glances out the window, at what's left of the piers. They are, indeed, in ruin, if still somehow functional. Royce, at the time the hurricane hit was 81. After the storm passed, his trawler was upside down in Lazaretto Creek. His seafood supply shop ruined.

"We held a fund-raiser for him at the American Legion."

Impressive. Not just the spirit of the community, coming together to help a fellow seaman in distress. But that he was still on the water, operating a working shrimper at 81.

"It's the life," she says.

Did ever she work a trawler?

"No. But I did grow up shrimping and crabbing Shem Creek."

Impressed again. This time with reverence. I was face-to-face with a bona-fide, flesh-and-bone, avatar: a true "17-er." A returnee.

"I went to school with the brothers that now own R.B.'s. Son of the man owns The Wreck too."

R.B.'s—formerly The Trawler, one of the original restaurants on Shem Creek—and The Wreck, along with Red's Ice House, are landmark restaurants in Mt. Pleasant, just across the U.S. 17 bridge north of Charleston.

I anticipate what she'll say next, and it comes to me like a vision.

"I've spent all but 10 of my 50 years on, or near, or traveling Highway 17."

The missing years off the highway were spent in Decatur, GA, where she enrolled in Agnes Scott College, majoring in Economics.

Agnes Scott ... smacks of privilege. And Shem Creek ... one of the most desirable and expensive residential communities in the Charleston area.

So here I am now confronting an even more rare type: A certifiable "17-er," yes, but one with the means and resources to flee the highway, and all it represents, who tries, who actually *does* get away, for awhile. But she comes back. She's an ex-pat "17-er." A returnee.

She has what many "17-ers" do not: a wealthy family with enough resources to send her away, to broaden her horizons, to show her that there is more to the world than small town cultural pretentions or, inversely, anti-cultural animosity—both modes prevalent along the Lowcountry corridor, that contradictory strip-mall and haute couture southeastern coastal belt served by U.S. 17. She spends a year abroad, does the Occidental tour, returns, takes a summer job in a restaurant off 17. But she writes her sevens with a line through the stem, and people complain. What's that? A nine? I can't make out the bill. Food's good but the server was snooty. She has seen the world and returns to insults and reverse snobbery. So she retreats again to Sweetbriar or Hollins or Agnes Scott. Nowhere like the genteel mountains of Virginia or the pastoral quad of one of the Seven Sisters of the South to shake off the stigma of the eastern Carolinas. Where the students' last names mirror family corporations (yes, that Hunt), where alumnae include advisors to presidents, best-selling novelists, Jacqueline Kennedy's mother ... she graduates with her MRS degree, scores a Washington and Lee law school future super-partner, would if she could, escape ... but she comes back, lives her Southern Living *life in the Lowcountry, in Lowcountry style.*

Opting not to return to Charleston for "personal reasons"—technically, Shem Creek—but desperate to get back to the Lowcountry, to live off 17, the bartender at CoCo's, a privileged ex-pat "17-er," settled for what she considered the next best place: Lazaretto Creek, Tybee Island, GA.

CoCo's Sunset Grille, Lazaretto Creek, GA. Along Lazaretto Creek, they take shrimp seriously.

"And became a piscaterian," she says.

Piscaterian: a person who eats seafood but no other animals.

It was easy, in her mind, being a piscaterian, given the abundance of fresh seafood around the area.

Favorite style of shrimp?

"Boiled," she says, without hesitation. My disappointment must register, because immediately she reconsiders. "Actually ... I like 'em pickled."

Pickled? She opens a jar from beneath the counter.

"You peel 'em, then you par-boil—you know, *under* boil 'em—then marinate 'em with capers and peppers and..."

And ... what?

She won't say. It's her father's secret.

"In the bar here we use 'em for garnish on Bloody Mary's. Try one."

Crunchy, sweet, sour.

"My dad says you can't properly pickle 'em unless you're on Shem Creek."

Impressions of U.S. 17?

"I remember," she recalls, "when I was a child, riding bicycles on 17. Playing kick ball. Now..." She trails off. "I think some of it's lovely. I like taking it all the way to Key West."

I don't have the, what?—spite?—to spoil her memories and tell her U.S. 17 does not go to Key West. But I know what she means.

Favorite section of the highway?

"Murrells Inlet," she says. "Hands down."

Why Murrells Inlet?

"Lots of fun bars on a beautiful creek."

Ah ... spoken like a true "17-er."

≋4≋

Beaufort to Little River

That unpretentious, old-fashioned retro-charm. That kitschy Americana. Trinkets and arcana. Sights like the smallest church in America, outside Darien, near Eulonia. (Now a replica of the original building, rebuilt after being destroyed by an arsonist in 2015.) That marshy, coastal estuarial essence ...

All lost, spoiled as U.S. 17 approaches, and then by-passes, Savannah, crosses the Savannah River and enters South Carolina.

The Coastal Highway north of Savannah is an afterthought, much of it obliterated by I-95. An interesting wasteland without much "coastal" to recommend it. After Hardeeville, U.S. 17 merges with U.S. 278 and follows the interstate north until Ridgeland, where traffic is diverted back onto I-95. A remnant of the original survives as a frontage road, which runs parallel to and just west of the interstate, until the highway regains its identity as Kings Highway, the route through the ACE basin to Charleston. The road from Ridgeland to the turn-off to Charleston is a straight, unrelentingly shade-less, sparsely populated stretch that seems to mirror the railroad aligned with it.

Not exactly a route conjuring the cries of seagulls. The lure of shrimp or any of the other leisurely pursuits associated with the beach.

The highway through this region is ghostly in its lack of character. Unless lack of character could be considered, well ... character.

Of course, when this segment of the highway was originally built, the motif was not to provide access to what was then considered the spoils of the coastal wasteland; it was simply a main road, a conduit for motorists, both tourists and commercial interests, a quick, safe and easy transit between Savannah and Charleston. The draw of the coast—and its accessibility—is a modern phenomenon. The first bridge out to Hilton Head, for instance, wasn't completed until 1956, finished, not coincidentally, the year Charles Fraser began developing the island for wealthy vacationers. Likewise, until the late 20th century, Beaufort, now a tony retirement venue, was known mainly for the Marine recruit training center, Parris Island. The coast between Myrtle Beach and the Golden Isles off Brunswick was swampy, mainly good for hunting and fishing but not particularly suited for the fashionable beach-goers more interested in drinks with umbrellas and boutique shopping. Surfcasting was trendier than jet-skies, volleyball and boogie-boarding.

The route the designers chose for U.S. 17 cut about as close to the coast as it could given the propensity for flooding in the areas east of the highway, the relatively sparse population (at the time) of the coastal plain, and, perhaps most importantly, the difficulty of constructing a continuous highway across the marshy arms of the Harbor River and its many tributaries.

Similar to the situation in Georgia, where U.S. 17 divides into "before Brunswick" and "after Brunswick," the shrimp-scape route in South Carolina can also be divided into zones of "before Charleston" and "after Charleston." The area south of Charleston includes Bluffton, Beaufort, Edisto, and the West Ashley District outside Charleston, while the area north of Charleston includes Mt. Pleasant, McClellanville, Georgetown, and the Myrtle Beach Strand, including Murrell's Inlet and Little River.

From South Carolina's border with Georgia, to its border with North Carolina, the landscape changes noticeably and significantly. As you move north, the shallow coastal waters and bogs that define the coast from Savannah to Edisto, and again from Isle of Palms to the southern tip of North Carolina's Outer Banks, the ocean close to shore becomes deeper. Below Frying Pan Shoals, the shallow coastline is more hospitable to shellfish nursery areas, promoting juvenile populations. Approaching the North Carolina border, the ocean becomes more treacherous, and above Wilmington a major transition occurs, impacting how shrimp are harvested. The nature of shrimping in the zone around the Outer Banks becomes distinctly different from the dragging style south of Bogue Banks.

The area below Wilmington is associated with Myrtle Beach and shares a similar topography, as the coast through this region gradually becomes more traditionally "beachy." In fact, there's a rule-of-thumb shrimpers in North Carolina live by that illustrates the difference between the character of the ocean between Myrtle Beach and Fernandina and from Wilmington to the southern border of Virginia: most of the shrimp in the Tarheel State need to be caught before they reach the open ocean.

In short, if shrimp in North Carolina make it from the sound to the sea, they're basically gone, lost in the deep waters offshore.

The ACE Basin portion of U.S. 17 connects with several direct access roads that lead out to individual clusters of beach communities like Edisto Beach and Folly Beach. One especially rewarding route before the run to Charleston involves another looping itinerary that bypasses the dead zone of U.S. 17 between Hardeeville and Coosawhatchie but still retains the spirit of the Ocean Highway: the drive out to Beaufort, SC.

Immediately over the bridge from Savannah, as it enters South Carolina, U.S. 17 heads into a high-contrast no-man's-land before essentially dissolving in Ridgeland, SC. This cultural disparity is evident first when the road rolls past two gentleman's clubs—Temptations and Karma—then again when it passes signs promising a chance to fire fully automatic machine guns, and then again as it runs past the horse stables and riding grounds for wealthy SCAD students. The contrast continues after the turn east, onto SC 170. It winds through a landscape of natural beauty spoiled in spots by saturation housing, scrunching ageless rural local communities up against new developments—mini Hilton Heads—linked by a spidery web of new roads and old byways crossing fingers of the Harbor River, before the detour finally spills into the Port Royal Sound area of Beaufort County.

Beaufort is the second oldest city in South Carolina. (The name is pronounced "bew-fərt," not to be confused with Beaufort, NC, pronounced "boh-fərt," a former 18th century whaling village some 300 miles north.) Beaufort, SC, began as a shipbuilding center in 18th century, evolving, like much of the surrounding region, into a slave-based agrarian economy, and later, during and immediately after World War II, a shrimping center. Until the late 20th century, the town was considered a hayseed backwater associated with rowdy Marine recruits and small town southern despondency.

The truth is that, historically, Beaufort has always punched above its weight class, vying with Charleston and Savannah for cultural relevance and political influence. Before the Civil War, rice and cotton plantations created an affluent class of landowners, and this prosperity drew the wealthy and well connected to enjoy the charm of the Lowcountry and the elegant social life available to the well-heeled in antebellum Beaufort.

Though it never regained its early 19th century status, and suffered a major economic and social decline after World War II, modern Beaufort is now a desirable destination for a hip set that value nostalgia and a conservative constituency with a genuine appreciation of history, fishing, watersports and ecology, even if it can't quite shake its reactionary roots.

The difference between an attractive town catering to heritage tourism and a community once disparaged and derogatively associated with the Marine "boot camp" has not been lost on Hollywood. Along with popular military and action flicks like *Full Metal Jacket* (1987), *The Fugitive* (1993) and *GI Jane* (1997), Beaufort has served as the backdrop for baby-boomer films like *The Big Chill* (1983) and *The Prince of Tides* (1991), as well as that perennial favorite (and shrimp boat classic) *Forrest Gump* (1994). The town hosts an annual film festival, and locals still traffic in rumors of celebrity sightings.

This sprawling collection of neighborhoods is anchored by Bay Street, a bustling strip of shops, bars and restaurants along the waterfront lining the Beaufort River immediately west of the Richard V. Woods Memorial Bridge. A concerted effort by interested parties has produced tourist-friendly policies, promoted preservation and restoration initiatives, and showcased some of the best examples of antebellum architecture in the southeast, efforts which have created a small town with a trendy sensibility. The scene now is much more upscale and modern, considered posh by lifestyle magazines, its sophistication muted only by its reputation as a socially conservative enclave of white privilege and affluence.

One enamored local—a pert, fit, energetic hotelier, history buff and a former shrimper—recalls the years when Beaufort was still a fairly important shrimping venue, and fondly talks about her time on a trawler. A Beaufort native, she also loves to talk about the history of the area, current and past. She's a wealth of arcane knowledge. She knew the owner of the Miss Sherri, the boat used in *Forrest Gump*, and where it lies now. She can also explain why trawlers don't operate in local waters, sticking to off-shore grounds, by dredging up stories about how, during the Civil War, there were ships anchored across the bay in a blockade, and, according to her, they were left moored in place so long the anchors frequently rusted off, so today, when contemporary shrimpers try to drag the inland waters, their nets are shredded from all the scraps of anchors littering the bottom.

One of her favorite stories is how to catch shrimp without trawling. Illegal now, the strategy involves cutting bamboo stakes and driving them deep into the banks of Harbor River east of Parris Island. Then she creates mud patties from marsh soil mixed with fishmeal and sets them at the bottom of the bamboo poles. The shrimp burrow down into the mud to eat the fishmeal. When the tide is right, she shines a light on the water, and when the shrimp explode into the glow, she throws the nets against the poles, sinks them into the mud, and nets a "mess" of shrimp.

"When those shrimp would pop up out of the water, it's like a ballet," she says. "It's the most beautiful thing. We'd catch so many you couldn't walk in the boat."

One variation on this approach uses red clay pies mixed with fishmeal, but, she claims, "The kinda clay we used killed the catfish."

The most lasting impression she remembers is that of the "butterfly," which is how she describes the spread pattern of the trawler nets as they are lowered into the water. Another impression is the fun of riding the spreaders attached to the otter trawl. The process was fairly simple. The arms with nets are lowered into the water. The weighted nets drag along the bottom, while the wooden "doors" plane along the surface to keep the nets open. The nets close as they are hauled up, and the shrimp are dumped onto the center table on the rear of the boat. To "ride the spreaders" she would stand on top of the trawler cabin, climb out onto the arms as they swung out, drop into the water and swim back to the boat.

A child's game, she says ... but obviously for a select few.

She was fifteen years old when she worked on the trawler, so her job was limited to "heading" the shrimp—popping their heads off—sorting shrimp from by-catch, scooping the shrimp into the ice hole. Back then, in high school, working on boasts for her and her friends was a rite of passage. Considered part-time work for some, she recalls how many others dropped out of school to shrimp full-time.

"Everybody was either shrimping, gigging, or crabbing," she says.

She also fondly describes a tasty dish she cooked while on the boat at sea called "poop," a concoction of hot mac and cheese, green peas, and canned tuna stirred into cream of mushroom soup. There she was, on a boat full of fresh fish and shrimp, serving "poop" on platter.

"The cooking facilities were limited," she says. "And besides, we were out there to work."

Any memories of U.S. 17?

"I use I-95 to go to Florida. When I'm going, all I want to do is get there. But US 17 is the only way to get to Charleston, so ... it was nicer in the old days, when it was a two-lane. It was quieter, before all the traffic. Back then, I could go to Charleston in 30 minutes. It's more convenient now, but ... when Hilton Head took off, that changed everything."

One thing hasn't changed: she still likes "poop."

From Beaufort, the only way back to civilization, heading north, is to rejoin the Ocean Highway via U.S. 21 at Gardens Corner. As the road swings inland around the marshes and estuaries of the Lowcountry between Beaufort and Charleston, the various veins running east off the U.S. 17 artery venture out toward the Atlantic across a series of barrier islands that make up the ACE Basin.

A quick thirty miles from Beaufort, the first significant turn leads out to Edisto Island, and after another, slower thirty miles, ends in Edisto village. Made famous, sort of, with the bildungsroman of the same name by Padgett Powell, the area was once, probably, more than a diversionary sandbar playground for the smart set from Charleston, although it seems to have always been a recreational fishing retreat with little else to offer. Its history involves a mix of 17th century Spanish and "Edistow" Indians, and later slaves, of course, and a plantation commerce support by rice, cotton and indigo. When the cotton crops were destroyed by an infestation of boll weevil, the residents turned to fishing and the town gained a reputation for its seafood, especially shrimp. The commercial fishing improved during the 1920s, helped by both the dredging of the Intracoastal Waterway and the improved access to the mainland thanks to a new drawbridge.

U.S. 17, A.C.E. Basin. A.C.E. is an acronym for an area where the confluence of three rivers—the Ashepoo, Combahee and Edisto—forms one of the largest estuaries along the Atlantic Seaboard.

Today, Edisto Beach consists mainly of resort cottages built between the oceanfront and sound, strung along a road that loops from the end of the island back to the main road. Tucked in among the cottages are a handful of novelty shops and restaurants, a fuel dock, bait and tackle stores, an arcade. To be fair, this is a trend everywhere, displacing indigenous populations around mountains and lakes and various desirable vistas—in this case, the beach—where "people of means" go to pretend to be rustic. Developers in Edisto have modeled the toy town at the end of the island on Hilton Head, which has, throughout the southeast, become the Ur archetype for gated resort living, with designer homes surrounding a lush (if, in Edisto, minuscule) golf course and other resort amenities with pathways for cars and golf carts, docks with davits for fishing boats. Strict building codes stress conformity.

If the village itself is an upper class enclave for those who can afford seaside cottages, and to play among the poor, who can transform inconvenience into the merely quaint, the road out to the tip of the island follows a long road of dispossession and poverty, and it's that stretch of the turn off U.S. 17 that best expresses the beauty and truth of the ACE Basin.

Urbanization transforms neighborhoods as well as livelihoods, especially where waterfronts are transfigured, from commercial enterprises into tourist accommodations and recreational venues. Edisto illustrates this phenomenon nicely. In the actual town of Edisto, for instance, according to the most recent consensus, the number of people listing their occupations as shrimper is zero, even though the community is situated on an island located in a prime shrimp zone. White shrimp is listed as the number one species landed in terms of local quotient, well ahead of Blue Crabs. Similarly, the number of residents involved in professional careers like finance, real estate, law, education and "art" is over 60 percent. The median household income is over $65,000, while the number of people living in poverty, not coincidentally, mirrors the unemployment rate: under 3 percent. Ethnicity is nearly 100 percent white, non–Hispanic. Median age: 64.

So for those looking for social diversity, or a youth culture thriving on water sports, or a beach town full of clubs catering to young professionals, or a commercially viable, working waterfront, Edisto may not be fill the bill.

No question that the posh set prefers Edisto, the vacation slash retirement beach-life scene of choice between Hilton Head and Folly Island. But it's a long drive out to Edisto, and the island, once it shed its seafood harvesting culture, offers a smidgen of style, basically a-cut-below-frou-

frou, given its imitation Hilton Head couture, golf-couture culture, and rustic pretense.

Back on U.S. 17, the highway crosses a few miles of nondescript scenery before approaching the choke points that clog the highway into Charleston. Just south of West Ashley, incessant jams serve as a rude introduction to the even more snarled traffic ahead.

But an eastern detour sends the curious traveler into part of the Lowcountry that rarely appears in the Chamber of Commerce tourist brochure.

More bizarre and "removed"—an antidote, in some ways, to Edisto—and less a resort than a working shrimp enclave, Rockville, SC, sits on the north bank of Bohicket Creek, a tidal arm of the Edisto River at the end of Maybank Highway, SC 700, accessible from U.S. 17 via SC 1020 just as it enters into the West Ashley neighborhood southwest of Charleston.

Rockville, as a town or village, doesn't exist. Each branch of the main road into the area is fronted by a sign that says, "End of the Road," or "Road Ends 2000 Feet."

You get the idea.

In fact, the only reason to drive out there, unless you happen to prefer docking a yacht in the middle of nowhere, or having decided that this sort of isolation purifies the soul—there are more than a handful of small, tastefully rural and manicured churches in a community with no convenience stores, no restaurants, no, well, anything except a few boat slips—is to visit a storied seafood outlet—Cherry Point Seafood—famous for its fresh local shrimp and enduring if dwindling fleet of shrimp trawlers.

(Once at 40 boats, the number is now down to less than a half-dozen.)

The whole scene has a "religious retreat" feel to it ... for the wealthy. Secular encroachment is evident in the stratifying contrast of real estate in the area: mansions mixed with ramshackle cottages, a manor house beside a trailer on blocks with rusting remnants of cars or ghosts of appliances in the yard. From the Cherry Point Park Boat Launch you can see the upscale condos of Seabrook Island across the waterway. On the road to Cherry Point Seafood—the sign adorned with a Christian fish symbol and a quote from St. John—a well-appointed plantation-style estate sits on the water across from a derelict wreck of an old trawler.

The main draw of this outback—besides the hunt for fresh wild South Carolina shrimp—seems to include architectural historians that like to study playthings of the privileged. Magazines gush about the raised foundations and spacious porches and live oaks draping Spanish moss over the paths through the thick stands of palmettoes.

Cherry Point Seafood, Rockville, SC. The end of the road. There's only one reason to come this far away from anywhere. Fresh shrimp, right off the boat.

But ask Charleston locals about Rockville, and, if they remember where it is, it will be because of the Sea Island Regatta, a once noble and even legendary sailboat race turned into a excuse for an alcohol-fueled bacchanalia that might well, in late August, frighten even the spawning shrimp.

Following SC 700 away from Rockville leads back to a semblance of civilization in the form of Folly Beach, a seaside playground of Charleston. Catering to the kitsch-and-touristy set desperate for a more pedestrian beach experience than the patrician *plein air* attitude associated with Isle of Palms, Folly Beach clutters one of the few inhabitable barrier islands along the southern coast of South Carolina. The history of the island is insignificant, with all due respect. When the Europeans showed up, in the 17th century, they found the area populated by the Bohicket Tribe, which later mysteriously disappeared. Aside from the rumors of activity by Blackbeard—common throughout the Carolina banks—and minor skirmishes associated with the Civil War, the most significant recorded historical event was a visit by George Gershwin while he was hammering out *Porgy and Bess*.

Top: Mural, Cherry Point Seafood, Rockville, SC. *Bottom:* Trawlers, Rockville, SC. With the price of waterfront property skyrocketing, shrimpers operate, and often live, along lonely stretches of rivers and creeks, hoping not to get priced out of the areas. In Rockville, the contrast between the affluent and working class is obvious and acute.

More significant than the exploits of pirates or American folk opera is of course the availability of wild South Carolina fried white shrimp. And the scenic village main street in downtown Folly Beach offers a welcome respite from the *haute cuisine* elegance and *Chef de partie* aesthetic of Charleston's French Quarter.

Located just out of the main village, Crosby's Fish and Shrimp is about as local and authentic as it gets. The spawn of Captain Horace Crosby, Sr., a former taxi cab driver in Charleston with a serious penchant for fishing, Crosby's has been in business since 1973. By the time the family took over management, in the late 1980s, Crosby's had become an institution famous for the trawlers docked out back, selling fresh shrimp and seafood from its market, and hosting the occasional dock party, serving beer, shrimp, crab cakes and fish stew.

(The parties—when they occur—are announced with a sign by the highway, about a week in advance, with no set schedule, depending on, among other factors, the tidal pull of the moon.)

The strip through the core of the village, Center Street, offers a casual selection of choices for sampling the local catch. One of the most celebrated of these eateries is The Folly Beach Crab Shack, on the corner of Erie Avenue and Center, a cramped, intimate space with inside and outside seating. The walls are covered with murals, scenes of local interest, like the pier and the lighthouse, with the crab motif played up—more tastefully than the Tybee Island iteration, more fun and less exploitative. (No space for bus parking.) The outside tables are arranged in a porch-like setting, with open air seating on a deck along the sidewalk. Their small menu focuses on quality, not quantity, and though the theme is crabs, the offerings are heavy on local seafood: except for the snow crab legs, and Chesapeake oysters, they use Crosby's exclusively.

I learn all this from the bartender. She's proud of the shrimp—actually brags about how *local* they are. Then a guy at the bar chimes in: "The local oysters are better."

He's a self-described "Army Brat." Lived in Folly Beach for 37 years. Right across the street from the Crab Shack. Served in the 101st Airborne. Now retired. Spends his time fishing, crabbing, hunting and shrimping.

Here is another type of "17-er." Retired military. Given the abundance of military bases along U.S. 17, and the rugged wetlands and forests it cuts through, the U.S. 17 corridor from Camp Lejeune to Parris Island has long been a haven for career military types who separate from the service but retain the mentality. The former mercenary outfit Blackwater in Moyock,

NC; Marine Base Camp Lejeune in Jacksonville, NC; the Air Force Joint Base in Charleston, SC; Marine Training Camp at Parris Island, SC; Hunt Army Airfield in Savannah; the Sub Base at St. Mary's; the Naval Station at Mayport, FL. The U.S. 17 route travels a landscape the military considers its own theme park. Restricted air zones, off-limits training areas, barracks, hospitals, off-base housing ... from Norfolk, VA, to Jacksonville, FL, the Coastal Highway rolls like Main Street through the southeastern military-industrial complex's private reservation.

These ex-service members define the character of the region as much as any other subset living along the highway. The isolation offered by forests and wet-lands, along with the abundance of game and seafood to accommodate self-sufficiency, seems to succor the allegiance of group-think among like-minded "patriots" who tend to agree with the right wing political agenda ... the U.S. 17 corridor often promotes even more radical affiliations: self-identified white-supremacists, survivalists, militias; loners suspicious of government agencies, "city-slickers" and people who do not fit the White Christian Separatist ideal, commonly referred to as the Aryan Brotherhood. More troubling, perhaps, are the crypto-racists that act just within the boundaries of accepted political discourse and tactics. They operate behind the veneer of propriety, but their motives are precise, direct and effective. These ex-soldiers and militia types of Alt-Right fanatics are as much a part of the social fabric of U.S. 17 as the partiers and vacationers and retirees settling into their rentals units, hotels and ocean front villas.

This is a region, after all, even into the mid–1970s, that sported signs featuring a hooded figure on a horse, holding a burning cross, blaring the legend: "This is Klan Country. Love it or Leave It." The ghost of that horseman plagues the route, and the vociferous denials by apologists tend to underscore, rather than undercut, the reality of this phenomenon.

Not to say this man in the Crab Shack enjoying his noon cocktail— whisky soda—on a cold and blustery day at the edge of the continent between the sands of the Atlantic and the marshy creek separating Folly Island from the mainland is a racist political operative determined to undermine the constitution and return the country to an idealized Jim Crow past....

Far from it. He was born on a U.S. military base in Germany but raised off 17. He's been around the world, as a child and a soldier ... and yet, he has come back, like so many others, come home, back to the familiar world of The Coastal Highway.

Outside Wooten's Drive Inn, nursing a can of Schlitz in the parking lot, the young "17-er" has some decisions to make, or at least to seriously think about. Never been involved in sports. No social clubs. Bit of a loner. Likes to hunt and fish. Drives a jacked-up pickup, cab-mounted spotlights, oversized tires, dual pipes. Girlfriend he's already thinking about marrying, especially if he graduates next year—yes, he's underage, surreptitiously enjoying his beer—based on his passing English, which does not look likely, or biology, or history, or general math ... and entering a post–Vietnam cooldown (say, mid–70s), the military option looks good. But every day, less like an option, more like ... the only option.

"These are "creek" shrimp," the Army Brat explains, pointing to the entrée. "They're caught inside, not in the ocean. And they're big this year."

As proof, the bartender brings out a plate of butterflied beasts, jumbo "creek" shrimp. Medium coating of batter, deep-fried to an orangey brown. Succulent, firm, plump and sweet, they taste as fresh, meaty, and clean as if they were caught miles offshore.

"Most of the inside shrimp are nabbed with cast-nets," he says.

The bartender laughs. "You can use cast-nets, set-nets, drop a basket off the bridge ... toss in a crab pot. It don't matter. Shrimp'll swim right into your boat around here."

"Trawling inside is tricky," the vet says. "Lots of trash on the bottom."

I recall the lady in Beaufort, her story about the blockade boats, how those derelict anchors shred nets.

"But that ain't the worst of it," the guy says. "Mainly it's the oyster beds. Tears up the trawler nets. Plus, the channels are so narrow. Outside, it's open, wide and flat. Inside, you got to stay between the buoys, and that's a challenge, even for skiffs with the small drag nets."

The bartender listens, leaning on her elbows. It's a winter crowd, sparse. She is open, friendly, celebrates what she calls her "Irish roots"— auburn hair, freckles, deep laugh. She sings to the music she's programed from her cell phone: Christmas pop.

"You listen to this stuff all day, it's not long before you memorize it, even though it's a nice break from the normal theme music we're supposed to play: steel drum stuff, you know, Jimmy Buffet."

I commiserate, and join into the spirit of Darlene Love singing "Jingle Bells." (I'm guessing.)

Any thoughts of U.S. 17?

She and the Army guy answer in unison.

She: "Auto Mile."

He: "Motor Mile."

She: "Buncha car lots."

He: "All owned by the same guy."

Impressions?

"Traffic," he says, without hesitation. Then comes the inevitable qualification. This happens frequently. It's a pattern with "17-ers." The first response is a quick negative, usually concerning traffic. (Or, in the outback, killer deer.) But then, slowly, they reevaluate their initial response. Reconsider their snap answer.

"Well ... I do like the south side," he says. "Hell, I grew up going to River Baptist Church, right in the heart of the Motor Mile. And now that I think about it, US 17 takes me where I need to go to launch my boat. But I do not like Mt Pleasant."

I consider this Army brat "17-er" and, to be fair, recognize another type of retired military member that occupies the U.S. 17 corridor. A true conservationist, lover of activities not restricted to hunting and fishing and the mythical pursuits of self-sufficiency, but of water-sports, kayaking, paddle-boarding, sailing, surfing—a connoisseur of natural beauty and the resources that make the landscape around The Coastal Highway so desirable. This kind of noble warrior—just as lethal, maybe even more so—returns to the land east of U.S. 17 either as a non-ideological non-partisan preaching co-habitation, or, more rarely, as a progressive enthusiast, actively operating against his radicalized brethren, countering the Alt-Right view of the world fostered by so many fellow veterans....

On the other side of Wooten's Drive-In, nursing his can of Schlitz among the popular students, he wears stylishly faded jeans, pressed cotton shirt, leather loafers, another Army Brat wasting his Wonder Bread years off 17. He has good hair. Drives a classic MGB. Dates his way through the cream of the cheerleading squad, without even playing varsity sports. Makes the debutant circuit. Graduates high school. Gets accepted to West Point but turns the scholarship down. Turns it down. Flabbergasts his parents. Amuses his friends. Slips in and out of state universities. Prefers the surfing life. The fringe of the townie scene. One day decides to clean up, runs 10 miles a day, signs up for BUDs training, joins the Navy SEALs, conducts missions in exotic locales around the globe. Retires. Settles off 17. Comes back. Home. To U.S. 17.

These two types of military "17-ers" reflect, metaphorically, the current American political situation: just as the country is teetering on a direction forward or backward, U.S. 17 is poised to lead into a progressive new century or backslide into a reactionary past.

I shake off the reverie. Pull myself out of this philosophical miasmic muck. The bartender wants back in the conversation. To talking about U.S. 17.

"Me too," she says. She's remembering the south side of U.S. 17 through Charleston. She used to travel with her grandfather out past the Motor Mile, to Wappoo Road, which runs from the Coastal Highway to Edgewater, between Stono River and Wappoo Creek, to a park her grandfather cherished.

A "born and raised" Folly Beach girl, she allows her story to unfold like the highway she cannot escape: another "17-er," she leaves for a while, in her case a few years, to live with her family in Ashville, NC. But she comes back too, enrolls in College of Charleston, majors in business, is now working on her real estate license. She left, but she came back, plans to stay. U.S. 17 is in her blood.

Like the former soldiers: The draw of the highway is just too strong.

So many "17-ers" have no choice. They stay because they can't leave. Family. Jobs. Limited imagination. Limited funds. But those with resources. The ones who leave. Who travel. Sample other cultures. Other highways. When they come back, and fuse their new experiences with the old, they are the future of U.S. 17. They will be the diplomats that drag the outdated worldview characterizing much of the highway into a more inclusive, tolerant future. They are the ones that will shape the course of the 21st century highway.

One more time I escape the high-minded socio-political musing and order another half-dozen jumbo fried "creek" shrimp.

I bite back into the "17-er" life.

Fan-tailed, local, wild.

The stretch of U.S. 17 from Charleston to Georgetown connects two shrimp-mad consumer regions—Charleston and Shem Creek at the southern node, Georgetown and Myrtle Beach to the north—passing straight through the heart of wild-shrimp harvesting country in the northern sector of the South Carolina coast, the nexus of which is located in McClellanville, one of the main port and processing center of the South Carolina shrimping industry.

In South Carolina, the waters off Beaufort, Shem Creek, McClellanville and Georgetown make up the trawling grounds for the delicious white shrimp indigenous to the area. And while the shrimp are basically the same from Hilton Head to Little River, the ports-of-call differ. More importantly, the processing plants, and the docks where the shrimp are unloaded, both separate and unify the various conglomerate suppliers and independent trawlers.

Processing shrimp landed in South Carolina mainly involves two plants, one located near McClellanville and one near Pt. Royal, the latter serving the haul taken from the Beaufort area north to Charleston, the former drawing stock from the Georgetown docks, McClellanville and south to Shem Creek. Many of the shrimp taken from Shem Creek north are processed out of state, adding to the scarcity in the area and elevating prices. Shrimpers in the affected areas argue that improving the existing plants and perhaps adding another plant around McClellanville to keep the processing local would increase the yield and supply the loyal customer

Shem Creek, Mt. Pleasant, SC. One of the most popular party and recreational destinations around Charleston, Shem Creek has evolved from a traditional shrimp dockage and processing area to a major tourist attraction, drawing equally from visitors and locals. Many residents have resisted the transition, but even in an area like this, with a deep-rooted and powerful historical preservation society, money talks. The volume of shrimp the restaurants go through forces most of the kitchens to rely on imported shrimp, but most claim the shrimp are nevertheless harvested from wild Atlantic and Gulf waters.

base with wild shrimp, because, surprisingly, many restaurants, from the Lowcountry around Hilton Head to Charleston and Myrtle Beach, still serve both imported and farmed shrimp, especially national chain restaurants, buffet-style diners, and those catering to tourists seeking all-you-can-eat budget platters.

While clients of restaurants serving local shrimp extoll the taste and texture of local wild caught shrimp, many cooks suggest that when it comes to shrimp—especially fried shrimp—even a consumer with what might be described as a seasoned palate has a difficult time discerning wild from farmed. A study by Robert Moss, conducted for *Charleston City Paper*, in its February 25, 2015, edition, illustrates this slippery reality, the nuance of the distinction between local and farmed. While the experts in the test (including famed Charleston chef Brannon Florie), "could certainly notice subtle differences in flavor and texture … amid all the seasoning, breading, and the time the shrimp spent in extremely hot oil, the end differences in flavor and texture were subtle at best."

This notion is not popular, or even accepted, among "seasoned" locals.

Especially among those who flock to the legendary restaurants lining Shem Creek.

A legend among the pioneers of the modern shrimping industry in the area, Shem Creek traces its roots back to the post–World War II glory days of the shrimping industry in Mt. Pleasant. Two names most famously associated with Shem Creek and the industry it supported for so long are Ronnie Boals, who opened the first restaurant on Shem Creek, The Trawler, and Lewis "Red" Simmons, who opened one of the first ice houses and packing plants for local shrimpers, which later evolved into a contemporary restaurant, Red's Ice House.

Descendants of these early shrimp industry mavericks, and the customers who continue to patronize the Shem Creek restaurants, might claim to be able to expertly recognize the sweet toothsome bite of local Atlantic shrimp, in contrast to the rubbery, flavorless long-frozen product common on most menus, but it's the ability to recognize that "subtlety" that separates the buffet diners and dilettantes from the serious enthusiasts that know where to find wild shrimp and why it's worth the effort.

The popular restaurants along Shem Creek cater to wild shrimp connoisseurs and tourists alike, and this appeal to both camps sometimes creates a problem. Tourist traffic keeps the businesses in business. But when the appeal for volume leads to compromise, well, that leads to friction.

"Keeping it local" implies satisfying natives that know the difference between lemons and lemonade, as it were, and others that perhaps lack the refined Lowcountry taste for authenticity. But sorting out the pretenders from the genuine can be tricky, even in Shem Creek.

The Mt. Pleasant area, like most of the Charleston region, is steeped in antebellum history. But its history begins, as does so much of the continental east coast, with colonization. Populated by Sewee tribes, the land was first settled by whites when the British landed in 1680, where they established an outpost to defend the early northern colonies from attacks by the French and Spanish. By the time the Carolinas had become two states, with South Carolina deeply involved in the machinations of the slave state politics of the mid–19th century, the township now known as Mt. Pleasant embraced secession, and was instrumental in prosecuting the Civil War. After defeat, the freed slaves from the plantation economy counted for over three quarters of the local population, and original segregated communities created, developed and controlled by African-Americans just after the Civil War exist today. The most prominent of these communities is Scanlonville, named after the freed-man carpenter who first purchased the plot, Robert Scanlon, which lies just to the northwest of U.S. 17 as it crosses the Cooper River.

One of the most popular attractions in Mt. Pleasant, at least with the flag-pin-on-the-lapel crowd and Greatest Generation buffs, is Patriots Point, home to the museum ship USS Yorktown, a World War II Essex-class class aircraft carrier. Other history buffs point out that the area was used during the Civil War for testing the Confederate submarine, H.L. Hunley, action many locals still consider a heroic act of patriotism.

For those of a more epicurean bent, true patriotism consists of munching fried, locally processed, wild South Carolina white shrimp. If you can find them ... a paradoxical statement given the reputation of Shem Creek. But the ugly truth is that, with the volume of diners invading the several restaurants by the Coleman Boulevard bridge, it's impossible to serve local shrimp year-round, in and out of season.

So finding the real thing in the cluster of restaurants along Shem Creek calls for vigilance. In fact, although its reputation is built around the local shrimp industry, and the restaurants that pioneered bringing them to hungry customers, these days finding local shrimp along Shem Creek is problematic. The commercial heart of the waterway is built along the banks bisected by the actual creek flowing east to west. The upper part of Shem Creek, cut off by Coleman Boulevard, has limited access beyond the bridge to all but small craft, kayaks and paddleboards. Actually, many visitors come to Shem Creek not to eat but to stroll the planked walkway built throughout the park, perfect for viewing the marshes and observing the wildlife: manatees, dolphin, pelicans, coots and cranes. They come for the sunsets. The views.

The food, often, is secondary.

The Shem Creek Bar and Grill, in business since 1982, occupies a space on the north side of the bridge (given that the winding creek through this immediate area flows north to south), overlooking a marsh and abutting a small craft storage and dock facility, Shem Creek Marina, and Coastal Expeditions, a canoe and kayak charter tour business. The inside dining room features a typical table and booth set up with lots of plate glass facing the creek, framing awesome views of the marsh, the creek and paddle-boarders, although the majority of the heavy boat traffic perforce remains on the other side of the Coleman Boulevard bridge. Outside, tables situated on the wooden deck offer umbrella shade and a nice breeze when the weather's right. A pier leads out to a sheltered bar at the end of the pier, with strings of lights along the railing.

While the metal sculpture in the parking lot is a nice touch, the overall effect is that of an aesthetic that can't decide if it's going for camp, kitsch or just plain pandering. Touristy touches like the huge gator on the roof, photo-op props, the aquarium, a slew of nautical figurines and hanging knickknacks, the inside bar shaped like the prow of a yacht, the oyster bar out back strategically cluttered (decorated) with fishing gear, the self-consciously Key West pastels and calibrated funkiness ... all of these cheesy artifacts echoes Tybee Island's Crab Shack, on a smaller scale.

The menu might be evidence of, unfortunately, even more pandering. It reads like an encyclopedia: trendy sliders and shooters, stews, soups, salads, wings and fingers, dips and seafood tidbits, mussels, clams, oysters, shrimp—steamed, fried, grilled—salmon, dolphin, flounder, lobster, gumbos, pastas, sautés, sandwiches, chicken, burgers, tacos, okra, collards, red rice, cole slaw ... and, you guessed it, Newberg over grits.

But there's more, including a Sunday brunch, with omelets and Benedicts and waffles and French toast and nachos and oysters Rockefeller, baked oysters, fried oysters, raw oysters on a half-shell, and prime rib, rib eyes, plus a kid's menu and a Happy Hour menu and cocktails, and wine and beer and specialty drinks....

The shrimp comes adulterated: spiced with garlic and Tabasco, swimming in gumbos, riding a steak, adorned in sherry cream sauce or simply boiled, grilled or peeping from beneath a salad leaf. But, yes, the shrimp also comes fried.

On the south side of the bridge, Shem Creek offers a deep-water haven for trawlers and large recreational craft, with direct access to Charleston Harbor and the Atlantic Ocean. The west bank is anchored by the Shem Creek Inn, an upscale hotel on Shrimp Boat Lane, sided on the north by Water's Edge restaurant, and on the south by Vickery's Bar and Grill. Across the creek sits Tavern and Table, Red's Ice House, and R.B's Seafood. Further along toward the mouth of the creek, squeezed in between those warehouses and the adjacent dry dock marina, the bare-bones Wreck of the Richard and Charlene survives, famous for serving seafood on paper plates in a singular, patented no frills environment.

After World War II, most of the shrimpers unloaded their catch in the basin along what is now Ben Sawyer Boulevard in an area known as Simmons Pointe (yes, that Simmons). During the season, with all the boat traffic, the mouth of the creek remained deep enough to keep the passageway open, but during the off season the mouth would fill with silt. To remedy the silting-in, shrimpers used dynamite to blast the channel open, which over time was banned by regulators for the amount of fish kill associated with the blasting.

To keep the shrimping industry in the neighborhood, as it were, "Red" Simmons moved his operations to Shem Creek, and soon the wharfs along the creek became the epicenter of shrimping in the Charleston area. Commerce bloomed: the area saw the incursion of boat building companies, seafood processing plants, fuel docks, a serious fleet of offshore trawlers, and of course restaurants selling fresh catch right off the docks.

A few trawlers still line the shore, moored in front of a dwindling number of seafood companies that seem to go in and out of business, depending on the weather. Which is the way it goes these days, especially for an industry as stressed as wild shrimp trawling. In Shem Creek, where, at its peak, eighty shrimpers lined the wharfs, barely ten now call it home. One supplier, Wando Shrimp, shuttered its doors in 2014. The same year, the iconic business, Magwood and Sons, for 65 years synonymous with Shem Creek shrimp, sold to Simmons Marine, part of the Simmons dynasty that basically developed Shem Creek the way J.R. developed the Ewings' family ranch at Southfork.

Similar to the machinations on the fictional TV hit *Dallas*, the politics of the Creek are complicated, yet simple too, as far as small town politics go. In one camp is the Simmons family, active in the Mt. Pleasant seafood industry since the late 1940s. They decided to build an office complex along the wharf to increase the viability of the other businesses sharing property along Shem Creek. In the other camp are the residents of the upscale neighborhood surrounding the area, known as The Old Village, which resisted the office complex.

Many Mt. Pleasant denizens blame the Simmons family for what they consider the denigration of the traditional Shem Creek ethos. Since the 1950s, the family has been instrumental in transforming Shem Creek from a rough working boatyard to a waterfront recreational zone that features the restaurants and parkland the Creek is known for today. While the residents argue over the perceived increase in traffic flow and noise, the Simmons camp points out that the Creek has always had a business presence, and the office complex doesn't change the "character" of the Creek but continues the tradition of combining tourism with local business, providing restaurants to the residents as a bonus and preserving the shrimp industry tradition.

(One bumper sticker reads: Save Shem Creek. The question is, these days: What's to save? The original establishments, the "soul" of the Creek, sold out long ago.)

And after all, these days, the surviving trawlers look more like movie props, providing a picturesque backdrop for postcard-styled photographs, Facebook postings, and advertising copy for the heritage tourism market. If still barely authentic, the industry is slipping into nostalgia. For instance, Shem Creek Inn claims the rooms overlook "the Charleston Shrimp boat fleet." Sure, a few decades ago the trawlers were tied off three deep, nets and rigging cluttered the piers, and shrimp were sold right off the boats. Today, pleasure craft and tourists outnumber locals and working trawlers. And yet ...

Of the restaurants along the east bank claiming to serve fresh seafood, two stand out, while two others seem to be outliers at polar extremes of style. At the "low" end, the ostentatiously unpretentious Wreck, nearly indiscernible when viewed from its access road (Haddrell Street), takes its name from the fate of a derelict trawler moored next door at Wando's, wrecked by the wrathful winds of Hurricane Hugo, the eye of which, in 1989, passed directly over Mt. Pleasant. The main dining area is an enclosed patio style room, cooled in the summer by ceiling fans and warmed in the winter by a fireplace The waterside deck, available for special events and the occasional oyster roast, is literally on the docks shared with assorted craft from sailboats and power yachts to skiffs and trawlers.

At the other extreme, what might be called the "high" end, Tavern and Table pretends to a class more in line with the French Quarter restaurants around East Bay Street in downtown Charleston. The interior is minimalist modern chic, intimate lighting, artsy chandeliers, small wooden tables paired with a sofa style booth along the wall, lots of glass, natural lighting, airy floor plan. The establishment highlights an "Executive Chef." Not what comes to mind when you think of a fried shrimp basket with cole slaw and fries. During a recent visit, the chef du jour was a graduate of La Cordon Bleau Scottsdale, Arizona, which is about as white-bread as the Hilton Head Tennis Club, about as Lowcountry as Aspen (or Scottsdale, where she was working her kitchen magic at BB's, before being seduced into service at Tavern). And the menu reflects the chef's pedigree and aesthetic: Blistered Shishito Peppers, Roasted Poplano and Cilantro Hummus, Goat Cheese Polenta ... shrimp dishes include peel-and-eat, a reluctant Shrimp and Grits entrée, shrimp dumplings.

The two remaining eateries on the east side of the creek are legacy establishments. The Simmons' family roots in Shem Creek are evident at Red's Ice House. The restaurant was named after an ice shed "Red" created on the property to store shrimp fresh off the boats before shipping out the catch or selling them to locals. That cooler from the shed is now the bathroom at Red's. The restaurant rests on the original concrete slabs that served as the floor of Red's old seafood business.

Red's Ice House is rough. In a good way. It maintains a barroom feel even as the dining area spills onto the patio and the pier out over the waterway. The fashionably limited menu is heavy on shrimp and various local seafood—oysters, scallops, fish—with an emphasis on fried baskets. The shrimp do come sautéed, in a marinade, grilled, barbequed, served in a Lowcountry boil, in a sandwich. Buffalo style. Coconut. Skewered. This is bar food in a raw environment. Lots of beer. $20 bottles of wine. An oyster roast going off on the back deck. Live music. Dog's welcome. Young people on a tear. Rowdy. Crowded. Loud.

Not a place for foodies.

The key to Red's transcends its reputation and pedigree. They claim to rely on local products and freshly caught seafood, and to concoct their own sauces, dips and beverage mixes. Everything custom, fresh and basic. Given the honest approach to food and service, it's easy to see why Red's is so popular with the sundeck crowd. Even the imported shrimp (yes—in those fried baskets) are properly crunchy, tasty, and breaded in the spirit of clean deep-frying.

Immediately adjacent to Red's is another, well ... *once* classic eatery, R.B.'s, based on the original restaurant opened by long-time restaurateur, Ronnie Boals. Boals is responsible for a list of Shem Creek legends such as The Trawler (Shem Creek's first restaurant), The Lorelei, and The Mousetrap. The original R.B.'s burned down in 2002, but a new building opened on the site with state of the art facilities just one year later. The new establishment, according to long time residents, provides an entirely different experience from its former incarnation. The original R.B.'s operated out of a tin shrimp-heading shack with 35 seats. The reincarnation—Boals' Phoenix?—spreads over 10,000 feet of dining space, with an additional 2,000 feet upstairs.

But with a neon Blue Marlin over the entrance, the slick R.B.'s logo, the faux Key West architecture, the "nautical" interior décor replete with hanging ferns and dark wood paneling, the small colorful bar with coordinated trinkets and trim—all adds up to a restaurant that cannot shed its touristy core, an appeal that might indicate a contagion from other "downtown" Charleston properties owned by Boals, including The Noisy Oyster, a Market Street staple catering to tourists and refugees from the cruise ships docked at the Port of Charleston terminal.

(It must be stressed that even the most tourist-oriented restaurants in the Boals' lineup claim to serve, when possible, wild caught shrimp, usually acquired from the McClellanville docks).

Though it's not really fair to compare the two, as they tend to attract different clientele, Red's is intimately fundamental, even Spartan, while R.B.'s is spacious and more commercial—a strange epithet—"commercial"—given the heritage and evolution of the name and reputation. Hardly the bar scene that Red's flaunts, R.B.'s offers more formal if relaxed dining with, for those so inclined, open air seating under a covered porch by the water. The menu, less basic than Red's, is crowded. The entrées range from essential to frilly, from sandwiches to pasta pomodoro, from fried chicken tenders to baked stuffed mahi. When you dish up all the usual suspects—New England clam chowder!?—trying to please every taste, the interesting local items—oyster stew, steampot—tend to get lost. Lobster, pasta, snow crabs, Caesar salad ... the menu becomes interchangeable with the last chain restaurant you pulled into off I-95.

Given the history of Ronnie Boals, and the authentic, straightforward legacy of his early restaurant, with the focus food more than volume, maybe R.B.'s can be forgiven for its present state of affairs, but for many old timers, or those schooled in the culinary tradition that made Shem Creek's reputation, R.B.'s comes off like a betrayal.

The two west side restaurants do not share the colorful grunge of Red's, the historical reverence afforded R.B.'s, or the scruffy no-nonsense authenticity of The Wreck. They do, however, indicate the direction Shem Creek is headed: a faux rustic corporate style banking on scenery and sunsets more than the simple truth of local seafood.

As if to complement the pretentiousness of Tavern and Table, Water's Edge sits directly across the creek. Although the restaurant promises to bring what it calls "Downtown Dining" (meaning French Quarter, Charleston) to Mt. Pleasant, it stresses its local roots and connection to the area, mainly thanks to the owner—also an "Executive Chef"—Jimmy Purcell. The extensive menu, if generic, claims to be heavy on local seafood dishes with Lowcountry themes. In reviews the phrase "fine dining" crops up frequently, a concept offset by the Cabana Bar, a downstairs dock area that can accommodate a limited number of boaters. According to his bio, Purcell, after spending his youth as a waterman—surfing, fishing and boating—honed his trade in the gastronomic arts around some of the upper end establishments (and at the Culinary Institute at Johnson and Wales University).

The schizophrenic nature of the restaurant is endemic to the locale. On one hand, there is a demand by locals and tourists for an upscale dining experience, but on the other hand, both factions demand a laid-back patio-party feel. The possibility of hanging out by the water on a pier and knocking back drinks while watching boaters, dolphins and buff bodies is a seductive draw—what many consider the essence of Shem Creek—and suggests that formal inside dining is a tolerated, necessary option anathema to the spirit of "the Creek." Whereas the shrimp on the menu are mostly disguised in scampi, sautés, grits and paellas, there is a fried seafood platter available, but with a menu crowded with non-native fare, the fried shrimp seem like an afterthought. Incongruously, the bragging rights at Water's Edge seem to rely not on the honesty of their food but on the perceived prestige of their Wine List, selected for the Wine Spectator Award of Excellence every year since 2003.

Vickery's, at the other end of Shrimp Boat Lane, is a native Atlanta-based outfit, partial to cheeseburgers, that moved to Charleston in 1993, opening in a spot off Beaufain Street, an area downtown between Calhoun Street and Broad Street near King Street south of College of Charleston. The owners opened in Shem Creek in 1999, and have established an identity distinct from the other restaurants along the strip.

The downstairs patio seats patrons on both a wooden deck and literally on the sand beside the marsh and the plank boardwalk running along the creek bank toward the mouth of the creek. The views from upstairs are impressive, looking in one direction over the yachts and trawlers and all the action at Red's, and in the other direction toward the extensive marsh grass and spoils to the northwest.

The building combines a modern look—huge plate glass windows—with rough-hewn wood accents. The inside dining area upstairs features a classic combination of red vinyl booths and wooden tables, a colorful bar; the strategically shabby Sharkfin Bar outside provides cushioned stools, aluminum siding, lots of wood and metal railings. A predictable craft beer and no-nonsense wine list match the food menu, which trends toward sandwiches and fried plates, although there are funky appetizers like fried green tomatoes and artichoke dip, while the full meals include oddities like Cuban Black Bean Cakes along with southern staples like fried chicken and blackened shrimp. Even though the entrées have a Cajun flair, along with spicy Lowcountry themes, and the shrimp can be abused, in Bourbon, sautés, served over pasta or with Andouille, the fried servings are fairly straightforward.

Given the corporate sheen of the restaurants—they all share a certain gimmicky vibe, designed to appeal to a calculated variety of tastes and clientele—I decide on Red's. The bartender, when I ask if he got his shrimp from a trawler not two hundred yards from his deck, replies, "We do, but they go through Bull's processing first."

That would be Livingston's Bulls Bay Seafood, in McClellanville. A tricky, qualified answer ...

For wild shrimp aficionados, the fan base along Shem Creek—that mix of locals, homegrown and loyal—and tourists—from the larger Charleston environs, "17-ers," out-of-staters ... all seek authenticity. But so much of the shrimp come pre-packaged and processed. People who "know" are right to be suspect. Shem Creek, once a good place to find authentic wild shrimp, now finds its main draw—local fresh seafood—compromised.

When you ask servers or bartenders—"Where do you get your shrimp?"—part of the confusion, in a place with the volume of Reds or R. B's, is that they aren't sure because, depending on the product and the availability, they use so many different wholesalers. Further confusion stems from the difference between "local" and "wild." Local usually means from trawlers that have a home base in the immediate area, whereas wild simply means not farmed, and usually not imported. By most accounts, 90 percent of shrimp consumed in the U.S. is either imported or farmed.

Luckily, for those shrimp lovers along The Coastal Highway, a big chunk of that remaining 10 percent is hauled in from waters off the edge of the highway. The point is, even if the shrimp isn't "local," harvested from a trawler down the street, it might still be wild, caught between Norfolk and Mayport ... or even harvested from the Gulf of Mexico. Those shrimp are wild, just not exactly local.

(Maybe they should designate the catch "US 17 wild," which could also describe lots of the people who eat them.)

I ask a chef from one of the neighborhood's finer upper-crusty restaurants, The Old Village Post House, built circa 1888, a restaurant and guest house (six rooms) a few blocks east of the Creek, in the heart of the historic section of Mt. Pleasant.

"'Local' can mean from any state from the Carolinas to Key West," she explains. The real distinction, according to her, is the difference between wild shrimp taken from ocean waters versus farmed shrimp, headed, peeled, deveined and frozen, ready to thaw and cook with little preparation. Freezing peeled shrimp is a guaranteed method of stripping out flavor and freshness.

Which leads to another source of confusion. Never frozen but iced is, of course, ideal. But lots of wild shrimp are fresh frozen, and all the catch has been on ice. Usually, shrimp are headed right of the boat, then iced in the hold before being unloaded, where the shrimp are sold shells-on, or processed and frozen for delivery. Obviously, the closer to the source, and the less time on ice, the better. But local, "off-the boat," is a bit of a myth ... after all, as the manager of Crosby's told me, even the man selling shrimp off the back of his pick-up needs a license.

"Otherwise," she says, "How do you really know what you're getting? You wouldn't purchase ground beef from some guy selling it out of the back of his truck. Shrimp ... no different."

The problem, the bottom line, is volume. Shem Creek has grown from a strictly local, small outfit of shrimpers, wholesale suppliers and solo restaurant entrepreneurs to a full-bore, corporate identity, high turnover trademark. The reality of its development from a seasoned spot for those-in-the-know to a flagship tourist draw on the Charleston to-do list for visitors is, perhaps, now best reflected by that huge, multi-storied office complex dominating the east side of the creek, complete with a covered parking center.

The bartender at Red's explains that because of the volume of shrimp they need to serve year-round, for their bulk dishes, like fried baskets, they are forced to use imported shrimp. The only local shrimp they sell is boiled, for peel-and-eat plates and their signature Lowcountry boil. These shrimp are small, firm, slightly earthy, with a mild muddy taste. But in the boil, the natural shrimp flavor is overwhelmed by pepper.

I pick out the shrimp and push the dish away.

The bartender shrugs. He's a throwback to the early seventies, sporting shaggy shoulder-length hair, a scraggly beard, wrap-around shades. With his wiry blondish-red hair and matching beard, he looks like an extra in a Hollywood movie extravaganza about Vikings. He admits he's from Charleston. Born and raised. Went to high school "downtown." Attended College of Charleston. Grew up in The French Quarter. Implies he comes from a family with, well, assets ... but he quickly plays down this factor, his wealth, and shifts the conversation back to his morning surf, out on Folly Beach. An unusual southern swell has been pouring through for nearly a week. He's been "stoked" for days. Turns out, his surfer look is more than just a pose. Costa Rica, Bali, Australia, Hawaii, Europe ... he's surfed many of the more exotic locales on the planet.

"Spent some time in New York City, too," he says, to balance, I assume, his worldview.

But more importantly, I ask: Does he like shrimp?

"I do," he says. Then he quotes Forrest Gump—the first time, in all my talks with people in the industry.

(Except for the woman in Beaufort who had memorized every scene from every movie ever filmed in the swamps of Port Royal.)

I immediately forget the quote. But basically, the Viking likes shrimp any way you cook them. More importantly, and telling, for this self-sufficient global trekker, he adds: "You get a boat, a $15 fishing license, some nets, and shrimp are free."

Free. I try to frame what "free" means to this affluent Viking from College of Charleston School of Anthropology, study the context of "free" that involves a boat, an outboard motor, launching costs or dock fees, a license, the gear, the energy, effort, time involved ...

Meanwhile, he prattles on, friendly, outlining the Mt. Pleasant seafood scene, the general Shem Creek vibe, arctic surfing, the knotty state of geo-political mayhem in the era of Trump.

I try to bring him back to the immediate context. Ask him what it means to be "from" U.S. 17. To be a "17-er."

A noticeable change comes over him, an immediate shift in his demeanor. He's suddenly defensive.

"From?" Hostile pause. "That doesn't make any sense," he says. "Nobody says that."

I try again, asking if he lives near U.S. 17, hangs around it, uses it to get from here to there.

He shakes his head. The notion seems to trigger some Pavlovian aversion.

I remind him, "Charleston's on US 17."

"But nobody associates Charleston with that highway," he says. "Charleston was here before the highway. Know what I mean?"

Here was a new type of "17-er": a denier.

The bartender, this "trustafarian" Viking, did not want to be identified with U.S. 17. His identity was built around Charleston. But he preferred to be associated with the global community, and for him the distinction was essential.

"Highway 17 is just not a reference point for me," he says. "We don't even call it US 17. It's the Crosstown Highway or Savannah Highway."

How about going north from Mt. Pleasant?

Another hostile pause.

"That's US 17," he says.

Another bartender pipes in. "I live on James Island. Across two bridges. I don't play on this side. I stay on that side."

Suddenly, the city is being parsed into kaleidoscopic pieces holding ontological clues to sociological class affiliations. I suggest that U.S. 17 might be a unifying factor connecting various factions of the city. At least, on a north-south grid. West Ashley and Mt. Pleasant, for instance.

The Viking shakes his head.

"Nobody thinks like that. It's just a another road through town."

Then, as if dismissing the entire region north of the Ravenel Bridge, the Viking says, "My grandmother calls this area East of Cooper. She never says, 'Mt. Pleasant.' It's always, 'East of Cooper.'"

"You don't find many locals here or there," the guy from James Island says, referring to Folly Beach, at the tip of James Island. "Charleston is a metropolis, now. The economy is booming. It's like the eighth largest tourist destination in the country."

The Viking considers his situation. As if to convince himself that, after traveling the world, he has returned to Charleston, not U.S. 17, he says, "Charleston is just such a super-nice place to live. The quality of life is extremely high."

Here was an archetype: a "downtown" Charleston nationalist. A native, which, he offers, makes him a rare bird—bred and schooled in the heart of the city—but obviously not from a Spring Street neighborhood. He's traveled. Europe. Latin America. Southeast Asia. Lived in New York City. A young man of assets … about which he's vague. Embarrassed by his wealth. About the highway coursing, even as he denies it, through his blood. About his … pedigree.

"Anybody who grows up in downtown Charleston is going to have … some…." He searches for the accurately ambiguous term, settles on, "means."

He's a man of the planet. Into co-habitation. Majored in Anthropology and Religious studies. Considers himself worldly. Surfing an expression of his harmonic intimacy with nature.

I feel an urge to remind him that the key to traveling is not where you go but what you learn while you're there. But I'm not here to teach. I'm here to learn. And I'm intrigued with this new prototype: A rich kid, denying his wealth. A "17-er," denying the highway.

But, after all, he *did* come back. Traveled the world. Surfed the oceans of the earth. Ends up at back at Red's. Slinging PBRs and seafood platters.

A young blonde server in a Red's sweater jacket elbows up to the bar and orders two umbrella drinks for her customers.

Is she from U.S. 17?

"Myrtle Beach," she says, and then it hits her: the truth of the highway in her life. What it means to be "from" U.S. 17. "Yeah … guess I never thought of it like that."

And now you live…?

"In Charleston."

So…?

She draws the conclusion.

"Wow. I'm a '17-er.'"

She's excited. She likes the idea. As if it anchors her.

"Eighteen years in Myrtle Beach. Four years here. That's my whole life."

She too is a College of Charleston graduate, double major in Dance and Arts Management.

Her idea of fun?

"Competitive dancing."

Shag?

"My parents love shagging."

Parents ... I let it go.

She slips away before I can ask about shrimp.

"She likes 'em," says the Viking. "Boiled."

He calls after her. "You like shrimp, don't you."

"Yeah," she calls back. "Cold."

The ice machine buzzes. The Viking shrugs.

Sham Creek?

Seems harsh ... I retreat to The Old Village Post House.

East of Cooper.

Off 17.

McClellanville occupies a weird black hole along U.S. 17 as it cuts through northern coastal South Carolina. Leaving metropolitan Charleston, the highway runs through Awendaw, famous for the Gullah weavers selling sweetgrass baskets from wooden stalls along the road; past the SeeWee Restaurant, once a general store dating back to the 1920s; the Center for Birds of Prey, a museum and medical treatment/research center specializing in exotic birds; the tiny, uber-local McClellanville Diner; and finally arrives at the eastern turnoff toward McClellanville proper.

Originally incorporated in 1706, what exists of the village of McClellanville dates back to the 1860s, after the plantation era, when the economy, like so much of the coastal south, shifted from farming to fishing, eventually establishing the town's reputation as a shrimping center. With its proximity to the open ocean, its safe harbor, and its easy access to U.S. 17, McClellanville remains one of the several ports aligned with The Ocean Highway that continues the tradition of "blessing the fleet" in the spring. Here, the ceremony actually means something beyond a tourist draw dreamed up by the Chamber of Commerce.

After the isolated affluence of that conservative, sterile redoubt, Edisto Beach, and the calculated charm of Charleston, and the ensuing congestion around Shem Creek, there's something genuine about McClellanville that defies gentrification. And yet ... there is also something specious about the place that causes people to inflate its significance, as if to protect and confirm their own need to believe in it.

Exactly halfway between Charleston and Georgetown, directly off 17, the town reeks of authenticity, probably because no matter how many posh houses retirees build along Jeremy Creek and the Intracoastal Waterway, the village economy is still dependent on harvesting shrimp. The commercial fishing fleet of trawlers dominates the wharf at the corner of Morrison and Oak streets.

U.S. 17 between McClellanville and Georgetown. Wild flowers in the Francis Marion State Park, near the Center for Birds of Prey.

McClellanville's resilience was sorely tested in 1989 when the eye of Hurricane Hugo passed directly over the area, destroying the village. When the wreckage was cleared, the residents set out not only to rebuild their primary business—its shrimping fleet—but also its past, its heritage and reputation as a working fishing village, just as it had been since the late 19th century.

But something's missing ... mainly, a semblance of a town, even a village. Similar to Rockville, SC, but without the strange "Church" kookiness, little identifies McClellanville as having a "center." There's a restaurant, a couple of shops, schools, churches, the spacious, often stately houses standing in their luscious lots surrounded by live oaks dripping with moss—and of course the busy, crowded docks, the throbbing heart not just of the town but of the entire area.

The impression is of a loose federation of components with no nexus, almost like a sprawling gated community, a compound of sorts, certainly more residential than commercial ... except for the fleet, the splendid line-up of working trawlers striking out to sea or moored along the picturesque creek.

Above: Shark art, Coastal Highway, McClellanville, SC.

The schools serve the larger community, the surrounding township, but the students do not necessarily reflect the reality of the residents residing along the waterways or the adjacent neighborhoods. Among the residents, there's an "art colony" vibe, tempered by a working underclass that seems oddly out of place, residing like misfits in their own community.

Left: Sweetgrass Gullah baskets, Coastal Highway, near McClellanville, SC. Sweetgrass baskets woven by Gullah natives have a long history in the region. The vendors line the Coastal Highway between Charleston and Georgetown and sell their wares from wooden stalls. Motorists simply pull off U.S. 17 and browse the handicrafts.

The commune called McClellanville retains an enigmatic identity. Like Marlow, in Joseph Conrad's classic *Heart of Darkness*, trekking up the Congo, hearing rumors of Kurtz, a traveler searching U.S. 17 for wild local shrimp between Charleston and Myrtle Beach will hear the name "McClellanville" uttered with the same mysterious reverence, like the incantatory echo of a sacred deity. But aside from its fleet and its wholesale seafood industry—the "ivory" shrimp—its reputation is larger than its reality. The trawlers are splendid. The houses impressive. The restaurant, T.W. Graham & Co, lodged among the oaks and resurrection ferns and five-leaf ivy, is fairly famous. (Its website features a photo of Mill Murray eating there, a segment on *The Food Channel*, a mention in *Southern Living*, and a *Forrest Gump* connection.)

But somehow I seem to have talked myself out of the aura of McClellanville, not the fact of the place but the myth, before I even got there. Marlow discovers the frail humanity of Kurtz, reduced from a God to

McClellanville, SC. The main drag, anchored by T.W. Graham, Inc., Seafood Restaurant. Picturesque, isolated but still close to Charleston and Georgetown, the village promotes a "traditional" lifestyle that underscores the split between haves and have-nots in the region. The community consists of a cluster of cottages, splendid houses, lush flora, and an impressive shrimping fleet.

a petty nihilist, the same way I find McClellanville underwhelming. The feeling is admittedly counterintuitive. Of all the towns and hamlets and holes-in-the-road that define the essence of The Coastal Highway, McClellanville *should* be revered. Up and down the coast, the very mention of the name conjures the quintessence of a "shrimp mecca." The trawlers are real, as are the crews that work them. But the town ... it all seems too precious, somehow fabricated, as if whoever was in charge of making McClellanville what it is, and what it became, betrayed what it was.

Its character relies more on reconstruction than preservation, and by playing on its past, its present has become a simulacrum, more semblance than fact.

I acknowledge the props—along with the truths, those that persist—and roll on, more at ease once I cross the South Santee River and catch the stench of Georgetown.

The third oldest settlement in SC, and its second largest port, Georgetown is famous for that stench. The locals call it "the smell of money." To them, it's the smell of jobs at the paper mill.

But between 1936 and 1969, Georgetown was best known for the Sunset Lodge, one of the most famous whorehouses in the southeast. My

The fleet, McClellanville, SC. Like Darien, GA, McClellanville is an actual working shrimp village and one of the major centers for the commercial shrimping industry on the South Atlantic Coast.

U.S. 17, between Charleston and Georgetown, SC. View of the North Santee River, looking west.

father remembers the establishment being written up in "the flying magazines." (He was a private pilot, member of the Aero Club.) The "lodge" was out near the airport, about three miles south from downtown, right on U.S. 17. The proprietor, Hazel Weiss, was rumored to have mob connections, ties to professional baseball, wealthy industrialists, the most important politicians in South Carolina ... the stuff of legend.

Off 17.

Today, still scarred by its reputation as a depressed (and depressing) mill town, its acidic pong permeating the community, Georgetown is, along with the nearby Murrells Inlet, perversely, a last gasp of fresh air before the mayhem of Myrtle Beach's Grand Strand. Actually, the infamous stink from the paper mill plagues the downtown village only when the wind is from what the locals call "the right direction."

Otherwise, the main drag, Front Street, has a city marina and anchorage along a riverside boardwalk lined with restored buildings filled with novelty shops and restaurants. The revitalized section of town by the waterfront is surrounded by a neighborhood of dignified antebellum mansions and Victorian homes, manicured lawns and shady Live Oak trees (one of which, on Prince Street, is over 500 years old). The shrimp trawlers unload at the end of Cannon Street, where it's still possible to buy fresh seafood right off the boat—or, at least, right off the counter once the catch is shifted from the boats. Brown shrimp thrive in the summer, often caught "inside"; the larger white "roe" shrimp caught "outside" are plentiful during late fall and early winter.

Big Tuna, Georgetown, SC. Rustic chic on the waterfront, serving some of the best local fried shrimp in the region, usually procured from the Georgetown docks or McClellanville.

The historic waterfront caters to an eclectic mix of heritage tourists, sailors, bikers, shoppers and assorted day-trippers, plus the spill over of residents from Murrells Inlet and Litchfield. Among the novelty shops, art galleries, antique stores and boutiques, the strip supports nearly a dozen restaurants, from hole in the wall delis and ice cream parlors to the pseudo-posh River Room with its imposing panoramic windows and indoor reef aquarium. While most of the eateries in the prime, "revitalized" waterfront lack the pretentiousness of the country club-styled restaurant near the marina, a few places still seem out of place with the gun-rack-in-the-pickup locals. Others seem overly touristy or chain-themed.

The gem on the strip is a diamond in the rough, the ramshackle Old Fish House, also known by its original name, Big Tuna. The restaurant's rustic décor only hints at artifice. A rotted skiff hangs from the ceiling. Wooden tables line a rough brick wall. Outside, a water front deck provides a close-up view of the river and boats in the marina. In a corner near the door, a 26 year-old Scarlet Macaw named Sassie meditates in a huge steel cage, occasionally screeching out some incomprehensible advice to amused diners. On the wall behind the wooden bar, a Pabst Blue Ribbon sign sports a bumper sticker that reads, "Friends Don't Let Friends Eat Imported Shrimp." A souvenir t-shirt for sale hanging beside the beer sign reads, "Yankees Served Fresh Daily" with a silk-screened image of a tourist hooked on an oversized rod and reel.

If the faux dereliction might seem, to a practiced eye, semi-authentic, the restaurant serves some of the tastiest shrimp off 17.

The menu offers requisite "Specials"—e.g., fried pork chops, rice and gravy—but it is heavy on local seafood, especially fried shrimp and oysters. Other exotic staples include shrimp and smoked sausage gumbo with okra, tomatoes and peppers.

I gobble a plate of fried shrimp and a bowl of gumbo. The shrimp are crusty with batter, but firm and sweet, the heavy coating less a disguise than a tasty adornment. In the gumbo, the flavor of the shrimp is barely camouflaged, blending nicely with the mellow spices.

My primary assignment finished, I troll for "17-ers."

The youngest employee is a local high school girl about as communicative as a pluff mud clam. A sultry, petulant teen, she lives just off the highway. And probably will for the rest of her life, even if she doesn't yet know it.

What does U.S. 17 mean to her?

"Nothing special."

Does she like shrimp?

She shrugs and walks outside to clean the windows.

Another young bartender claims she "grew up between Greenville and Morehead City," both communities in North Carolina that lie within 30 miles of The Ocean Highway.

How did she find her way to Big Tuna?

"My Mama worked here," she says, nonchalant. "I followed my mama."

Where is her mama now?

"In the Keys."

She is glowing with youth and optimism, wearing her effervescence as easy as her jeans and sneakers. I wonder why she is not in the Keys, but ask instead if she likes shrimp.

"I like hot dogs," she says. "I used to drive a half hour, all the way from Greenville to 'Little Washington,' to eat at a place called Bill's, right by the river." Bill's being for her a significant landmark on U.S. 17 and her allusion to "Little Washington" clearly mark her as a Coastal Highway local.

The fleet behind Independent Seafood, Georgetown, SC.

In contrast to the two teens—the one moody and preoccupied, the other chatty and bright-eyed—the bartender is a seasoned woman with an honest laugh. Her husband moved to the area after graduating from Charleston College. His family owned a cottage on Pawley's Island, a quick run up the highway, just south of Myrtle Beach. He owns a light tackle charter business, specializes in "flats fishing" throughout the Keys and the Bahamas.

Clearly a "17-er."

"And a fishing fool," she says.

Two facts that, I note, are not mutually exclusive.

But did *she* grow up on U.S. 17?

"81," she says, crafty.

I nod. She means Interstate 81. Roanoke, VA.

Favorite kind of shrimp?

"I wouldn't turn down a fried shrimp," she says, filling two glasses from a jug of Pinot Grigio. "But I like to taste it. I prefer my shrimp steamed."

Impressions of U.S. 17?

"When I was younger, up in Roanoke, US 17 meant, Woo-hoo! Myrtle Beach! Party! But when you get older, everything loses its luster."

She looks away, wistfully....

"Nowadays, US 17 don't mean nothing but traffic and tourists."

The Macaw screeches. The young bartender pours rum on ice. The woman from Roanoke winks at me, says, ruefully:

"That bird'll bite the shit out of you."

Crossing the Waccamaw River outside Georgetown, U.S. 17 enters Pawleys Island, a sliver of a barely inhabitable sandbank that was once a fish camp famous for oyster beds and bird watching but is now a playground for the economically set who can afford the exorbitant real estate prices associated with cottages lining the seashore. Separated from the commercial district along U.S. 17 by a tidal creek and marsh, the actual village of Pawleys Island is unique in that it has banned industrial buildings on the islands, except for a couple of low key inns and one colossal mistake, Pawleys Pier Village condominiums. The character of the area is well preserved and strictly residential, especially in the south end, the north end being wider and more populated.

Of course, all this preservation means most of the decent local restaurants are bunged in with Waffle House, McDonald's and Sonic Drive-In along the dense and busy U.S. 17 as it channels the northbound traffic toward Myrtle Beach. Lumped in with all the pretenders, the few exceptions

Birds of Georgetown. *Left:* **Wilber, a regular at Independent Seafood.** *Right:* **Sassie, Big Tuna.**

are easily stifled by the corporate chain vibe dominating the four-lane through the area. Without local guidance, even an astute diner might not feel compelled to hazard a visit. The saturation is simply too overwhelming.

Continuing north, the highway fronts the western edge of Litchfield, one of those communities invented to provide a generic life for people who think convenience is a virtue. Exclusivity—especially to coastal property—is, after all, a right of the privileged. Litchfield-by-the-Sea—the preferred signature—is modeled on the sort of pre-fab, interchangeable, sealed-off communities popular in south Florida but perfected in Hilton Head. This is white bread America, where year-round-golfing is more than a life-style: it's an existential quest. Slipping through Litchfield without being recognized by the local constabulary is as easy as it is advised, as there is little to recommend this self-described "upscale" neighborhood unless you thrive on leathery folks riding around in convertibles, dressed in age-inappropriate attire, for whom shopping is an occupation.

Pushing through the often bottleneck traffic clogging the highway as it approaches the outskirts of the Grand Strand, U.S. 17 Business shifts east off the Ocean Highway bypass to Murrells Inlet, a throwback to a simpler era of modest cottages, small motels and family-style diners mixed in—threatened, actually—with some new-fangled over-sized pastel homes and a strip of bars and restaurants that share more than a passing resemblance to Shem Creek, or, equally synthetic, the line-up of tourist traps along River Street in Savannah. It's not that these establishments are so horrible ... it's that they pretend not to be. Their claims to authenticity are just so inauthentic.

Recall the quote from the bartender at CoCo's, Folly Beach, the "17-er" born near Shem Creek, whose fondness for U.S. 17 zeroed in on Murrells Inlet: "Lots of fun bars on a beautiful creek."

This is the place. Her reference now makes perfect sense. They've turned the waterfront on the edge of Ocean Highway into a counterfeit version of Shem Creek, right down to the boardwalk, the boat slips, the neon plastered night skyline, the affectation—"Seafood Capital!" "Right off the Boat!" Along this tarted-up strip of tidal mud, that bartender from CoCo's would be right at home. I envision her behind a couple of drinks, deep into a fish taco, on the deck with a live biker band, a sunburn, the wind, the gulls, the smell of outboard motor exhaust mixed in with the redolence of pluff mud ... and the difference between Shem Creek and MarshWalk evaporates like a prism of oil spilled in the briny water.

The history of Murrells Inlet reflects similar historical facts up and down the coast from Florida to Virginia. The colonial years begin with land grants, baronies, plantations, agrarian slave economies—in this case, a farm owned by John Murrell (or Morrall)—growing cash crops of rice and indigo. After the Civil War, the shift from farming to the rise of tourism for wealthy industrialists looking for seaside resort opportunities parallels other areas in similar situations, when "Yankees" discovered the charms—and the warm climate—of southern coastal living, further promoted in Murrells Inlet by the paving of U.S. 17 in the early 1930s. After World War I, like other areas of the southeastern coast with a navigable inlet and an abundance of protected harbors, and where plantation farming could not be sustained without slave labor, Murrells Inlet developed a vibrant seafood industry geared to satisfy a growing demand for fish, oysters, clams, shrimp and crabs to a newly affluent and discerning clientele. The recreational fishing industry followed and, where the commercial ventures declined, charter boat fishing continues to thrive.

This idea that recreational fishing displaced the commercial industry is a familiar sentiment throughout the southeastern coast, and it is a fact that underscores the hype common to Savannah's River Street, Charleston's Shem Creek, and the Murrells Inlet MarshWalk. In the case of the restaurants along U.S. 17 Business in Murrells Inlet, they advertise seafood taken "right off the boats," but of course the boats don't haul in enough seafood to supply all those restaurants, so even if some of the fresh catch of the day might actually come through the marina, on average the seafood is bought from a bulk supplier servicing the majority of restaurants in the vicinity.

This schizophrenia—between its past and present, its modesty and obscenity—is evident in the claim, in promotional literature, that Murrells Inlet is The Seafood Capital of South Carolina, while in the same breath (or sentence) claiming the nation's finest golf courses. One can imagine the herbicidal and fertilizer runoff collecting in the estuaries from all those manicured lawns in gated communities, the putting greens and trim fairways of the dozens of links in the area, combined with the sewage and seepage from the all yacht basins lining the waterways, flowing through the gills of spawning fish, crabs and various species of bivalvia like oysters and clams....

The ease with which restaurants and seafood distributors can import seafood from other, less spoiled waters—especially if the catch is advertised as "local" or "right off the boat" in the "Seafood Capital of the World"—further illustrates the dissociative identity disorder common to the region: on one hand, an abundant and constant supply of seafood satisfies the cravings of people that love eating seafood, and it keeps those restaurants flogging seafood dishes to their faithful punters in business; at the same time, that easy access to, and plentitude of, imported seafood— along with the occasional and ever scarce truly local right off the boat catch—creates the impression that the local waters are healthy, that runoff pollution is a hoax, and the seafood industry is sustainable ... just look at all the fish and stuff in the local market!

Actually, "right off the boat" means a limited supply, when they can get it, as long as it lasts, and you pay for it ... thus the catchphrase, "market price," which is, of course, worth it if you want real line caught grouper, dolphin, tuna, or seasonal local shrimp. Fresh means as fresh as the restaurant can get it. Otherwise, enjoy the hushpuppies, sauces, and the view. This ain't cheap real estate. The scenery is beautiful. The crowds often can't tell one white fish from another, and with enough booze and sunburn, they don't care. MarshWalk turns Murrells Inlet into the kind of place where volume supersedes quality, and the ocean breeze, live music, a bit of canned romance, plus a few rum drinks, tends to dull the palate.

One helpful and unusual feature on the menus around Murrells Inlet is that the cooks specify whether the shrimp are Fantail or Creek. The fantails tend to be larger, and can be from local Atlantic waters, or the Gulf of Mexico, or even New England, for that matter. They are wild, but not necessarily local. (Back to the meaning of "local.") Creek shrimp, however, do vary in size, depending on the season, evident in other areas like Folly Beach, SC, and Morehead City, NC. In Murrells Inlet, the creek shrimp are smaller and often tastier but more expensive. In Shem Creek, the local creek shrimp are reserved for gumbos and peel and eat platters, because frying them would deplete the supply. According to most chefs, the flavor is too delicate for frying.

At MarshWalk, what you see is what you get. Bovine's is a steak house (no kidding.), but a bonus is its brick oven pizzas. Creek Ratz (don't speculate) and Dead Dog Saloon (ditto) cater to a younger crowd more interested in fancy drinks, live music and wild buff bodies than wild South Carolina shrimp. Even so, some of the establishments along the Marsh-Walk, which runs nearly a half-mile along the saltmarsh from Crazy Sister Marina to Bovine's, bank on their reputation for quality. For instance, Drunken Jack's features renowned chefs, one of which was awarded the 2015 South Carolina Chef of the Year by the South Carolina Restaurant and Lodging Association. The menu is heavy on shrimp, with some fairly high end, even interesting, entrées, given the basic fare. Wahoo's Fish House offers a surprising—and refreshing—limited menu, straightforward and unpretentious, which adds to its class and complements its sushi bar. The Claw House is unique with its connection to New England seafood suppliers, taking delivery of live Maine lobsters twice a week. Owned by the same family as The Dead Dog Saloon next door, The Claw House hopes to distinguish itself from the other eateries along MarshWalk by its raw bar approach to dining, stressing chowders and lobster rolls and the New England feel—along with a light wood interior and a 3,000 gallon saltwater standing fish tank. The menu is a busy collection of standard fare, but they take their oysters seriously, and of course, those live lobsters are a draw.

The social schism operating in Murrells Inlet is also evident in its geographical features. The town was established, like so much of the coastal areas along the U.S. 17, before the craze for beach property, during a time when living on the beach was undesirable. Property owners in those days were skeptical of the isolation, the inaccessibility, the threat of storms and the instability of the landscape. As a result, most of the people seeking a coastal lifestyle built on the west side of the tidal creeks and sounds separating the beach from the mainland.

But the new economy drove a new aesthetic. Desire for beachfront living, regardless of the risk, transformed what was historically cheap fish camp acreage into multi-million dollar sandboxes. The contrast between the working class mainland side of the sound and the newfangled luxury of oceanfront dwellers expresses a split between the traditional sense of coastal living, based on a reverence for aquatic life, the quietude of

MarshWalk, Murrells Inlet, SC. Similar to Shem Creek, MarshWalk hosts a collection of restaurants that line a wooden pier running for half a mile between the sound and the edge of old U.S. 17. Even with the proliferation of new businesses, cottages and restaurants along the strip, this brief stretch of the Coastal Highway feels like a throwback to the 1960s, before traffic shifted over to I-95, when U.S. 17 was the major north-south route along the southern East Coast. A few of the motels and restaurants date from the 1940s.

wetlands, and the contemplative serenity at the edge of the continent, and the amplified party life of aquatic toys—runabouts and jet-skis, parasailing and rollercoasters—with people running amok in the lights and flash and sun-cooked brilliance of abandon.

U.S. 17 can deliver the action as quickly as it can offer an escape from it. Along the coast, the Ocean Highway is the entrance and exit to lifestyles both frenzied and tranquil ... for instance:

An old timer joins me outside the porch bar at Drunken Jack's. He's wizened but fit, lean and wiry for a septuagenarian. He fires up a cigarillo. We sit on the dock bench overlooking Main Creek, and, in the distance, Weston Flat. Three-story cottages, condos and developments blot the landscape along the beach strip across the sound. His smoke dissipates in a cool wet wind fanning the marsh reeds to the east.

"I remember," he says, "when there was nothing over there but mosquitoes."

He's a self-avowed "escapee" from Myrtle Beach. What he refers to as "up north."

"Life moves slower down here," he says. "Why I moved."

Myrtle Beach, I remind him, is about 10 miles away.

"Night and day," he says. "Look."

A huge grizzled osprey lands on an elevated post beside a plastic crow meant to scare off sea gulls from the deck. The hawk is unfazed, his talons prodding the wood, lithe and seriously deadly.

"We got eagles too," he says. An amateur ornithologist, he points to a dredge operating in the inlet and explains how the pelicans and gulls have figured out that fish swim away from the scooper. He admires the feeding patterns of the shore birds.

Turns out he's also an old "17-er" who used to roll U.S. 17 north to surf the Outer Banks.

"As soon as I got my driver's license," he says. "There weren't nothing out there back then but good waves. Last time I looked I didn't recognize the place."

For him, U.S. 17 was always "the road to anywhere." Mainly, he says, before I-95, the highway was "the way to Florida."

He remembers the advent of the "Motor Court" motels, before the various U.S. 17 bypasses were introduced in the late 1960s, stressing how the motels had to be directly off the highway because the crowds were transient. They were loathe to deviate off the straight line to their southern—ultimately Florida—destination. The beach property at this time in

South Carolina had not been developed, and was not particularly desirable, as the traffic stream was part of the New York to Florida artery flow, and stopovers along the way were mainly for one night.

"After I-95 opened," he remembers, "the seaside areas began to develop. Mom and Pop hotels moved off US 17 to the Strand, catering to seasonal beach-goers; they started out with the same flat motel design, but then built on extra floors. They couldn't spread out because the lots were expensive. So they built up, starting the high-rise craze. Wasn't long before it all gave way to corporate America. There's places on Ocean Drive where you're lucky if you see the sun till after noon."

One issue was beach access from the mainland, feeder roads off I-95. Very late in the development of the current state of Myrtle Beach, only three bridges spanned the Intracoastal.

"Plus the one at Georgetown," he throws in.

"Back then Myrtle Beach, going north," he says, "stopped at 62nd Avenue. US 17 was the only road we had. You had to take it to go anywhere."

To shag?

He smiles, as some deep image surfaces from the dark mnemonic recess of his youth.

"Men these days don't dance. But back then, you had to dance to pick up girls."

The bands?

"Tams. Drifters. Billy Scott and the Prophets."

Where?

"Beach Club. It was all PBR in those days. They didn't sell Anheuser Busch products until the owner moved down here and noticed there wasn't no Bud sold on the beach."

Or Schlitz? (Shades of Wooten's Drive-In, New Bern, NC.)

"You know what they say? 'When you're out of beer, you're out of Schlitz.' Because that was the last beer people bought when they ran out of beer."

He laughs. His hack turns into a cough. He relights his cigarillo. The sea hawk ignores us, kneading the wood.

At the south end of the Strand, just past the Air Force Base, he recalls how, when U.S. 17 was first expanded, the freshly paved four-lane was perfect, during the winter, for drag racing.

Did he race?

"I had a 'may start,'" he says. "Had to push it and pop the clutch to get it going. Wasn't much of a street rod."

He gazes at the osprey, seems to connect with the bird. The composition suggests some sort of poetic analogy, but the old man pulls me back to the restaurant, specifically to shrimp.

"The problem these new restaurants have is consistency. When you're buying shrimp from the local boats, you can't "grade 'em out."

Grading—to "grade 'em out"—is the process cooks rely on for buying bulk shrimp, referring to a dependable count of shrimp to the pound. The problem is, if you have jumbo shrimp mixed in with small prawns, when you toss a batch into a deep fryer, the small shrimp will be overcooked and the large shrimp will be undercooked. In a restaurant on a busy night, the cook can't adjust the volume on the fly, so the batches tossed into the fryer have to be consistent.

Most processing plants use a conveyor belt device with rollers of various sizes, hinged so they oscillate and sort shrimp by size. The smaller shrimp drop through the wider gaps as the belt rolls toward a hopper that receives the sorted product.

"These local shrimpers," he says, "refused to play the game. They just wanted to catch the shrimp and dump 'em on the market. They did not want to grade 'em out."

This situation created a conflict between what the cooks needed and what the local suppliers were willing to provide, and the problem grew so acute that, for a long time—no matter how the shrimpers frame the gripe—the restaurants buying from wholesalers shifted to farm-raised imports and processed shrimp from the Gulf to insure consistency in the count. Things have not changed much since then, and bulk packaging glitches continue to be a challenge for local shrimpers: no matter how much shrimp they catch, there are not enough processing plants to guarantee the shrimp are properly headed and "graded out."

"Hell, local shrimpers didn't even want to head the shrimp."

At some point, the only way the local owners could market their shrimp was through seafood markets or retail stalls, if they had a license—the so-called "off the boat" sales or "highway stand" option. Large distributors who wanted to improve the quality of local shrimp, and who basically wanted to help keep the local shrimpers in business, stepped in and established policies where the local trawler owners delivered their catch to major processing plants like the ones at McClellanville and Georgetown, where the shrimp could be graded and headed and tailored to the need of restaurants for different counts—21–25, 16–20—depending on the needs of the various restaurants. But then the shrimp blended with all the other loads and it became impossible to source the shrimp. From a processing plant, the shrimp could be labeled "Atlantic," but that could mean they were caught anywhere from Florida to the Carolinas, or New England for that matter, and specificity—like labeling them "Mayport Shrimp"—was impossible to verify.

"Take this guy," the old-timer says, indicating the long time owner of Drunken Jack's. "He's been here nearly 40 years. Started out with a small restaurant. Had his own seafood market. His own boat. Several other local trawlers he depended on for fresh catch. He got out of the trawling business as soon as he needed more volume. Had to find big distributors that could guarantee consistent deliveries."

Did the shift away from local trawlers to major wholesalers hurt the quality?

'It's a tradeoff," the man explains. "Given the volume, you couldn't rely on the local fleet. And given the seasonal nature of the business, it's tough to keep a fresh supply."

Obviously, what began as an economy based on a reputation for fresh local seafood has outgrown the reality of that standing: another parallel with the situation at Shem Creek. What started—in both Shem Creek and MarshWalk—as an authentic attempt to continue the tradition of home-grown natural resourcing and food traceability has devolved into retail ethics, a marketing model based on volume, where scenery supersedes the quality of the cuisine. It's an outlet mall mentality, where the ambiance, the experience of the event, overrides the standard of the product. Volume at a discount, with good drinks and a great view.

Then the reality check:

"Think about the headaches," the man says, as if anticipating my complaint. "First, the vagaries of the market. If you have too much supply, you have to ship to Baltimore or New York, somewhere willing to pay for good seafood, but the decision has to be made fast or the load will spoil. And think of maintaining the trucks. Drivers. Refrigeration. It's a nightmare. And the boats? Imagine, along with all the other variables, you got to worry about a starter on the fritz. A winch needs a rebuild. Captain's in jail...."

The bartender delivers a plate of fried shrimp. They look beautiful: plump, butterflied, lightly breaded, served with the fantails on. I let 'em cool.

"There was a time when this guy (the owner) would let people browse his seafood shop, pick out what they wanted, and he would cook it for 'em, on the spot. Used to be charter boats, too, come in here with all this fresh fish, and he would invite 'em in, cook what they wanted ... those days are gone, man."

The old man is clearly in his element. I indulge him, ask about the name: Drunken Jack's.

"It's a true story," he says, a little too quickly, which makes me skeptical. "There was this pirate..."

This pirate ...

"I know," he says, reading my face. "But listen. He was just a mate. Not famous. He and his crew found this cask of rum, and they brought it ashore along the beach here, starting partying, cooking fish and whatnot, and drinking the rum. At some point, they spotted a Spanish ship, and she started chasing 'em, so they had to rush off, but they couldn't find Jack. He'd passed out somewhere on the island and they couldn't find him, so in their haste they left him behind. The Spanish chased them down to the Bahamas or somewhere down south, and it wasn't till two years later they managed to get back up here to try to find Jack. All they found were his bones, under a myrtle tree, with the keg of rum, empty, beside him."

Why not, I think, fiddling with the shrimp.

"Notice that light cracker meal batter," he says, admiring the plate.

I consider the osprey.

"That light batter let's the shrimp speak for itself."

Except these shrimp are silent. Tasteless. Rubbery. Looking out over the flats and marsh, I think of what could have been.

The osprey flies, silently mocking my despair. His meal will be fresh. Traceable. Local. Free.

After Shem Creek, I should have been shy. Should have known to resist the pull of the crowds, the romantic views, the chance to spot miscellaneous aquatic creatures and birds that somehow thrive in the muck ... MarshWalk and Shem Creek ... the parallels are too similar, the bustle, and the hustle, too close to the bone....

I slip away. But I don't get far. I pull into a vacant lot off "the strip." The view across the sound is spectacular. In the parking lot a waitress is taking out trash. It's an awkward moment. She looks hard and soft at the same time. Her eyes are young. Her face tired. She seems to perk up when she stops to consider the view over the creek. A cool mist bathes my face.

I tell her I'm recovering from a bad shrimp experience.

She doesn't snipe, run, or call 911. She fires up a cigarette, leans against the railing, acknowledges the view, almost religiously, and commiserates with me.

She agrees about the shrimp, and hazards a guess as to what went wrong.

"Those shrimp have been frozen the whole time we've been closed for the season. Forty below zero. And then they defrost 'em in water. Kills the flavor."

She explains the proper way to defrost frozen shrimp: leave them in a plastic bag and then dip the bag into cool water.

"You can't let water run through them," she says.

She grew up on the Jersey shore, so she knows seafood. She's also lived in Pawley's Island long enough to recognize a split between the Georgetown sensibility and the MarshWalk ethos.

"They've sold out up here," she says, referring to the restaurants lining U.S. 17 as it slices the coast from Pawleys Island to Myrtle Beach. "I buy my shrimp off the boats in Georgetown, from Independent Seafood, bottom of Cannon Street. All the other stuff, fish and such, I get at the shop on Highmarket."

She frequently "pulls" her own oysters. Nets shrimp in season, using the fish patty and bamboo pole method. She brags that on her day off she caught 36 blue crabs. Held a crab boil for the neighborhood.

I try to draw her back to the disappointing shrimp. She hesitates to bite....

"I don't want to say anything bad about any restaurants around here that claim to serve local seafood. But everybody knows these days they're serving frozen imports. They're doing what they can. The tourists don't know the difference, anyway."

She crushes her cigarette with her toe and picks up the butt. Eco-friendly.

"Did you know there are 18 kinds of grouper? That's one thing we still get around here. Fresh Carolina grouper."

The light drizzle picks up, chills the lot. She moves toward the back the restaurant, pauses on the porch, holding the screen door open.

"I want to learn more about groupers," she says. "The ones we serve were swimming yesterday."

I heard the same line in Fernandina, about shrimp, from the girl who loved to watch the trawlers from the beach at night.

A cry of love, from a neo "17-er."

⟫5⟪

Calabash to Elizabeth City

The dual personality of The Ocean Highway is readily evident as it runs through North Carolina. The landscape along U.S. 17 in this region underscores and illustrates the problematic nature of the highway, its name as well as its temperament: coastal and landlocked, ugly and resplendent, plagued with poverty and nurtured with excess. U.S. 17 through here cuts across working class areas mingled with leisurely holiday retreats, crosses a tarnished industrial landscape fused with attractive refurbished town centers, connects despoiled acres with scenic waterscapes, and passes occasional funky oddities bent on resisting the franchised homogeneity plaguing the highway from one end to the other.

The sector of U.S. 17 running north through Brunswick County basically separates the coastal zone from the Piedmont. It forms the western edge of the Eastern Carolina coastal plain, lipping the Inner Banks and separating, essentially, the shrimp from the barbeque.

Nationally, North Carolina ranks second in hog farming, which is concentrated in the eastern sector, along with chickens and turkey farms, and is rightfully famous for its barbeque, a finely chopped dish seasoned with minimal pepper and vinegar frequently served on a plain hotdog bun garnished with coleslaw. The historical cash crops in this region used to be tobacco, sweet potatoes and beans. The tobacco fields are being phased out, replaced (ironically) with cotton. Corn still thrives in the area, as do cucumbers (for pickles) and soybeans. This confluence of agri-business and livestock farming with tourism and the seafood industry along the coastal plain segment of U.S. 17 defines the landscape, which varies from featureless farmland to picturesque seascapes, from rural exurban sprawl to areas of intense historical preservation, much of it dating to the colonial era.

Just as it does in Georgia and South Carolina, U.S. 17, as it enters North Carolina, connects to a series of access routes leading east to a string of interconnected beach communities. It forms a cobweb of roads weaving through the coastal landscape, and they all tie back into U.S. 17 as it threads the landscape between the Little River and the Cape Fear River, and then further north, as it skirts the Pamlico Sound. These communities strung along the Intracoastal Waterway and lining the creeks, inlets and rivers that cut through the coastline, represent the dilemma of both The Ocean Highway and the shrimp industry as each exists today: gentrification and displacement, reallocation of resources, pollution, restricted access to once public lands—all these underlying factors contribute, as much as rising operational prices like fuel, labor and upkeep, and competition from foreign farm-raised commodities, to suppressing the market for independent shrimpers.

Like most of the highway as it wends through southeastern North Carolina, a lot of U.S. 17 has become merely a four-lane bypass for vehicles moving from point A to point B, splotched with generic convenience stores and sterilized by chain restaurants. Any charm the Coastal Highway once promised a leisurely traveler tooling through the southern section of the state has been subjugated by the raw business necessities of transport priorities. Meaning, in this region, U.S. 17 is no longer a scenic route. As an integral part of this commercial-recreational schism, the shrimp industry is likewise pressured to produce quantity, not quality, in a market with diminished profit margins and a corporate business model that promotes anonymity at the expense of sustainable lifestyle for a colorful, dedicated few.

And just as U.S. 17 divides Eastern North Carolina into an east-west bifurcation—the coastal plain cut from the Piedmont—it also connects two distinct north-south coastal sectors: the seacoast route just below and just above Wilmington, and the more inland route crossing the waterways around the Pamlico Sound. Its main function is to serve as an operational link, first through the transitional stretch connecting Calabash to Cape Fear, and then as a feeder linking the Inner Banks to Hatteras Island.

North of Shackleford Banks, offshore fishing can be treacherous; the waters are deep but plagued by shoals, with the Gulf Stream running close and fast, adding to the turbulence. Most seafood harvesting in South Carolina and Georgia is done offshore, in the relatively calmer waters associated with the Lowcountry. But because of the prevailing ocean conditions off Hatteras, the shrimping—and fishing, for that matter—is a different game. The barrier islands of North Carolina are known as the Graveyard of the Atlantic, and for that reason, most of the shrimp harvested in the northern half of the state are taken from Pamlico Sound and the myriad inland waterways that flow together to form the second largest estuary in the United States.

(A fact that, in the minds of commercial seafood operators, underscores the importance of keeping the waters between the Inland Banks and the Outer Banks open for trawling).

South of Wilmington, the coastal landscape is more closely associated with the topography of Myrtle Beach than the more inhospitable and savage land out on the Outer Banks. Between the "drowned coastline" below Pawleys Island and Cape Fear, the coastline is shaped like a bay, formed and protected by Bald Head Island and Frying Pan shoals, where the Cape Fear River empties into the Atlantic. The marshes along Murrells Inlet slowly give way to sandy stretches of beach that persist up through Little River, Calabash and on to Southport, at the mouth of the Cape Fear. Much of the beach strand through this area faces south, and this posture helps keep the shore immune from the punishing northerlies that cause so much damage to the shoreline. The coastal communities below Cape Fear, cut with navigable inlets, open out to a fairly gentle seascape.

Similarly, the coastal area from Wrightsville Beach to Atlantic Beach, from Cape Fear to Cape Lookout (the names alone indicating the menace of the northern sector of the Carolina coast), forms Onslow Bay, framing another shoreline tucked between protective banks. South of Shackleford Banks, the south-facing beaches are similarly protected from north swells, allowing offshore navigation to remain relatively tame. Although commercial fishing through this region has mainly given way to recreational sport fishing and charter boats, trawlers still operate offshore, especially out of Snead's Ferry and Beaufort (NC), without worrying too much about the sort of rough seas encountered around Diamond Shoals and the Hatteras Bight.

Those islands collectively known as the Outer Banks form the eastern edge of Pamlico Sound, and they clearly mark the area where shrimping and fishing interests shift from offshore harvesting to dragging inland waters. The conditions along Diamond Shoals simply create too much of a navigational hazard for incautious "outside" dragging.

Life on the Hatteras seashore remains wild.

The mosquitoes are murderous. The sun unrelenting. The sky brittle, hard as glass. The overhead surf feathers in the strong offshore wind....

A raw dawn on Hatteras Island.

The plan, like every important decision in a small town along the

Coastal Highway—long-term, short-term, life-changing or petty—had taken shape over illegal beers in the parking lot of Wooten's Drive-In. The air is crispy. An early fall brisk westerly wind is tinged with a whiff of smoke from a lingering fire in the Croatan forest. A front is moving through. The NOAA weather radio reports a long dominant wave period and increasing swell heights from Oregon Inlet sea buoys. The Outer Banks is going off ...

The hardcore surfer in the lot at Wooten's will graduate this year, not just from high school, but also into the life of a "17-er," resigned to the reality that his surfing life will be limited to the Carolina coast, with occasional excursions to more exotic locales—if his dreams and expenses allow it. For now, he keeps his jobs flexible. Options open. For him, nothing matters but chasing youth in the form of waves peeling off a stretch of isolated beach on the easternmost edge of the state. Tomorrow, the conditions press an imperative: head out at four am, roll up U.S. 17 north to U.S. 64 east to NC 12 ... from there, instinct, surf wits, will determine where he enters the water. He arranges his life so that, when a swell pumps, he can hit it—north to the Lighthouse, south to Masonboro, a boat out to Shackelford—his future inextricably linked to where U.S. 17 can take him. Tomorrow, it's north, to connect with the land route to Nags Head. The alternate itinerary involves taking the ferry from Cedar Island, but he's too impatient, the delay too tense.

He considers others in the lot. The ones that will escape the highway— if escape is the right word—the highway that will define the rest of his life: U.S. 17. He scoffs. Professional careers are reserved for the dilettantes, the hobbyists on the other side of the lot, who dabble at surfing like a pastime, not a lifestyle. They will go to college. They will be doctors, lawyers, accountants ... and they will look back (with regret, he hopes) at missing this night of possibilities, tomorrow's ephemeral session: tasting the best surf (in his mind) the east coast can offer.

And that next day, when he rolls toward the beach, he admits: he never gets used to it, the way the farmland and pastures edge right up to the bridge, and then, crossing the sound, the sudden blinding glare of the rising sun, the wide open expanse over the dune line, the sea flecked silver in the harsh light, and the surf, overhead, glassy, breaking in perfect sections over the inside sandbar, the scene delivering him a million miles from the fields and meadows and countryside behind him, his job, the stricture of his life, that definitive highway ... he is as far east as he can get, and sees nothing but wet space, freedom, roiled into a white foam by those mystical, glassy tubes of energy, peeling into eternity....

A dream from the sixties. Before the influx of money and tourists and permanent transplants that somehow managed to relocate to the Outer Banks. Those refugees from the northeast that made the turn off 17 and cut themselves even further off from whatever they left behind beyond the Coastal Highway. Weekenders. Vacationers. Day-tripping surfers from Virginia Beach, their Madison Avenue wave-of-dolphins decals giving them away. Even visitors slap an OBX sticker on their Land Rover. Everyone's a local.

These days, most "17-ers" cannot afford to live on the Outer Banks. Some "17-ers" got in early, before the boom. Made the transition and cashed out, nicely. Others simply have the money, often family money. The "trustafarian" class. ("Yankee money," my old man called it.)

But no matter how hard real estate agents and their wealthy clients try to domesticate the coast, building million dollar "cottages" along the dune line, nature continues to take its revenge, wreaking havoc on the fragile strip of sand from Frisco to Duck. The towns, once tight-knit remote fishing villages, have been transformed into vacation destinations. The camps and shacks have been replaced with beachfront cottages, sport fishing marinas, condos and golf courses. "Surf shops," boutiques and upscale lifestyle entertainment complexes now form census-designated, pre-planned communities, promising a "charming" small-town experience as if it were a pre-packaged commodity sold off the shelf at a "big box" store.

To illustrate the fragile ecology of the area, consider the Herbert C. Bonner Bridge spanning the Oregon Inlet and connecting Bodie Island to Pea Island and Nags Head to the Hatteras Island National Seashore. Created by a Hurricane in 1846, the inlet has, since its formation, moved two miles south, and it continues to migrate. The strong currents destabilize the pilings, causing frequent closures and constant repairs. A new bridge, begun in 2016, will be subject to the same whims of nature that undermined the old one: shifting shoals and channel fill requiring constant dredging, and, of course, the occasional hurricane that might tear a new inlet through the sand dunes. The highway running the length of the island, NC 12, has been severed several times, once by Hurricane Isabel in 2003, which created a new inlet that had to be filled in before the road could be repaired; a storm in 2007 flooded the road, again shutting down traffic; Hurricane Irene cut the road in two spots, causing construction of a "temporary" bridge (six years old and counting); Hurricane Sandy flooded the road and stranded residents for weeks. The story continues, with every nor'easter and "September storm" posing a serious threat to the architectonic integrity of the island.

As U.S. 17 enters North Carolina from South Carolina, running south to north, the first outposts are the modest towns of Calabash, Shallotte, Varnamtown and Southport. These once pristine landscapes, downstream from the Cape Fear River, now face ecological disaster. All the septic, lethal muck flowing out of the Cape Fear River at Southport is discharged into the Intracoastal Waterway and the estuaries associated with the Shallotte River. Logging and construction activities release toxic sediment into the watershed. Industrial waste and raw sewage from pig and chicken farms create fecal bacteria and algae blooms. Fertilizer runoff depletes oxygen levels. To shore-up property values, sand re-nourishment projects— dredging or trucking-in sand to pile up in front of cottages—displace the muddy bottom shrimp need to feed and mature in.

To some, these areas represent contemporary success stories. Thanks to retirees, vacationers, beach enthusiasts, fisherman, and golfers, the area between Little River and Southport has seen a resurgent tax base. Businesses fueled by tourism have contributed to skyrocketing prices for beach real estate. To others, these towns are casualties, their "assets" the problem: overcrowding, nonpoint source pollution, habitat endangerment, overfishing. Where shrimp fleets once flourished, now only a handful of boats continue to work the home waters for wild local shrimp.

In addition to the usual difficulties associated with the costs involved in maintaining a fleet of trawlers—or a single trawler, for that matter— other factors beyond market economics have deteriorated the shrimp grounds in this region. Some of the factors are familiar: unregulated seafood imports, labor shortages, tighter quotas and harvest restrictions, increased fuel prices and regulatory compliance costs. But one overarching factor having a negative impact on the commercial seafood industry is directly related to the massive increase in tourism and retirement industries: the repurposing of waterfront property, from industrial to commercial, and from commercial to resort, from resort to residential.

The problem of seafood industries being priced out of access to coastal property isn't unique to Brunswick County, although the situation along the Southport Estuary is acute. Land once perfectly situated for a dock or processing house is now more valuable as a spot for a waterfront condo, a restaurant or a hotel, and these residential or retail waterfront properties typically exclude marine industrial infrastructures as well as, in most cases, the general public.

The fleet along Lockwoods Folly River, Varnamtown, NC. Like Rockville, Varnamtown, just north of Calabash, is truly the end of the road. Hard to find, but worth the effort. Nothing here but mosquitoes, trawlers and fresh local shrimp.

The Coastal Highway, as it plows through Brunswick County as a four-lane throughway, seems to be as much a casualty of the gentrification as the beaches are. In long stretches through Georgia, and a significant swath of South Carolina, U.S. 17 retains some of its original character, meriting in spots its "Scenic Highway" designation. But the section running through southeastern North Carolina is a soulless stretch lined with golf courses and tract housing developments carved out of pine forests and defunct tobacco fields, an unsightly assortment of auto shops and tire dealerships, convenience stores, storage units, pop-up churches, chain restaurants, gas stations, strip malls ... here, U.S. 17 is a functional, generic, savagely utilitarian strip, efficient, at times, where the speed limit even increases to 65 mph, a rarity on U.S. 17. The effect, for the holiday driver pursuing a "Coastal Highway" experience, is dry and depressing.

The turnoffs toward the coast, however, as crowded and cheesy as they are, do serve as an easy emollient to the open wound that is the reality of U.S. 17 as it cuts through this wasteland.

The first turn, onto NC 179 just across the state line, runs into the heart of Calabash, whose city limits border with South Carolina. This nondescript town on the edge of the Calabash River, a tributary of the Little River and an arm of the Intracoastal Waterway, bills itself as "The Seafood Capital of the World." The town was originally known as Pea Landing, named after the abundance of peanuts farmed in the area and shipped off to market via the river. Local lore suggests that the name is derived from the shape of the river, that early settlers, or native Americans, thought the river was shaped like a gourd, for some reason, and so the town was christened with the native name for a gourd—Calabash. Other lore involves Jimmy Durante, who used to sign off his radio show, "Goodnight, Mrs. Calabash, wherever you are." For years, people argued about the identity of "Mrs. Calabash." Many residents claimed it was their mother, or their sister, or a singer from the area who joined Durante's band for a while as a singer. Nobody knows, but Durante did stop in for a meal, probably on his way to a gig in Myrtle Beach, and mysteriously invented his signature "Calabash" phrase.

Most of the action is along River Road, which terminates at Waterfront Seafood Shack where a line of piers supports what's left of the Calabash Fishing Fleet. The restaurant "fad" began in the 1940s, when Lucy Coleman opened The Original. Her sister opened Becks. Their brother started Ella's. Others followed. The one thing they all had in common was the Calabash style of deep-frying seafood. Mostly the style involves dipping the seafood in evaporated milk, then raking it through cornmeal seasoned with salt and pepper and deep frying it, quickly, usually for two minutes, in very high temp vegetable oil.

One of the most popular restaurants, Captain Nance's, sits just above the docks—famous primarily for its location than it's food because, let's face, the Calabash style is the same all over town. But the phrase—"I just love sitting right there on the water"—crops up frequently when diners around the region think of Nance's.

For instance, I'm trying to find that tiny fishing hamlet, Varnamtown. No easy task. I hit a minimart on a road that, I assume, leads out to Holden Beach. The lady behind the counter—a large, friendly blonde seemingly at ease with the world—drew directions to the dead end river port on a blank piece of register receipt paper.

"What you want in Varnamtown?" she asks, not exactly suspicious but genuinely curious.

Shrimp, I tell her.

She nods, knowingly, satisfied. Then she begins to reel off the names of the half-dozen or so trawlers that dock there. "There's the ... and the..."

I state the obvious: she must be local.

"Been here 32 years," she says. "My husband's from Shallotte. I'm originally from Lumberton. Took me a while to get used to life down here. Now I love it. But when I first moved, my husband would leave the doors unlocked, even at night, when we went to bed. I could hardly sleep. In Lumberton, I lived in town, and there's no way I'd ever go to bed without first locking the doors. Out here, he leaves the screen open. There."

She hands me her "map," a series of squiggly lines with vertical hash marks for stop signs.

"You pass this church. Then turn left at the fork with a brick house in the middle. A quick right, another quick left"—she stabs at the squiggle—"take you right to the river."

She seems amused at my quest. I test her. Ask her what she thinks about U.S. 17.

"I don't get out there much," she says, wistfully, as if the highway is somewhere to go. Her world seems confined to the back roads of Brunswick County, bordered by the Lockwoods Folly River, the Atlantic Ocean, and NC 179. Her life is the store, the steel building minimart, and shopping in Shallotte.

Does she go to Calabash?

"I love Nance's," she says, recalling some afternoon she passed blissfully munching fried seafood by the docks. I hear it coming: "It's so nice sitting right by the water."

Location, location ...

After a few false moves, I manage to find the docks at Varnamtown. The dead end is lined with small houses and a few backyard businesses— mostly related to seafood or mechanics—and most bedecked with American flags above Confederate Stars and Bars. Plenty of signs show a pistol pointed directly at the viewer with the legend: Nothing Here is Worth Your Life. Trump signs rule.

A cluster of seafood shacks surround the main lot and dock area. Garland's on one side, Beacon 1 on the other, High Rider Seafood dead ahead. Most of the several trawlers are small boats that look like inlet trawlers. But a huge wooden trawler sits at dry dock on a trolley track,

Spring maintenance, Varnamtown, NC. *Top*: A trawler, dry dock, being prepped for the season. *Bottom*: Last-minute touch-ups.

Beacon Seafood, Varnamtown.

being prepped for the season. A huge shark bursts from Beacon 1, but otherwise the buildings are all business, no frills, just like the trawlers.

A crusty local offers a few comments. His skin is like crinkled leather. He never found the teeth he lost. He's as reticent as he is rugged. Says between seasons he works on heavy equipment, mainly dredging operations. He's never far from the water, and never far from U.S. 17. He's waiting in the lot for a chance to affix a winch to his trawler. He's anxious to haul his boat—a 57-footer—out on the rails in the yard to paint it.

"Gimme three weeks," he says, looking over at the 45-footer up on the rails at Beacon 1, sanded and ready for its early spring painting. He's unaffected but clearly proud. "My boat'll look like new."

Just across the near channel, built in among the marsh reeds like a water rodent's nest, a lone shack with a dock sits in the middle of the river, a hermit's haven. Across the way, million dollar vacation homes grace the edge of the river. The contrast is as obvious as it is striking.

Similar to Pelican Point and Rockville, Varnamtown is not a place for a curious city slicker to be poking around asking nerdy questions. You come here—if you can find some of these places—to buy seafood. The locals are hostile to outsiders. No trespassing signs are prevalent. Welcome signs rare. Those "Forget the Dog. Beware the Owner" signs are not campy jokes. You have to marvel at the paranoia. The Info Wars mentality. What provokes it? Racism? Bred from what sense of white resentment? They want to be "left alone." But who wants to bother them? I imagine the crime rate in this neighborhood is zero. It's a simple life, far removed from civilization and all the corruption that, one assumes, civilization represents to the mind of a serious recluse. And as if just living off the grid in Varnamtown proper wasn't remote enough, someone felt compelled to build a shack on an island in a marsh in the middle of nowhere—accessible only by boat. Paranoia runs as deep as the main channel, a mere 10 miles from that cosmopolitan pipeline, U.S. 17, flushing Yankee elites and affluent progressives right past this rustic outpost and its militant citizens, a resistant delegation of peckerwood renegades.

The essence of Varnamtown, NC.

Scenery, loyalty, people you know … the variables that go into choosing a seafood restaurant in Calabash are not associated with the food. Calabash style is Calabash style, no matter which setting you decide to indulge.

Nance's, right on the main town dock, is surrounded by charter fishing boats, small trawlers and sundry recreational and commercial craft. You can buy fresh seafood right off the docks—it's not unusual to see buckets of fresh fish and shrimp just a few hours, as they say, from swimming in the sea.

Inside, tables are arranged in a square room with lots of glass to frame views of the creek docks, boats and tourists. Plain is an understatement. Just the one room. No bar. No deck. No ambiance. Focus is strictly on the food.

Several other eateries line the river and River Street, most with more character and attention to décor … barely. The restaurants along the main drag in Calabash are all about selling "the style." Most hawk some sort of "heritage," claiming to be the "original" or family-owned or "authentic."

I settle on Beck's, mainly because it has an actual bar with stools and bottles and draft beer. Two young girls are covering the bar and working the floor. Physically exact opposites—one is a full-bodied blonde with gray eyes, the other a radically thin brunette with viciously blue eyes—they are culturally homogenous, hailing from a place called Ash.

"It's not on the map," the brunette says, obviously delighted with its obscurity.

"It's on NC 130," the blonde offers, as if that helped. "West of US 17."

Their accents mark them as authentic. Both just out of high school, they are now students at Brunswick Community College studying to enter the medical field, one as a nurse, the other hoping to become a hygienist. Both grew up in, and still live in, Ash, N.C. They are "17-ers," preparing for a future that will not exclude U.S. 17 from their lives. They cross the Ocean Highway without considering its importance in their socio-economic cultural reality. Their high school: off 17. Their community college: off 17. The hospital where they hope to intern: off 17. To get to Wilmington on a shopping spree, they ride U.S. 17. Out to eat in Myrtle Beach, or to a concert on North Ocean Drive: U.S. 17. The highway funnels locals and tourists, transients and transplants alike, into their diners, onto their charter fishing boasts, their knick-knack stores. Without U.S. 17, the crossroads that exists, improbably, as "Ash, NC," would not sustain Babson Auto Salvage, located just across from a copse of pines known as (no kidding) Possum Branch, just down the road from Outback Gun Range.

Given those demographics, I wonder aloud where they go for fun.

"We don't stray far," the brunette answers, without a trace of irony.

The blonde adds, "We're too busy."

I try the Calabash shrimp. The order comes back as a simple plate full of small shrimp—what might commonly be called popcorn shrimp— tiny bits lost in a crispy jacket.

I tell the girls the shrimp are small. Like prawns.

"I never heard of a prawn," says the brunette, scrunching up her face, like the word had a foul flavor. The shrimp were pitiful.

I ask: Why are they so small?

The blonde takes this one: "They shrink some when you cook them."

She explains that the "little ones are natural. The big ones, they put all kinds a stuff in 'em."

No tails?

"They peel 'em first."

The docks, Calabash River, Calabash, NC. The small fishing village of Calabash bills itself as "The Seafood Capital of the World." "Calabash Style" seafood has been appropriated by restaurants up and down the coast, but this is where— according to local lore—the original deep fried, batter-encrusted shrimp recipe was first commercially developed.

I consider this answer. I try to imagine Ash. West Brunswick High School. Seven years as a server at Beck's, Calabash, N.C. I convince myself that I am not being condescending. I'm being honest. The shrimp suck.

I keep scooping into the pile, hoping for a burst of flavor. But the more I munch these tiny tidbits of fried pancake batter, the more I conclude that Calabash style is merely an excuse for people to eat fried cornmeal that is not an actual hushpuppy, so they think they're eating something chic, of substance, when really the miniature morsels are mainly good for slathering on condiments.

NC 179 reconnects with U.S. 17 near Shallotte, where NC 130 runs out toward the beach and Varnamtown. Stone Chimney Road leads back toward U.S. 17 along the Lockwood Folly River, connecting to NC 211 as it continues along the other side of Lockwood Folly back to the coast and Southport. NC 211 crosses the Cape Fear as a ferry over to Fort Fisher and transits a series of city avenues until merging again with U.S. 17 on the north side of Wilmington. The other route back to U.S. 17 is to double back out of Southport using NC 133 and hitting U.S. 17 on the south side of Wilmington, crossing the river over the Cape Fear Memorial Bridge.

Heading into the southern region of the Outer Banks, I contemplate the dead zone of tasteless shrimp I just encountered. I think of the territory between Georgetown and Sneads Ferry as a transition zone, a once undeveloped area recently inundated with tourists hungry for nostalgia, convinced they can find the sort of pristine beauty promoted in real estate brochures and postcards. They seek the casual slow pace promised by southern small-town life and ruin it by finding it. Like the bird that fouls its own nest. Yes, the pilgrims who first settled the area netted fresh seafood and cooked it however they could. That's not the way it is anymore. Tradition in this zone is a selling point, a marketing ploy.

Authenticity in this zone has been hollowed-out.

Then I consider the several restaurants in Mayport and Fernandina, Darien, Tybee, Folly and Georgetown that still source their product and continue to serve the most delicious honest fried shrimp on the coast. For them, the catch is traceable. The diners get a good product—scrumptious local wild shrimp—the restaurants get respect and turn a decent profit. But in the tourists centers—many spawned in areas once deserted, that cannot sustain the obscene crowds these places now draw—the volume is indecent. The expectation for "real" food is low, conditioned by the view, the hype, the fancy drinks, or the "reputation," "tradition," concepts whose value are like old coins with the faces worn off, the demarcations indiscriminate, their value reduced to a fabricated legend on the back of a plastic menu.

Above Sneads Ferry, however, I enter a different world. The landscape changes. The beachscape changes. The culture changes. And more importantly, the nature of the shrimping industry changes.

Throughout this area, much of the coast is developing beyond sustainability, especially in the northern and southern extremes of the Outer Banks. But the area between the tip of Bogue Banks to the ferry to Ocracoke Island seems to have reached a saturation point. The local resources are not overwhelmed ... yet. A delicate balance exists between sustainability and consumption. How else to explain the plethora of restaurants in this region that manage to serve "real" shrimp? Or the chefs that still go to the source. You see "Market Price" on menus and know the phrase actually means what it says. The selections change daily based on what's available, and the prices fluctuate accordingly. The area still promotes a community that makes a living in the seafood industry in harmony with conservationists. There is tension in the region, between commercial fishermen and the retirees, between the people who fish for a living and recreational sport-fishermen. But as things stand, a sort of balance has been achieved, allowing shrimpers to deliver a quality product at a fair profit to an appreciative fan base that supports conservation but demands, and is willing to pay for, fresh locally sourced seafood.

Not to say the area is immune to shoveling piles of tasteless frozen imported seafood onto the platters of tourists who don't know a local shrimp from a chum clam. If volume is the enemy of value, the strip from Sneads Ferry to Sealevel is ripe for spoiling. During the season, families flood the zone. Vacationers swarm the beaches. Crowds overwhelm the parking lots, jam the roads. Jacksonville and Havelock, on U.S. 17 and U.S. 70, respectively, host huge military bases. All of which invite a proliferation of chain restaurants and motels, budget feeding troughs, all-you-can-eat buffets, drive-thrus ... businesses deemed anathema by lovers of locally sourced, wild, fresh seafood.

Still, at the moment, the availability of excellent shrimp in this region is encouraging.

Especially in Sneads Ferry, the most authentic shrimp stop above Wilmington. The ferry alluded to in the town's name is real: the crossing was an integral link on the original colonial highway called Post Road connecting Norfolk and Charleston—the precursor to the Coastal Highway. Sneads Ferry actually began as "Ennet's Ferry," named after the early colonial entrepreneur Edmund Ennett, who created the ferry service at New River back in 1728; it operated until 1939, when a bridge spanning the New River was completed.

With its economy once almost totally dependent on the seafood industry, like so many of the areas served by U.S. 17, Sneads Ferry diversified during the late 20th and early 21st centuries, and as the shrimping industry continues to decline, the town has become dependent on golf courses and retirees looking for a mild but seasonal climate to kick back in, plus jobs associated with the Marine Base at Camp Lejeune. The rise in property values due to the influx of tourists and residential communities monopolizing waterfront acreage has invariably put pressure on the fishing industry, as much as new regulations and costs associated with the commercial aspects of business.

Trawlers, Sneads Ferry, NC. Sneads Ferry, just off 17, abuts Camp LeJeune, near Jacksonville, NC. Like so many of the small sheltered coves along the coast, the village is simply a bunch of cottages and houses clustered around a handful of creeks hosting a number of trawlers and a couple of wholesale and retail distributors. The trawlers operating out of Sneads Ferry, unlike the Pamlico Sound fleet to the north, must navigate New River Inlet, a relatively tricky cut leading to the open Atlantic just under the lower Outer Banks. During summer months, local shrimpers complain about sharks eating their nets.

Regardless of the economic stresses and diversification, the town still calls itself a "seafood village," hosts a blessing of the fleet, and celebrates an annual Shrimp Festival. The role of "seafood village" is a bit nostalgic, and the festival is more of an arts and crafts show than a true food-fest, but all the civic fun, along with several fishing tournaments, does serve to remind the community of its rich fishing heritage and celebrates its current state as one of the few classic working seafood ports associated with the Coastal Highway.

About a decade after the bridge from Topsail Island to the mainland was completed, Davis Seafood opened on Wheelers Point, selling fresh local shrimp hauled in by the family trawler. The family members that currently own the business continue to operate a fleet of commercial trawlers, and the seafood available in the store is mainly stocked from what comes in off the boats—especially fresh Carolina shrimp.

Entering Sneads Ferry makes it easy to understand why these shrimpers seek such remote harbors—Darien, Rockville, McClellanville, Varnamtown ... now Sneads Ferry, plus other nowhere ports to the north like Engelhard—and why they live such isolated lives. It's simple: the price of coastal real estate. That's why Sneads Ferry, as a natural harbor, makes sense, why it harbors one of the largest clusters of trawlers on the Carolina coast: cheap real estate.

Things *are* changing. The smattering of coves and dockage areas along the river are littered with trawlers, crab shacks, fish huts, machine shops ... but houses pop up in unlikely locales, along New River, for instance. The river views are spectacular, but the water is dirty and muddy and there's very little navigable channel for deep draft boats. Most of the upscale houses along New River are owned by retirees and ex-military officers seeking a laid-back, leisurely coastal lifestyle, removed from the hubbub of the tourism and retail traffic along the commercial strip of Bogue Banks. Other denizens are connected to the military or the seafood industry.

But the main problem persists: it's hard to get here, and once you're here, if you don't like small craft fishing or burning up the water on a jet-ski, there's not much to do.

From U.S. 17, there's one road leading in, another road leading out, limiting the volume of thru-traffic. There are no hotels. No cute historic town center. Sneads Ferry does not cater to tourism. It's a working village. And to a point, this situation is a good thing: it maintains the authenticity of the village, its heart and soul, as they say. But it also stifles development, and keeps the economy depressed. The condos and apartments that sprout up off the waterfront, along the access roads leading in from U.S. 17, basically serve as base housing. The chain restaurants and businesses in this area service residents of these "barracks." For those with the means there is golf, fishing, boating ... the convenience of the base PX. But access to the waterfront is seriously limited.

(The northern route across the high-rise bridge, NC 172, runs through the edge of Camp Lejeune on the way to Swansboro, but after 9/11 it's become a restricted highway. You need a military sticker to use it. It's as if the N.C. Department of Transportation—the tax-payers—built the bridge solely for military personnel to use. Good for jobs and the tax base of Snead's Ferry, but a bad deal for the rest of us who have to double back through Jacksonville to get to the coast above New River.)

You can launch a boat. You can buy scads of fresh seafood. You can work on a trawler. Contract with the military. Sight-see. Otherwise, there's no reason to go to Sneads Ferry....

Except for the chance to rock at Blackbeard's, a hot spot for the groovy local party (and military) crowd, or to munch out at The Riverview Café, a small restaurant that has been in the same location since 1946. Blackbeard's occupies a colorful brick building, painted deep blue with an American flag embossed in one huge windowpane, a neon OPEN sign in the other. Inside a small resin-wood bar anchors a dining area with tables

Where the action is. Sneads Ferry, NC.

and booths, a stage for live music, some games, a pool table, a corner fire-place. It's a funky barebones bar with killer river views and an outside patio. And, of course, along with strong fancy (and plain) drinks, they serve fried baskets of seafood bought fresh off the docks.

The Riverview Café likewise has river views through lots of glass in its main dining room. Booths along the wall and tables are spread through-out. An old-fashioned pickup window separates the dining room from the bar. It's a classic diner with the focus strictly on food. The menu is plain and plastic. Daily specials deviate from the seafood party line but the seafood doesn't get any more straightforward. The hushpuppies are balls of batter with a hint of onion and sugar. The shrimp are plump, firm, with only a dusting of mix. Moist—juicy, even. They taste briny, with a hint of mud (for authenticity), bursting with flavor ... somehow they taste like the river smells.

The waitress has worked there for 27 years.

I ask her what she thinks of U.S. 17. The question throws her.

"It's just a way to go anywhere," she says, a bit confused. Her accent is impenetrable. I try again: Does she live near U.S. 17?

"I live on Old Folkstone Road," she says, as if I know where *that* is. "Near the J&B Crab Pot Company," she offers. "And Junebug's-by-the-Sea Grocery."

I nod.

"They're fixing to start construction on the road. Now, it takes me six minutes to get to work. When they start on that road, I got to go around. It'll take fifteen minutes, easy."

But what does she think of U.S. 17?

She shrugs, quizzical again. "You mean how busy is it?"

Your ... impressions.

She goes blank. The concept of considering U.S. 17 as more than a highway seems to escape her. Here is as new type. A "17-er" who doesn't grasp the concept. Who has lived her life between the Ocean Highway and Topsail Beach, New River and Alligator Bay. Who for 26 years has driving three miles from Old Folkstone Road to Hall Point Road. To work in a diner that serves about ten entrées all under ten bucks. To whom U.S. 17 conjures images of a mere functional anonymity.

"All I know," she says, mater-of-fact, "is when I'm out there driving 55 people are blowing by me going 80."

The other people working there take an interest in my "interview." They offer opinions, but seem to speak a foreign language. I pretend to understand what they're saying.

"They're from Down East," the cashier explains, declining my American Express.

I encounter the same accent by the trawler docks.

But not on my first try.

It's a crispy clear February afternoon when I pull into Mitchell's. They've been in the business for half a century. Recently refurbished the present building. Own their own fleet but process shrimp from various suppliers. The building sits at the end of a narrow cove filled with trawlers, mainly in the 60–80 foot range. No one in the parking lot or retail shop, but there's activity on the docks. Workers are loading ice onto a boat preparing to head out. I look like the one person who obviously doesn't belong there. I guess, in the narrow scheme of things, I don't. And they let me know it. These are not friendly people. "Reticent" doesn't do their frostiness justice.

I put down my pen and back away.

Davis seafood sits on the edge of a broader cove at the foot of the high-rise bridge. It's a small, semi-dilapidated building across from a barn-style tool shed and work station. Several trawlers crowd the cove. The family owned wholesale seafood shop and the few boats still in the fleet have been operating in the same location since 1948, although the Davis family has been fishing for generations. The family can trace its fishing routes back to the 1800s. Otherwise, the shop, the neighborhood, the waterway ... deserted.

Then I spot a crusty geezer fiddling with what looks like a weighing chute for packaging shrimp. Turns out his family operates several 60–80 foot trawlers out of Sneads Ferry.

"Got two boats out today," he says. His skin is crinkled like a crumpled paper bag. His accent is hard Down East, dropping his "H," his vowels emanating from deep in his throat. "I" comes out like "Oye." The most remarkable thing: he's approachable. Friendly. Almost chatty. He identifies family members by the number of boats they operate. Son, three. Son-in-law, two. And so forth. Down to second cousins....

"Shrimping's in the blood, I guess," he says. "My father, my grandfather, me, my family ... I don't know how to do anything else."

Most of the family trawlers are in the 60-foot range. But, he says, "I got a steel boat with a freezer down in McClellanville. It goes out for twenty, thirty days."

This month, he's been optimistic. Over the last three years, he says, "Shrimping's come back." He blames the slump on high fuel prices. But now the market's good, prices steady.

"There's boats all over now. Even Beaufort's coming back. Fulcher's got 'red boats' at the foot of the Beaufort bridge. There's lots of boats in Engelhard. Oriental too. Lots of boats unload at Oriental."

The Fulcher name is synonymous with the shrimp business around the Pamlico since the 1920s. Trawlers, processing plants, retail seafood markets ...

"It's not supposed to be a season," I think he says. "But a boat come in yesterday with 900 pounds." That would be shrimp. "They're all scrambling now 'cause the weather's been so bad."

During the summer, his boats move into the Pamlico, but for the most part his fleet drags the offshore waters off New River inlet, one of the trickiest inlets to navigate on the Carolina coast.

"You can't just go out when you want to," he explains. "You got to go out at high tide and come in at high tide. Unless you're drawing less than six feet. But these bigger boats, they got to go with the tide."

Part of the reason he moves to the Pamlico during the summer months is sharks.

"Of late, we've got more sharks out there than I've seen in years. When the water gets warm, they come in close. And when we're dragging, them little fish get gilled in the nets, you know, and the sharks come in and take a huge bite. Eats the nets up to no end."

He shakes his head, like this act of nature is too odd to fathom.

"Sharks," he says.

The Coastal Highway from Jacksonville to New Bern is a miserable stretch through scars of scattered steel warehouses, splotches of poverty, acres of housing developments set in treeless, repurposed fields, and a nondescript landscape curiously empty for skirting the edge of the often-picturesque Croatan National Forest.

A more rewarding route forms a triangular circuit, first veering off U.S. 17 onto NC 24 outside Jacksonville toward Swansboro, and then cruising the mainland side of Bogue Sound, merging with U.S. 70 at Morehead City, backtracking to U.S. 17 by picking up NC 101 in Beaufort, and finally returning along the banks of the Neuse River to New Bern.

It's possible at Beaufort to continue into the region known locally as "Down East," following U.S. 70 to its terminus, where the Broadway of America runs out of continent in a town called Atlantic, directly across from Core Sound Inlet and the Cape Lookout National Seashore.

Alternate routes lead on via NC 12 to the Cedar Island Ferry, which connects to Ocracoke Island, and then on to the Hatteras Island ferry, continuing through the Hatteras National Seashore, where, just below Nags Head, the route turns off the island onto U.S. 64 and runs south of Albemarle Sound, crossing the Alligator River and rejoining U.S. 17 near Edenton.

A northern traverse runs through Nags Head, Kill Devil Hills and Kitty Hawk, intersecting with U.S. 158 below Duck, exiting the island across Currituck Sound as the Wright Memorial Bridge, and intersecting U.S. 17 at Elizabeth City (or, following NC 343, hitting U.S. 17 at South Mills).

Technically, it is possible to approach Virginia without returning to U.S. 17. You can take a jeep along the beach from Corolla all the way to Sandbridge, outside Virginia Beach. A ferry from Currituck to Knotts Island enters Virginia on NC 615. But all the roads east of U.S. 17, even the rare remote few that don't complete the circuit back, spread throughout the North River Marsh Game Land and Nature Preserve like capillaries all linked to the main vein: U.S. 17.

From Elizabeth City, The Coastal Highway turns northwest and basically leaves the coast for good.

The turn off U.S. 17 onto NC 24 to Swansboro opens into a region defined by the Outer Banks, a strange mix of raw seacoast at the eastern edge of the continent and rich farmland on the western border of Pamlico Sound, an agrarian countryside where various waterways finger into the landscape.

Swansboro is the gateway to the southern corner of the Outer Banks. The preservationists who live there like to think of the town as a quaint antique village, but actually there's not much to it. Incorporated in 1783, Swansboro was literally Mr. Swann's borough, named after a speaker in the state's House of Commons. The historic downtown is clustered around a couple of waterfront blocks on Front Street. But aside from some featured waterfront property adjacent to the Intracoastal Waterway, and the boatyard at Casper's Marina, the contemporary township is composed of typical strip-mall commercial fare, tract housing occupied by lots of servicemen from nearby Camp Lejeune, and refugees priced out of (or grossed out by) the more commercialized towns further along NC 24 or the beaches around Emerald Isle catering to retirees and tourists.

But Swansboro is serious fishing country, home of the Mullet Festival, with a subgenre shrimping industry closely linked with Sneads Ferry just to the south, as the crow flies, and Beaufort, to the north up the Intracoastal Waterway. Bogue Inlet, which connects the White Oak River to the open Atlantic just east of Swansboro, is shallow with constantly shifting shoals; the inlet is marked but, like New River Inlet below it, tricky to navigate. Whereas most of the offshore sport fishing is centered in Morehead City, around Swansboro the recreational fishing focuses on the numerous shallow creeks, trout holes, sandbars and marshes between the mainland and Hammocks Beach State Park, up the White Oak River and around the waterways associated with Bogue Sound.

A local avatar of the era when the seafood industry was thriving, and shrimp trawlers crowded out pleasure yachts, Clyde Phillips Seafood sits at the edge of the White Oak channel bridge across the water from Front Street. A throwback to the pre-prepackaged seafood era, Clyde's inventory still depends on what is available "when the boat comes in." Spartan doesn't do it justice. Rough is more like it. Old school. It's a real fish market, with whole fish lying on cakes of ice, piles of heads-on shrimp and shellfish, a filet bench and sink behind the display case.

The distinction between the old Swansboro and the new is evident in the contrast between a business like Clyde's and the restaurant scene back across the Oak River bridge. In recent years, several new restaurants

Clyde's Seafood Market, Swansboro, NC. Stepping into Clyde's is like stepping back in time. An old-fashioned seafood market selling catch right off the boat.

The boat, at the docks behind the market.

have opened in Swansboro, and a few of the old ones have been revamped, and many of these refurbished establishments are catering to a different crowd from the ones that might find Clyde's more hospitable. Clyde's is not a restaurant, but it represents an "old school" mentality that seems to be waning in the revitalization project along Front Street.

Of the refurbished restaurants along Front Street, I decide on Boro, a named derived from shortening the Swansboro to four letters.

"So people can remember it," the bartender tells me.

She's an athletic thirty-something ash blonde, a self-described "foodie" who prefers her shrimp grilled.

"Our shrimp," she assures me, "are wild Carolina shrimp, but we only serve them in our shrimp and grits. We don't fry anything. You want fried shrimp, you need to go to next door."

Next door is The Ice House, Boro's sister restaurant, which sits out over the water on pilings and has a more traditional—read "fried food"— menu.

"Same owner," she says. "Different kitchens."

Born and raised in Jacksonville, she is a life-long "17-er" with mixed feelings about The Coastal Highway. The negative aspects center on the recent developments that, in her view, have depersonalized a once familiar, local highway.

"I remember when there wasn't a left-hand side (going north). Twenty years ago it was all woods. Now it's all Walmart and chain stores and car lots and stuff."

Her other gripe is the traffic, alleviated somewhat with the bypass, but still congested and slow-moving through the north side of town. She says she used to work in New Bern, and she remembers how difficult the drive could be when the local commuters merged with the "out-of-towners passing through."

She also laments that some of the areas have not been revitalized, or the property restored.

"Maysville is dead," she says. "And Pollocksville has so much potential, all those antique houses...."

She trails off for a moment, reminiscing.

"People let some of those beautiful houses just rot."

She waxes nostalgic for Old U.S. 17, as only a "lifer" could.

"There were some good restaurants on the old highway," she says. "The Marina, Shred Shack, Fisherman's Wharf—that one burned down ... it was my favorite. Right on the bridge crossing New River, downtown.

The building was an old ship. That was such a cool idea. An old ship as a seafood restaurant."

When she was in high school, U.S. 17 led to "field parties" held in the middle of a cornfield or soybean field with a bonfire and a keg of beer.

"With all the suds and beans, we used to think, plenty of protein out here."

She also recalls her time off 17 in Charleston, when she was a student majoring in restaurant management at Johnson and Wales, before the college moved to Charlotte.

"I remember the old narrow two-lane bridge over Cooper River. It was scary. Old people were so afraid of it they would call the police to escort them across."

Here was a soul mate. An unreformed "17-er." Spent her life rolling the highway. To home, to high school, to parties, to college, to several jobs. Back and forth from Jacksonville to Charleston. Familiar with the landmark cities. Met her husband off 17.

"I was there when they blew that bridge up. Every morning at 10 am we could watch from the campus."

Her life rhythm is inextricably linked to the highway. Proof: "US 17 is all about timing. "Coming home," she says, "I had to leave Charleston at just the right time or I'd hit Charleston traffic, Myrtle Beach traffic, Wilmington traffic, Jacksonville traffic…. I guess traffic is the one thing you have to get used to on US 17."

Continuing the loop toward the Down East region, NC 24 intersects with U.S. 70, a perennial and essential arm of the Coastal Highway, at Morehead, about 30 miles east of U.S. 17.

Unlike much of eastern North Carolina, preoccupied with its colonial past, Morehead City hardly bothers to promote its heritage. It was an early 19th century business venture, more a planned industrial park than a storied historic locale exuding colonial charm. The heritage tourists flock to New Bern for its Tryon Palace and the homes along East Front Street, or, following the railway through the dead downtown of Morehead, crawl around the waterfront of Beaufort, enjoying the gallery of early 18th century homes, the yachts crowding the City Docks or bobbing at their moorings in Taylor Creek, equally desperate for a glimpse of the wild horses roaming Carrot Island as they are for a seat at one of the several trendy restaurants along the waterfront.

Not to discount how cool Beaufort can be, at times, especially considering the sailing culture that now dominates the town. Established in

1709, Beaufort is the third-oldest settlement in the state, and Blackbeard's actual hangout, as opposed to all the rumored haunts up and down the coast where apocryphal tales about the pirate are as ubiquitous as seagulls. In 1718 Blackbeard actually ran his flagship aground in Beaufort Inlet (the remains of which have been discovered). He was killed less than 50 miles up the coast, on Ocracoke Island.

While the sport fishing fleet typically runs out of the Morehead City waterfront, the transient boaters traversing the Intracoastal Waterway tend to stop at picturesque Beaufort. The waterfront offers plenty of dock space, anchoring out allows easy access to ship chancelleries and shops, and for those heading offshore it is the first port south of the treacherous Hatteras shoals for a straight southerly run across the Gulf Stream to the Virgin Islands. During the season, Beaufort is bustling with sailing activity, and for those year-round residents, a sail out to Cape Lookout provides a perfect day trip or weekend get-away.

There is, of course, as with all the historic towns along the former coastal colonies, more to Beaufort than the remnants of an 18th century whaling village filled with landmarks so cherished by the historical preservation society, the novelty shops, restaurants and gift shops along Front Street, the scenic city docks and the scruffy, often wealthy sailing community, both those in transit and others moored in Taylor's Creek. The part of town off the waterfront is a residential, working middle-class community. Nothing historic about it. More significantly, and also typical, the once thriving seafood industry has been priced out of town—in the case of Beaufort, shifting further east, away from the touristy Beaufort.

This last point, however, requires a caveat. It's a romantic notion to think of Beaufort as a picturesque seafood village in the tradition of Sneads Ferry, or as an early 19th century port for whaling ships bound for the North Atlantic. In truth, Beaufort was the home of a far more prosaic industry: menhaden processing. The lowly fish, known also as bugfish and pogey, is ground up to produce plant food, or pet food, or it's squeezed by the ton to produce omega oil for paint, soap and dietary supplements. Schools of menhaden migrate off the coast every fall, and for years they were harvested in huge numbers. But for many reasons—some aesthetic, some economical—the industry fell out of favor and the last processing plant on Front Street along Taylor Creek closed in 2005. (The stench was gamey, and the tourists never cottoned to what the locals, as they do— see Georgetown, et al.—call "the smell of money.")

Because the fishing industry is often not an industry per se, but a family operated enterprise—and this is true for much of the coast—identifying where an industry might exist is problematic. Although fleets associated the Fulchers continue to operate out of Beaufort, docking at the foot of the old Beaufort Causeway draw bridge, most of the commercial action these days occurs outside of Beaufort, on the edge of the Inner Banks, in the Down East zone, along the inside shores of Pamlico Sound and its various estuaries, creeks and tributaries.

Lacking the allure of Beaufort, but offering its own attractions—especially its offshore sport fishing fleet—Morehead City, though it lies about 30 miles from U.S. 17, exemplifies the duality of the Coastal Highway as well any community the highway actually runs through. Morehead City began as an industrial commercial venture reliant on its natural coastal resources—specifically, a deep-water port serviced by Beaufort Inlet that would facilitate maritime shipments of timber products, handled at the time mainly by the port in Wilmington. But the town also has always exploited its scenic beauty and abundant recreational possibilities. In this aspect, Morehead City, as it morphs from a port city and adjunct facility for military establishments into a recreational playground, shares with U.S. 17 its twofold essence: business and pleasure, functionality and whimsicality, sterility and prosperity. The highway and the town are domestic and wild, composed of scenes both fabricated and natural.

After the Civil War, activity at the port declined, but the railroad allowed access to the charms of the southern Outer Banks, and soon the tourism industry replaced the port as the main draw. Accelerated during the Victorian era with the opening of the Atlantic Hotel, Morehead City offered guests abundant sailing and fishing adventures, and beach excursions to the nearby barrier islands. This conflation of industry and recreational pursuits was completed when the fishermen from Shackleford Banks moved to the mainland, populating an area of Morehead City on the shores of Bogue Sound known as The Promised Land, heralding the city's reputation as a fishing mecca for both commercial concerns and sport fishing.

The section of Evans Street between Eighth Street and Fourth Street exudes an authenticity that similar strips like Shem Creek or MarshWalk have spoiled. The restaurants and dockage at these other sites grew out of traditional seafood depots and processing plants, but like so many genuine projects they soon devolved into flashy tourist traps, their strolling platforms and limited boat slips more a conduit for party-goers to migrate from one scene to another than actual working docks. In contrast, the

Evans Street waterfront is the real deal, with a touristy element, certainly, but the promenade along the Harbor Channel separating the mainland from Sugarloaf Island reflects its tradition, unchanged since it was first developed in the 1930s.

As a commercial seaport, and then as a sport-fishing center, Morehead City quickly became one of the most important charter boat centers in the state. Fishing has always been at the core of the economy, and, more essentially, the soul of the city. Locals are fond of bragging, for instance, that people "down here" can eat a mullet and tell you where it comes from. The abundance and variety of the fresh catch—including, along with mullet, Spanish mackerel, tuna, amberjack and dolphin, plus game fish like blue marlin—naturally led to the establishment of seafood markets and diners built out on the docks beside the boats. These stands evolved into the two oldest restaurants in town, The Sanitary and Captain Bills, both established circa 1938, and laid the foundation for other more ambitious eateries that followed. Today the waterfront boat slips and restaurants share space with boutiques and galleries, a dive shop and yacht sales agents, condos and cottages, creating an eclectic mix that complements the city's past.

As one of the more manageable of the east coast ports between Hatteras and Palm Beach closest to the Gulf Stream (about 45 miles out), Morehead City cashes in on its reputation as the "Sport Fisherman's Paradise." Oregon Inlet on Hatteras Island is closer to the Gulf, but navigating that channel can get hairy (especially in a strong wind with a southeast swell); more significantly, perhaps, Morehead City, unlike Hatteras Village, is connected to civilization, is easily accessible from major population areas, and offers all the amenities of a "vacation" destination lacking in the hardcore, barebones Spartan sport fishing experience off the extreme Outer Banks.

But best of all are the Evans Street waterfront city docks, where the sport fishing fleet back in daily after their trips outside to display, unload and often clean on the spot their catch. Visitors and locals strolling the waterfront can stand right in the midst of fish blood and guts as the crews unload tuna, dolphin, mackerel, wahoo, cobia and assorted deep-water species. During the season, the Big Rock Blue Marlin tournament draws anglers from all along the coast, and it's not uncommon for competitors to record game fish weighing in at over 600 pounds.

And right in the middle of all this fishing fanaticism, several classic restaurants continue the tradition of serving a no-frills style of Down East seafood to a rapidly changing demographic.

The oldest surviving and most revered of the Morehead City restaurants is The Sanitary. Its walls are cluttered with black-and-white photographs of congressmen and celebrities, sports figures and business VIPs. For some, The Sanitary is best known for the longevity of its "no alcohol" policy, in effect from 1939 to 1995, popular with the church crowd that dominated the town.

(And still does, essentially, to some degree, although these days, well, money talks, but, historically that sentiment reflects some serious teetotalism, and is indicative of the prevailing cultural attitude still influencing the politics of the area.)

To compete with this frumpiness, and indicative of the changing nature of the once insular town, a chef born in Buenos Aires, Fabian Botta, and a business partner, opened The Ruddy Duck in 2008. Botta cut his teeth in some upscale establishments in Atlanta and Winston-Salem, catering to a haute couture crowd until, having had enough of the "city life," he decided to branch out and launch a place of his own, scheming to marry his flair for global cuisines to the no frills local seafood fare indigenous to the Carolina coast. A fairly new establishment, having played second fiddle to The Sanitary for years, The Ruddy Duck endures, and has come into its own as a prime eatery along the waterfront.

The semi-circle bar dominates the central dining room with table and booth seating available throughout, plus a back open-air deck with boat access. The full bar offers guest beers, an interesting wine list and offbeat specials concocted by the Botta, like a skate wing Ruben sandwich, bouillabaisse and gumbo dishes. Most important, they use fresh seafood from local sources and fishermen.

Speaking of … it was in The Ruddy Duck where I first heard of "greentail" shrimp.

The bartender explains that these are relatively large shrimp caught late in the season as they migrate from inland waters toward the open ocean, snagged before they get out of the inlet. I recognize this description as being the same as the "creek" shrimp I had in Folly Beach. They're also known as "Channel" shrimp or sometimes simply late season Whites. During rainy seasons, the shrimp leave the creeks early, before getting very big, but during droughts they stay "inside" and gain some bulk, and it's during these dry seasons that the greentails, or creek shrimp or channel shrimp, are best.

"Southern Salt (another restaurant, a block up Evans Street) just unloaded 4000 pounds of greentails," the bartender tells me, offering the info like an insider tip on Derby Day. "They come in around Wilmington, I think. He'll sell 'em by the pound, right out of the restaurant, if you want some."

The bartender, a dedicated jogger—"runner," she clarifies—is informed but curt. Her short dark hair and athletic build contribute to her all-business demeanor—which probably helps her deal with some of the more colorful transients (and locals) that might drop by. The restaurant certainly draws a mixed crowd, including affluent diners seeking fun fare at decent prices in a casual waterfront setting, young professionals (or retired young-ish professionals) unwinding after work (or a workout). But a lot of the bar habitués are "on the water daily."

Does she like shrimp?

"Anyway you cook it."

Does she shrimp?

"I fish."

U.S. 17?

"Don't know anything about it."

Her highways are U.S. 501, U.S. 301, I-95....

"I live on twenty four," she says. That's NC 24, between Swansboro and Morehead City.

I order a plate of greentails.

She moves off to serve a trio of fishermen just off the water, in for mid-afternoon drinks. Their conversation trends towards the natural elements of their lives.

One of the men, a swarthy, hearty unshaven man in a thick knit sweater is explaining some differences between the coastal waters around Core Sound and Beaufort Inlet and the waters off Oriental and the western edge of Pamlico Sound.

"The Neuse out there around Adams Creek gets rough. I've crossed it in the morning and by afternoon it's so choppy I couldn't get back. Not in my boat, leastways."

One of the other men, still wearing his toboggan cap, kicks in: "I've seen six foot swells out there tossing the ferry around."

He's referring to the ferry running across the Neuse River from Minnesott Beach near Oriental to Cherry Branch.

"I've never seen waves stop that ferry," says the third man. "Nothing stops it but fog and ice."

"It gets rough," the first man continues. "I got a double-vee hull, you know. Shallow draft. Breaks the waves. Still, I've seen it so rough with whitecaps my wife won't go."

They shift to trading fish stories, veering into water monsters like Asian Carp and sea snakes. The man with the toboggan recalls following Smith Creek at Oriental until his "trolling motor hit sand."

The third man notes: "Ain't no water in that crick."

He actually says 'crick.'"

My shrimp arrive, in all their golden brown glory. They're butterflied and fan-tailed—that is, split and fried with the tails on. Big. Plump. Sweet. No hint of mud. No briny aftertaste. The flavor is immediate and strong— snappier than normal Whites and more distinct than Browns. The green-tails tend to melt in your mouth compared to the tougher, crunchier Mayport variety, reminiscent of the Creek shrimp in Folly Beach, but even more delicate, more intense.

"It's a wind tide over there," the first man explains. "Here we got a lunar tide. Four feet, running around four knots. On the Neuse, they don't really have a tide. An east wind pushes the water out. West wind fills it in."

"Must've been an east wind that day," the second man concludes. "Weren't no water in the crick."

The bartender pours them another round. I feel "blown out," flirting with what the Buddhist call soteriological release.

Crick shrimp, I think. Greentails.

I pinch the last fat ort of sweet tail meat out of the fantail husk.

Alas, Wooten's Drive-In is long gone. Otherwise, New Bern doesn't offer much, as far as shrimp go, for the adventurous traveler along the Coastal Highway.

The town pretends to be famous for being the "birthplace" of Pepsi.

(My old man owned a business a block down the street from where the chemist, Caleb Bradham, concocted the original cola.)

Other old timers celebrate the day Elvis ate lunch in a diner on old U.S. 17 (now the Chelsea Restaurant) the day after a gig at the New Bern Sudan Temple.

The second oldest town in North Carolina, New Bern sells its history mainly in the form of Tryon Palace. The "palace" was finished in 1770, and served as the state capitol building after the American Revolution. The original structure was destroyed by fire in 1790, so the existing building is a reconstruction, serving mainly as a showcase for antiques and an opportunity for local history buffs to dress in period costumes. Like most of the towns lining the Inner Banks, New Bern thrived as a shipping center for timber goods and lumber mills in the 19th century, declined in the

20th century, and then began to rebound when the heritage tourism and retirement business rejuvenated the contemporary economy.

Today, New Bern seems more like any other normal small town filled with lower middle-class workers rather than a well-preserved museum town of historic remnants and significance. The natives are employed in various service industries and jobs associated with the Marine Air Corps Station at Cherry Point, fifteen miles way. Businesses cater to the slew of wealthy professionals who populate the riverfront property and retirees who have migrated in from colder climes. Even with its sharply divided socio-economical demographics and pretentions, New Bern does manage to offer what the tourist brochures call "small town charm," proximity to the Atlantic Coast, fishing and hunting opportunities, cheap coastal living and some of the best sailing in the United States.

It's this access to open water that perhaps most defines New Bern's historical profile and current viability as a boating center. But the town's location, as a prime navigable port at the western edge of Pamlico Sound, also has a commercial significance, a fact underscored in January 2017 when dozens of shrimp boats converged on New Bern to protest new regulations proposed by the North Carolina Wildlife Federation that would restrict trawlers operating in the estuaries, sounds, creeks and rivers associated with the Pamlico Sound. The new regulations would reduce the size of nets and the time they could be employed, eliminate night dragging and limit how many days a week shrimpers could trawl. But the fisherman and shrimpers view these new regulations as just another step in the process of closing the Pamlico to commercial trawling.

New Bern no longer supports fishing fleets, but the Fisheries hearing was held at the New Bern Convention Center, a waterfront building on the banks of the Neuse River. The setting offered a perfect backdrop for a picturesque protest with trawlers anchored off the banks of the river and cluttering the waterfront behind the center. North Carolina is the only state on the east coast that allows inshore trawling, and the practice has set recreational fisherman against commercial fishing and shrimping interests. Of course, it also sets scientific research against emotional and personal reactions. The proposals were designed to save juvenile fish that spawn in the estuaries before migrating out to mature at sea, to reduce the number of by-catch fish killed as a result of dragging nets, and to protect nursery areas where shrimp spawn, fighting depletion and insuring the species for future generations. Ironically, the regulations the fishermen see as destroying their livelihood are designed to save and protect their way of life.

The regulators might take the long view, trying to preserve the future of the industry. But in the short-term, the commercial fishermen see the regulations as a conspiracy by wealthy sport fisherman and bureaucrats to put them out of business. They argue that there are plenty of fish, the stocks are not depleting, they have no alternative work, and further restrictions will destroy an already fragile livelihood. It's an old fight, the preservationists against those immediately affected. Shrimping is a heritage business, family-owned, and usually handed down from one generation to the next. Change does not come easily, even when the environment, the natural conditions that create the basis for the business—in this case, a healthy and reproductive staple of seafood species—are under such serious threat, and long-term solutions tend to cause such short-term economic pain.

The key is balance. And the argument will not be settled any time soon.

But these fights over territory and replenishment indicate the fragility of the resources, and the unique situation of the seafood industry along the eastern Carolina seaboard. The Pamlico is finite. It is not open-ocean. Even where fishing and shrimping is mainly an "outside" activity, from Frying Pan shoals south to Florida, where the resources seems literally oceanic, the species for taking seemingly boundless, a misconception persists. Seafood stocks are not "boundless." Even in the open ocean many species are at risk; some already beyond recovery. The seafood industry is definitely being squeezed, as the availability of fresh stock dwindles and the cost of harvesting the catch increases. But given the particular landscape and circumstances of dragging the Pamlico and its adjacent waterways, these issues of depletion and sustainability are magnified, made more acute by the competing interests in an ecologically sensitive area of limited natural resources.

Such is the state of the industry as U.S. 17 enters the western boundary of the Inner Banks.

New Bern's significance as a hub at the intersection of U.S. 70 and U.S. 17, with waterway transit from the interior of the state out to the coast, has steadily diminished over the years and is now non-existent, although the logging business continues to play an important role in the economy, as Weyerhaeuser is a major presence in the community. Running north through town, U.S. 17 connects New Bern to "Little" Washington, Williamston, Edenton and Elizabeth City, forming a border that denotes the western edge of the Inner Banks. It is the easternmost direct route through the region, the highway to which all roads leading to the inside coasts of the Pamlico, Currituck and Albemarle sounds return. Even the one exception, NC 168, hits U.S. 17 in Chesapeake.

Oddly, New Bern fancies itself as the last outpost of civilization—of affluence and sophistication—as U.S. 17 runs north to the Virginia state line. Long before Nicholas Sparks moved in (and then left after being unceremoniously "black-balled" from the Eastern Carolina Yacht Club), and before Curtis Strange married a local girl and put New Bern Golf and Country Club on the map, New Bern was a destination for the well heeled and well connected. Linda McMahon (WWE) was born here. Jane Morgan lived on Johnson Street. Dick Pope, Jr., skied the Trent River. Tyrone Powers hung out at the Trent Pines Club. During the Fifties, New Bern was the place to be in Coastal Carolina. Today, most of the wealth is concentrated outside of town, in suburbs like Trent Woods and communities perched along the various riverfronts, but a neighborhood in the northeast quadrant of East Front Street facing the Neuse River still features some interesting early homes—many associated with the lumber barons of the late 19th century. And the action, these days, such as it exits in New

Middle Street, New Bern, NC. Two blocks off the now defunct U.S. 17 Business, a few stores down from where Pepsi was invented.

Bern, centers around the "historic" downtown, a refurbished section of once shoddy brick buildings and shops wedged between the Neuse and Trent rivers.

Although the fishing and shrimping concerns have long ago moved to the nether regions of Down East, New Bern still sports a few markets specializing in local seafood, and a couple of interesting restaurants that promote locally sourced products. Captain Ratty's is a convenient corner restaurant with rooftop dining and a dedicated wine program recognized by Wine Spectator for its listings. The ground floor is crowded with tables and a typical L-shaped bar. A huge window opens a view onto Middle Street. The menu is fairly predictable, heavy on southern dishes featuring steaks, pork and chicken. The seafood entrées favor Lowcountry style, but the selections are presented with an important tell: the fish and oysters are sold "at market price." This detail usually indicates that these items are selected daily and come from local sourcing.

I asked about the shrimp, which in Ratty's are offered grilled, fried, boiled, and sautéed in a scampi.

A server from Texas (read: military transplant) summed up the situation that pervades the restaurant scene in New Bern: "Our shrimp are usually brought in from Morehead City,"

One can only hope so. Only in New Bern would that be an asset.

How does she like her shrimp.

"Anyway."

Us 17?

"Pain in the ass."

Another restaurant a few doors up Middle Street from Ratty's, M.J.'s, bills itself as a raw bar, with "a hint of Maryland seasoning." It comes off more as a cramped sports bar, with a local beer drinking crowd. One of the diners must've picked up my vibe.

"Try Persimmons," she said, without really acknowledging me. "It's fancy."

Crosswire, I concluded. Mistaken for a gastronomical prig ... I let it go and roll on.

Situated on pilings out over the edge of the Neuse River, Persimmons Waterfront Restaurant at first seems out of place in this provincial outback. Its pretensions remind a curious traveler that New Bern tends to wear its gentrification proudly, like so much costume jewelry (saving the cultured pearls for special occasions). But Persimmons' farm-to-table style is inspirational, if trendy. Their eco-friendly business model—stressing geothermal climate control, energy efficient lighting, recycling and sustainable farming—is principled, if somehow too precious. They know where each leaf in your arugula and kale salad was cultivated. They can identify the rascal that butchered the hog for their crispy fried pork torta. They toss around terms like "chipotle aioli" that just a few years ago would frighten the locals, send them, perhaps, into a frenzy of ardent xenophobia.

(New Bern is clearly a tea-party deep red political land of resistance to most things considered "foreign." After all, the congressman serving this district renamed French fries "Freedom Fries" to taunt the French after they refused to support the war with Iraq in 2003).

Not to re-litigate that mess, but this particular *contretemps* illustrates the political climate that dominates the Coastal Highway in this part of the country, and explains why the bartender in M.J.'s described the menu as "prissy" and the portions "stingy," complaining that even the inspiration for the name—taken from rare persimmon logs, dating back to New Bern's 19th century lumber trade, dredged up next to the building during renovation—sounds affected.

Bottom line: Persimmons isn't big on shrimp. Actually, New Bern isn't big on shrimp—at least, locally sourced shrimp. Even so, given the political and cultural reality of New Bern and the surrounding *terrior*, it's refreshing that Persimmons continues with its in-your-face style of bringing progressive cuisine to a redneck enclave like Craven County.

From New Bern, two major loop roads run from U.S. 17 strategically out to the edges of Pamlico Sound where what's left of the dwindling fleets of shrimp trawlers continue to populate the western coast of the Inner Banks. NC 55 leads east and then south to the tiny community of Oriental. A nearby ferry runs across the Neuse River to connect with various routes towards the Outer Banks, and a northern loop rolls through the farmlands of Beaufort County. Retracing NC 55 from Oriental back to Bayboro, NC 304 continues east through the spoils of Goose Creek Game Land around Hobucken, then returns along the southern flank of the Pamlico River, joining U.S. 17 at Chocowinity, where the highway crosses the Pamlico River and Tar River into "Little" Washington. From there, a second loop begins east on U.S. 264, branching onto NC 92 that runs along the Pamlico through Bath (the oldest settlement in NC), up through Belhaven on the Pungo River, rejoining U.S. 264 at Engelhard. Limning the edge of the Croatan Sound, U.S. 264 passes through the communities of Swan Quarter, Engelhard, and Stumpy Point. Finishing at a junction outside of Manns

Harbor, the road becomes U.S. 64, with the eastern branch continuing across Croatan Sound as the Virginia Dare Memorial Bridge onto Roanoke Island, connecting to Fort Raleigh City and Manteo, before t-boning with NC 12 on the Outer Banks. The western run of U.S. 64 returns back to U.S. 17 at Williamston.

It says something about Oriental, a town of 900 souls, that the most interesting aspect of its founding, to some, is the derivation of its name. Ask half a dozen locals why the town is named Oriental and you'll get six different answers. One rumor claims that the postmaster's wife found the nameplate of a wrecked merchant ship on the beach, and her souvenir inspired the name. Another tale suggests that, in a public relations coup, she simply decided that "Oriental" was more exotic than Smith's Creek, and the name was adopted. Like many mysteries surrounding the Outer Banks—most involving ghosts and pirate lore (Blackbeard reportedly kept a "home" in nearby Bath)—evidence to prove many of the stories is scant. No mysterious nameplate from the doomed Oriental survives, for instance, but the exhibit at the local history museum includes a ship's porthole reputed to be from the steamer.

Once an arcane stop for travelers along the Intracoastal Waterway, and now a retiree destination littered with upscale housing, recreational craft and marinas, the town continues to maintain a sizeable trawler fleet. It bills itself as "The Sailing Capital of North Carolina," and there is some truth to that claim. The harbor opens onto the mouth of the Neuse River, the widest river in the United States, six miles across before it spills into

Oriental, NC, as seen from the bridge, looking out at the Pamlico Sound. Oriental is a major port and shrimp processing center for trawlers operating in Pamlico Sound. The town is also a major sailing center in Eastern North Carolina.

Pamlico Sound. The water is relatively deep, the wind steady, and the climate moderate. Several destinations are within reach for day sailing: north, to the Pamlico River communities; west, up the Neuse to New Bern; east across the sound to Ocracoke Island; an easy motor through the Intracoastal at Adams Creek leads to Beaufort, and from there to Cape Lookout and the open Atlantic.

Distinct from the more than 3,000 recreational craft that define the community, scads of fishing trawlers crowd around the city docks. Fulcher's seafood dominates the waterfront. The working trawlers often overshadow smaller recreational boats moored along the public pier.

And just off the harbor, within sight of the fleet, M and M's occupies a house converted into a restaurant. It's divided into two sections. A cramped but inviting bar on one side is flooded with natural light, a dining room fills the rest of the house. The menu is basic, offering a little of everything but nothing fancy. The specials favor the meat and potatoes working lunch crowd, but the seafood is served classic style, broiled, steamed or fried, with hushpuppies, fries and slaw. A small but full bar offers some interesting drafts, less interesting wines.

The bartender is a slight, seemingly gentle college-aged guy with shoulder-length hair, a beard, and a Down East accent mellowed by years of mingling with non-natives. He seems to be a bit "in the weeds," so reticent, although the bar is fairly empty. An upper-middle-aged man and a woman, obviously a couple, and obviously retired, munch on shrimp burritos. The couple has powered over from Broad Creek in their 32-foot trawler-style yacht to the restaurant. Turns out, he's a true shrimp aficionado who not only studies the species but also buys a 100 pounds of shrimp a season, in 50 pound bags, from Chris Fulcher (yes, that Fulcher), who owns several of the trawlers operating out of Oriental as well as the processing plant preferred by commercial Pamlico shrimpers.

The man is professorially discoursing on shrimp. The bartender tries to listen. The man's wife appears to have stopped listening years ago.

"The beauty of shrimp," the professor says, "is that they are a 100% renewable resource. Shrimp are like dandelions. They come up again every year."

The scene is Dickensian. The man holds forth like Brian Sewell chatting about art on BBC2. "As long as we protect the wetlands, the abundance of shrimp will be viable and thriving for years...."

The bartender, hustling drinks, tries to (or pretends to) pay attention. He's like a fidgety student trying to grasp a knotty concept. The wife, nodding catatonically, remains enraptured with her shrimp burrito. Now me, a stranger among them. The man acknowledges my sudden presence the way he would a student late for a lecture, pausing his oration just long enough for a cutting glance, but glad to have another member in the audience.

"I can predict," he assures us, "how good the shrimp season will be by how many larvae I can see at night off my dock when I flash my light on the water. It's a light I use to spot Red Drum, you know...."

I marvel at the situation. Right out of Casablanca: "Of all the gin joints in all the towns in the world...." I walk into a restaurant, totally on the fly, almost by mistake, looking for a different establishment, and find a man holding forth on the life-cycle of shrimp. Serendipity? Karma?

When I cut into the lecture to order a fried shrimp platter, the professor suggests that the best way to eat shrimp is not fried at all.

"Steamed in beer," he says. "Splashed with Zatarain's or New Iberia."

The bartender and I share a look.

"Fried," I say.

He puts the order in.

The professor scowls, returns to his lecture. "The larvae double in size every week. And when they mature they head for the open sea, where they spawn and die. They fall to the bottom, and become ... crab food, I suppose."

It's getting weird. His interest in shrimp seems to border on obsession. Might explain why he bought a trawler-style yacht.

"They don't live long," he continues. "Six, maybe eight months before they head to sea to spawn and die ... or, preferably, they are caught, cooked and served on a platter in a place like this."

Six months! That's not enough time, I think, to develop a bad attitude.

He seems to sense my snarky impertinence.

"It's a short life-cycle, not like some of these deep water fish that live 50 years or more."

Fifty years! It's going completely sideways. I check my scant fish education. Piscatorial longevity. Swordfish, around four years. Sailfish, seven. Maybe he means sharks ... they can hit 30. Or Koi?

The bartender cuts in, without raising his hand. Bad form.

"Unless they get attacked by a Giant Tiger Shrimp."

Tiger Prawns! We're entering a parallel universe now. Tiger Prawns, specific to Indo-Pacific waters, invading the Pamlico—and attacking our indigenous shrimp...?

The professor tries to restore order.

"Yes, this is often the case—"

But the bartender is intent on cutting in. On making his point. We've moved onto his turf now. He's like a student desperate to be recognized, waving his hand in the air while the professor ignores him. But he's not waving his hand. And he's not waiting to be called on.

"My friends caught one—"

"When foreign species are introduced—"

"Right out here, middle of Pamlico Sound—"

"Into a delicate ecosystem such as exists here—"

"They call 'em 'finger fuckers.'"

The bar goes silent. You can hear the hum of customers in the dining room.

"They got spikes on the sides of their body. When you go to pull 'em out of the net, they fuck your fingers up."

The professor stares at something lost in the distance. His wife stares at what's left of her shrimp burrito.

I wonder aloud, "How do they get here?"

The bartender wouldn't know a faux pas from a crab claw. But he discreetly slips off to the kitchen, leaving "finger fucker" hanging in the air like the smell of a dead rat in a heater vent. My question seems to have reignited the stalled mind of the professor. He answers it, his stare still a bit vague.

"They're brought into our native waters in the holds of ships, released into the environment when they flush their bilge."

Works for me. He begins to explain how it's the same with Japanese Beetles when my shrimp order arrives.

"In Japan they have birds that cull the growth of insects, but here..."

I lose track, munching the shrimp. They are typical of the region, very lightly brushed with batter, firm, a mix of sweet and salty, a bit overdone, but the crunchiness complements the bite.

The professor has moved on to the kudzu invasion when the bartender comes back out of the kitchen and begins polishing glasses. He cuts in again, irreverently: "I've seen Tiger Shrimp out there this big."

He indicates about a foot.

A discussion of size seems to settle the professor.

"During a heavy rainfall, the shrimp move away from the fresh water out towards the ocean and higher concentrations of salinity. These shrimp remain a normal size, as they are either caught, or they spawn and die.

Trawler, Oriental, NC.

"Or a Tiger Prawn gets 'em...." The bartender is clearly engaged. But the professor checks him.

"But..." Dramatic pause. "During a drought, the inland waters retain their salinity, and the shrimp do not migrate. This causes them to become abnormally large. I too have seen them at least this big."

He indicates the spread with his thumb and forefinger, what would be an incredibly huge shrimp.

His wife suddenly finds her voice. "They jump right out of the water and onto our dock."

The bartender and I exchange a glance.

"The dog bites them in his mouth, right out of the water." The wife looks pleased at the memory.

This seems too much for the bartender. He throws his towel across his shoulder, leans back against the counter. "Kinda dog is that?"

"Plott Hound," she says.

The professor explains, "Looks like a cross between a Labrador and a blood hound. Huge paws, floppy ears. Coat, brindle. State dog of North Carolina."

Who knew?

The bartender looks relieved. "Oh, yeah," he says. "We call 'em coonhounds." As if that explains a dog fetching shrimp out of a creek in Oriental.

The wife, again: "Don't try taking them out of his mouth."

The bartender tosses his towel in the sink. "Long as he don't bite down on no finger fucker."

Washington is the first town in the United States named after the first president. There's not much else to recommend it ... except for Bill's Hot Dogs, the favorite eatery of the girl working the bar at Big Tuna, in Georgetown, SC ... an establishment not to be so easily dismissed by its relative insignificance in the larger scheme of things, as it illustrates, quite neatly, how a long-standing, iconic "living" landmark creates a cultural cross-reference by which a true "17-er" defines herself.

Two blocks off "old" U.S. 17, Bill's has been serving hot dogs from the same location since 1938. (It originated in 1928, a few blocks further east, on Market Street.) The shop sits among a line of deserted low brick buildings, its red awning shading a screen door flanked by plate glass windows opening onto Gladden Street. To-go only. Steamed buns. Oil-fried dogs. With mustard, onions, or chili. That's it. Wrapped in thin white paper.

If your stomach's made of steel ...

But I'm after shrimp, and Washington is mainly significant because it's where U.S. 17 connects with U.S. 264, and that haunted highway lead into serious shrimp country. Thirty miles out, Belhaven, a popular port just off the Intracoastal Waterway, graces the edge of Pungo River. The downtown has one stoplight, and a deserted Main Street somehow maintains a lively buzz of dedicated locals trying to make a go of it. The community, like so much of the land sandwiched between U.S. 17 and the western edge of Pamlico Sound, is a mix of poverty and economic dead zones, and attempts at gentrification, or, more precisely, for those that confer a negative connotation to yuppie urban renewal, rejuvenation, are inexplicably resented by the locals. Belhaven, like much of the region, is below flood stage. In 2011, when Hurricane Irene hit the area hard, the police station had four-and-a-half feet of water in the building.

A Belhaven local explains that many area restaurants, just a few miles from major shrimp harbors and processing plants, don't serve local shrimp. But they don't serve farmed imports either.

"Off season, the shrimp supply is depleted, so most of the restaurants purchase shrimp in bulk frozen from various distributors. In the season, most restaurants get their shrimp from Swan Quarter, but even off-season, the shrimp are Atlantic, wild caught. No one serves imported farmed shrimp."

She should know. A sturdy brunette with thick glasses, an easy laugh and broad smile, she loves living near Pamlico Sound. Having worked "gill nets and crab pots" out of Columbia, on the northern loop of the U.S. 264/64 route, for 17 years—"catching striped bass in the gill nets, using nanny shad as bait for the blue crabs"—she now enjoys the recreational aspects of the region, celebrating its abundance of watersports, fishing, boating and kayaking.

"Columbia is low too," she explains. "They got No Wake Zone signs in the streets for when it floods. Our house was off the sound, but we had a dock on a small canal out to the river we launched from."

She remembers special areas near Columbia, where the Albemarle Sound, Pamlico Sound and the Alligator River converge, which were particularly fun.

"It shoals up fast out there. Very choppy. There's a place called Great Shoal. It's one foot deep in spots. We use to camp out there on a deserted island. It was so shallow we could walk right out to the edge of the channel. All these big yachts would be going by, and we would be standing right beside 'em. Must've look like we were walking on water."

Her views of U.S. 17?

"It sucks."

But then she reconsiders, admitting that, while she appreciates the "new parts," she understands how they have changed the character of the highway.

"Old US 17 is good for the scenery. Tobacco farms and cornfields and all those small towns you go through. People on the by-pass will never know how cool some of them small towns really are. And it's killing the economies. It's got all those four-way stop signs and caution lights, but it's a lovely ride."

She's old school, referring to "Old 17" and distinguishing between the new bypasses and the original that runs through all the small towns.

"Not a bad ride at all," she concedes.

As if referring to an old lover ...

U.S. 264 rolls from Belhaven into Swan Quarter, where a ferry connects with Ocracoke Island. The swans are real, for some reason migrating from the North American tundra to Lake Mattamuskeet to feed on wigeon grass and pondweed. They show up in early December and, according to locals, fly off after the first full moon in February. The highway continues east through farmland and low country, passing finally into Engelhard, the commercial shrimping base for the northwest sector of the Pamlico Sound. The village is seriously industrial, very locals only, and saturated with boat yards, repair sheds, seafood processing plants and. of course, a slew of trawlers crowded into the Far Creek harbor. The tiny inlet is a perfect shelter with direct access to the Pamlico Sound with a direct shot across the sound to Oregon Inlet and the open Atlantic. Plus, the area is so remote that the property values are depressed, and so attract commercial interests. There's nothing romantic about Engelhard. It's a working fishing town, along the lines of Sneads Ferry or McClellanville without the impressive retirement homes along the shoreline or celebrity restaurants or any semblance of holiday charm for even an ambitious vacationer. But if you're after fresh local seafood, this is the place.

The highway after Engelhard enters a desolate stretch of miles-long straights, where the road is simply a paved strip along an elevated grade between a drainage ditch and a swamp with only wildlife viewing spots

The Fleet, Engelhard, NC. Engelhard sits off the U.S. 264/US64 loop running out from U.S. 17 to the edges of the Pamlico Sound, to the Outer Banks, returning back to U.S. 17 along the edge of the Albemarle Sound. The village, along with Wanchese to the northeast, on the Outer Banks, and Oriental to the south, at the mouth of the Neuse, are the last outposts of true commercial shrimping on the Coastal Highway.

Trawlers, Far Creek. Engelhard, NC. This sheltered cove in the middle of nowhere offers safe harbor for the Pamlico fleet, direct access to the Pamlico Sound, and a straight shot across the sound to Oregon Inlet and the open Atlantic. And little else. No resorts. No golf courses. No vacation cottages. In its isolation and obscurity, it's an ideal trawler port.

to entertain the imagination—plus signs warning travelers that the area is a Navy bombing range. Surely the irony is not lost on the locals inhabiting the edge of the swamp, much less on the Department of Defense: Nature preserves and wildlife viewing areas in a zone frequently bombed to smithereens.

The next outpost of concentrated civilization is Stumpy Point, which is just that: a string of cottages and shacks built on the banks of tiny inlets leading out to the Pamlico. Among these cottages are more substantial, contemporary buildings—some very posh, large and well appointed—scattered along the shore of the sound: refugees, perhaps, from the commercial saturation of the Outer Banks, along with recreational fishermen and militant dropouts into a serious survivalist mode. As for yuppie infiltration: Lost Colony Brewery has relocated from Manteo to Stumpy Point. (Supposedly, the reverse-osmosis water system is a major draw for the brewer, along with, one assumes, cheap real estate.)

From Stumpy Point, the highway continues its deserted course atop the grade until finally T-boning U.S. 64. The sudden emergence into the "normal" world of tourist kitsch is almost shocking. East on U.S. 64 leads across Croatan Sound via the Virginia Dare Memorial Bridge—the longest bridge in the state, at over five miles—onto Roanoke Island, then out to Wanchese, the center of the commercial shrimp industry at the northern top of the Pamlico. A small community of boat builders and fishermen and chock full of huge seafood warehouses, boatyards, processing and shipping plants, Wanchese is all business. Whereas vacationers continue on to Manteo and the shores of Duck, Kitty Hawk, Nags Head and further south to Hatteras, the hard core offshore fishing crowd, professionals and wholesale seafood buyers head to Wanchese.

As the furthest point off 17 to which I would venture, Wanchese closed the circuit, to a degree, of the major shrimping points around the perimeter of the Pamlico Sound:

Oriental, Engelhard, Wanchese, with Morehead City and Sneads Ferry securing the shrimping grounds immediately to the south of Shackelford Banks. On Roanoke Island. Ft. Raleigh, site of the "Lost Colony" and home of Virginia Dare, the first English child born in North America, sits on the north end; Wanchese occupies the south side. Appropriately, Wanchese is thought to be the first fishing village on Roanoke Island.

O'Neal's sits near the end of a short paved driveway leading into a seafood industrial park. A self-service restaurant, the dining room is no more than an open space with booth and tables in the middle of a seafood market, paper napkins, a condiments stand, drink machine, sweet or unsweetened tea—no alcohol—an order window, a pick-up window—not a spot selling ambiance, just fresh seafood, not exactly off the boat but directly from the processing plant behind the restaurant. Nets hang along the walls, an attempt at wall art—plastic fish and "artwork"—blend in. A cooler offers a few pints of local fish dips. A photograph of the primary trawler supplying the restaurant adorns the wall beside the pick-up window.

One of the guys behind the counter assures me the shrimp have only been frozen once, after being on ice while the trawler was at sea.

"They usually go out for a week. Midnight Sunday they start dragging, come back Friday night. You can't drag weekends, so..."

The shrimp are small, deep fried into a tight ball, almost overdone, but lightly dusted with a crispy batter that easily flake off the nuggets. Crunchy, a subtle hint of brine, more salty than sweet, buttery aftertaste, no trace of mud or any hint of creek pong.

"These are Pamlico shrimp," the man tells me. "Although there might be some Atlantic shrimp mixed in there, too, because they were going outside a few weeks ago when the weather was mild, but even the offshore shrimp are from the immediate area, caught while they were heading for deep water here at the end of the season."

I finish my sweet tea. Pull out of the parking lot, admiring the sheer number of trawlers and sport-fishermen and warehouses ... follow signs back from the edge toward the other side of the Inner Banks, to the last stretch of The Coastal Highway that actually abuts the coast.

Head east on U.S. 64, the road back to U.S. 17, crossing the Albemarle Sound on NC 32 toward the town of Edenton and then turning toward the northern-most outpost on the Coastal Highway, Elizabeth City, before the road enters the spaghetti traffic stream into Chesapeake and Norfolk. Founded in 1794, Elizabeth City, like many early colonial coastal settlements, began as a shipping center for the logging industry and shipbuilding—along with oyster farming and fishing—before the inevitable incursion of modernity began the slow decline of the city as an industrial powerhouse, hastening its slide into an after-thought. Local polite history buffs like to connect the name of the town to Queen Elizabeth I, which is suspect because she died in 1603, and Elizabeth City was founded in 1794, and connotations referring to English royalty during this militant period of United States history would argue for the alternative theory that the name derives from the name of a local tavern owner, given that "tavern" in those days was probably a euphemism for a much older profession. Idle speculation aside, the name suggests the character of the city: older regal pretentions tempered by the essential character of a harbor city.

Once a main port with access to inland trade via the Dismal Swamp Canal and toward the open sea via the Pasquotank River and Albemarle Sound, the town began to lose trade once the railroad was completed, connecting the coast with more inland communities, and many industries began to relocate to the Piedmont, further eroding the significance of the town as a transportation hub. Resurgence occurred during WW II, when the Elizabeth City Shipyard was commissioned to build submarine chasers, but after the war that industry quickly evaporated, although the city's ties to the military continued with the establishment of the Elizabeth City Coast Guard Air Station, the largest station in the United States.

Off the tiny strip of waterfront that's been refurbished, and a small section along Main Street that has tried to restore the former charm of small town southern life, the town is a mixture of chain restaurants and shops and empty shells of houses. There are pockets of affluence, especially along the banks of the Pasquotank River, where retirees and a few prosperous folks reside in salubrious waterfront neighborhoods, but for the most part, the area is depressed and empty. Similar to the negative effects of the railroad, the completion of the U.S. 17 bypass further stifled the flow of commercial traffic through the city. Known these days for its Harbor of Hospitality, the town is a convenient stop for boaters along the Intracoastal Waterway crossing Albemarle Sound, which helps invigorate the tourist trade, but contemporary attempts at economical revival have not produced the sort of revitalization that will ultimately save the town.

The Chamber of Commerce likes to brag that its Virginia Dare Hotel and Arcade, a "listed building" on the National Register of Historic Places, finished in 1927, is the area's first skyscraper. The town also hosts an annual Potato Festival. These two facts seem to be the final word concerning the cultural flavor of the region.

I try Grouper's, a restaurant on the marina docks, thinking a joint on the waterfront—especially on the Intracoastal Waterway—would surely sell locally sourced shrimp. The place is not inviting, housed in a concrete complex that looks more like a Soviet era purpose-built "recreation" center than an Inner Banks waterfront eatery. It's dank, like a motel bar off a derelict highway, the raised bar dimly lit, the dining room spacious—read: cold—with generous windows opening onto the harbor.

First impression is not good. Then I ask the only guy at the bar, a middle-aged Asian with dark hair, a slight build, a bit shady—The owner? A manager? A bartender? A local thespian practicing street theatre?— "Where do you get your shrimp?"

"Sysco," the man says, without hesitation. "Depends on the price."

An honest answer. And reason enough to leave.

The other "recommended" restaurant is Cypress Creek Grill. The dining room is light and woody; the space feels new, with lots of windows. A simple bar in the back by the kitchen. The young manager is stylish. Tall, thin, white skin, dark hair, deep red fingernails, posh glasses. She's ready to talk but admits there's not much to say.

"It's a really small town," she says, apologetically. "I've worked here for 11 years." She ponders this fact. "Most of my life," she says, as if to herself.

I waste no time. Ask where they get their shrimp.

A guy from the kitchen, on break with his lunch, chimes in.

"Farm raised imported from Indonesia."

You have to admire this honesty. But the place is too comfy to leave, so I order a beer and try the U.S. 17 angle.

"It goes though here," the manager says. "I spend my entire life driving it, to work, to home, to wherever, but to me, it's just another road."

The guy from the kitchen cuts in again.

"I had some greentails last week."

This is encouraging. So far, I've got imported shrimp and a dead highway. Then, suddenly, a man who recognizes quality. Greentail shrimp.

"But not here," he says. "Cooked 'em at home. Sauteed, in olive oil, a little hot sauce."

"The fish are local," the manager adds, not exactly defensively but trying to restore some credibility to the kitchen.

"Sometimes," the guy says, as if to make her life difficult.

The girl ignores him. I suspect restaurant politics, but let it go.

"Around here," she says, "some of the most interesting stuff happens when people stop off the Intracoastal.." She indicates the bay across the street. "That's the Harbor of Hospitality. We get people going all over the world. Couple in here the other day heading to Australia."

They've got a ways to go, I think. But it's something. The manager returns to U.S. 17.

"Everybody's favorite these days is the wind farm. It's just off 17. There's over a hundred of 'em."

Certainly that's not what she does for fun, watch windmill blades spin.

"We go to the Outer Banks. Or Virginia Beach."

Any dreams for the future?

"To open my own restaurant," she says quickly, prepared for this one. But just as quickly, she adds, "Only, not here."

Any shrimp stories?

The guy comes out of the kitchen.

"I got a story," he says.

The girl looks disappointed.

"Guy comes in here right out of the hospital. He's not well, concerned about what he can and can't eat. The waitress says to him, "Get the shrimp and rice—"

"It's what we're known for," the manager throws in. I sense the competition.

"Yeah," the guy says. "Shrimp and rice … the server tells the man, 'Order shrimp and rice. That won't kill you.' Man's order comes out. Before he can eat it, he drops dead."

They all laugh.

I try one more place, Montero's. What passes for "fancy" in Elizabeth City. And it is nice. A stately home in a spacious yard—very southern and "piney." White. Huge. Ten thousand square feet. A large central dining room. Four dining rooms upstairs. Two banquet rooms accommodating over 300 people. El-shaped traditional full bar with excellent wine list and interesting beers.

The bartender, a short spunky blonde, is already in the weeds, shaking martinis and crushing fresh mojitos. I hate to ask her. But do. Where do they get there shrimp?

Freeze frame. She stops mid-shake. "I don't know. But I'm gonna find out."

She hustles off on her mission, and sure enough, the kitchen staff responds. One of the most informed is—which seems to be a pattern around here—dead honest. He explains that the trouble—echoing the issues in Murrells Inlet—is that the local shrimpers will not grade out the shrimp. He's held meetings with shrimpers, wholesalers, locals interested in buying local, to no avail. He claims he's forced to buy frozen bulk for strictly practical reasons. When he goes shopping for home cooking, he buys at the corner market, but when cooking commercially, buying in bulk is a necessity. He needs consistency.

"The restaurants on the Outer Banks," he says, "the ones that buy off the boat, they can afford to hire foreign labor to peel, devein and sort out the produce according to size."

If he buys local, he has to assume the labor costs. If he buys from a distributor—in this case, out of Hampton Roads—the shrimp are peeled, headed, deveined and sorted, which makes them "kitchen ready." Buying from small, local distributors becomes price prohibitive.

As for U.S. 17, he notes that the Coastal Highway is fast taking on the character of I-95. He agrees that the nature of U.S. 17 changes above New Bern. It becomes a bypass highway, destroying many of the towns it used to nurture. The snowbirds settle elsewhere. The draw of Emerald Isle and Beaufort and Duck doesn't exist for "Little" Washington, Bayboro or Chocowinity. The allure of the Carolina seashore doesn't travel far from the beach. No crush of glitzy kitsch or condo-saturation has spoiled the rural charm east of the Pamlico. Some of the areas are dying. The cities of the coastal plain are losing their children, especially the educated ones who go off to college and never come back. On the immediate coast, retirees often make up for the loss of productive young citizens, increasing the property tax base, but they tend to strain the medical facilities and demand more cultural and recreational amenities. With the manufacturing jobs in decline, these towns have fewer productive workers, fewer young families, and a rising population of people on fixed incomes.

The region north of Oriental and east of U.S. 17 to the western edge of the Pamlico Sound up to Elizabeth City, is, to be kind, still novel. To be accurate, the interior sections of the Inner Banks remain "country." At least, under-developed.

"Look at Washington, at Williamston," the staffer says. "Belhaven. All those towns are dying. Soon enough these once thriving, historical and often beautiful old towns between major cities will be nothing but a place to stop and pee."

I order a burger.

We consider our dying highway in silence.

Conclusion

The Highway

The Ocean Highway and the shrimping industry both represent the deaths of two traditions. The transformation of U.S. 17 from a personalized highway with a regional sense of identity to an impersonal bypass lacking in character exemplifies a transition from a simpler, more intimate style of travel to a mode of transportation thoroughly lacking in charm and charisma. This pattern of U.S. 17 shifting from a road expressing intense intimacy to an anodyne bypass of flaccid anonymity is made more acute as the highway runs from its southern coastal roots outside Yulee to its turn away from the coast in North Carolina, long before it exits the state above Elizabeth City.

During its short run through Georgia, just a few miles off I-95, the experience of U.S. 17 could not be more distinct. From Kingsland to Brunswick, passing the Whistlestop Lounge and Do-Dad's Seafood, then through downtown Brunswick and along the awesome approach to Darien, the highway continues to reflect the local culture. The crab shacks of Eulonia, the isolation of Riceboro and Midway ... the spoilage doesn't began to show until the outskirts of Savannah, and even then, if you avoid the bypass, the sense of U.S. 17 through that city still, in spots, mirrors the soul of the original highway.

As it traverses South Carolina, especially where it parallels I-95, U.S. 17 alternates between a close and personal highway to a cold and unfamiliar thoroughfare. When it manages to escape the shadow of the interstate, it regains its own identity. Below Charleston, as it crosses pockets of scenery associated with the waterways of the ACE Basin, and again, across the lowlands approaching Georgetown, the landscape of U.S. 17 offers vistas of the coast unavailable to drivers locked into the tunnel-vision tactic of negotiating traffic on I-95. Even the tiny strip through Murrells Inlet reminds an astute traveler of what once was, the brief stretch of road a living remnant of what's been lost.

In North Carolina, the highway begins to lose any charm it once afforded a casual traveler, having been transformed from a graceful two-lane road into an amplified four-lane freeway. From Little River to Wilmington, the road is nothing more than a straight shot connecting one urban center to another, with the only salvation the tricky by-roads out to the beach. Above Jacksonville the scenery is dull, with the extreme coastal routes along the Outer Banks a preferred option for a traveler expecting any sense of particularity. After New Bern, U.S. 17 quickly becomes a throughway, relinquishing its own sense of place to become a generic bypass funneling traffic past the Inner Banks, serving basically to facilitate access to the tourist industry that now defines the Outer Banks.

The road has become, in many spots along the coast, a mere means to an end, and the new routes mirror this sensibility. Instead of reflecting the tradition of the area through which it passes, it tends to cut off the culture from its source. Some old sections still exist, and they represent a sensibility more attuned to the hospitality of traveling, where part of the adventure is in the driving, experiencing the scenery, the possibilities of the landscape and the people. On the best parts of U.S. 17, you are close to the land you cross.

In stark contrast, interstates take on the character of a mall. They homogenize experience. Destroy authenticity. Traveling an interstate, like shopping in a mall, erases the uniqueness of a particular area. The function of an interstate, its essence, like that of a mall, reduces individual agency to a generic uniformity that collapses difference, to the point that con-formity is promoted as a virtue. On an interstate, comfort, familiarity, ease of operation and effortless transitions displace any sense of traveling, of going *somewhere*, not just repositioning oneself from Point A to Point B. The essence of actually traveling, as opposed to relocating, is to con-front—to *embrace*—dissimilarity.

Unlike traveling an interstate, a traveler on U.S. 17, even along its most generic sections, still has an opportunity, with a little planning, to witnesses the landscape changing, along with the people. You can still pull off the road. Hit that chicken shack. That barbeque joint. That back road to nowhere. In fact, the best strategy is to purposely avoid the bypasses and opt for the alternative business routes. This tactic will invariably involve confronting a nightmare of traffic lights and chain store madness, but at some point you will reach the middle of a town, a Main Street or Middle Street or Broad Street or Front Street, often along a riverfront, that opens a culture, leads to a sense of place. Unlike traveling an interstate, which nullifies the gradual geographical demarcations that define a culture, that make a region distinctive, driving U.S. 17 offers a chance not just to experience a meaningful change of scenery, but the change that scenery represents. Interstates, instead of celebrating differences, create interchangeability, reduce multiplicity, and unify diversity, amalgamate landscapes, cultural climates, annul the nuance of identities. At its best, its most intimate, U.S. 17 lends permanence to the flux of life, coherence to a country in mobility.

The Coastal Highway is best where it doesn't interrupt nature so much as it allows access to it. It's a highway that reciprocates, that reflects the rhythm of the locals, accentuates the vibe of the landscape. Rather than displacing the energy of the indigenous culture, interrupting the natural flow of the community, U.S. 17 complements the culture, especially if it traverses a landscape so fragile, sensitive and essential as the shrimp culture it cuts through ... or, more accurately, supports.

There's something encouraging about the stretches of U.S. 17 that resist development, that remain frozen in a less hectic, less dense, simpler style of life associated with "country," a term in this sense synonymous with rural. But, like Rousseau at his most hypocritical, I realize this sentiment might be a product of a middle class romance with simplicity, compounded by a convenient dissociation from the economic woes of the people residing in those lost sections of the highway. The moral implications are tricky in any situation where the privileged are allowed to regard poverty as a virtue.

Even so, with these philosophical caveats aside, the dual nature of the Coastal Highway, its urban character clashing with its feral alter-ego— might best be expressed in the parts of the highway I excluded from this study. To the north, as U.S. 17 emerges—or, really, survives—the Tidewater sprawl outside Norfolk, the left side of the highway along the York River is absolutely saturated with residential developments; on the right, forests and farmland. The highway then moves inland through raw, empty country, splitting the Richmond-Alexandria metropolitan I-95 corridor while side-stepping the madness of the Washington, D.C., area traffic, and then sliding into the anonymity of the Blue Ridge mountains. Likewise, in its land-locked southern incarnation, U.S. 17 leaves the minor congestion of Punta Gorda and crosses deserted stretches of interior Florida, rolling alternately through scattered but tightly centralized minor urban centers until bisecting one of the most densely clogged traffic nightmares in the state: Orlando. The highway survives—again—emerging outside Deland as it continues through the rural landscape of north central Florida before entering the metropolis of Jacksonville where it begins to skirt the coast.

The twofold nature of the highway is of course equally evident in the area I focused on. It runs through empty tracts of coastal Georgia grasslands, then into Savannah. It crosses the dead zone of Lowcountry South Carolina, then into Charleston. It rolls past the desolate estuaries along Winyah Bay, then into Myrtle Beach. It limns the sparsely populated Inner Banks regions of the Pamlico Sound, then dissolves in Norfolk.

This duality, a confluence of urban and rural, sophistication and simplicity, is reflected in the character of the people who live, work and play along off 17. Given the history of the highway, its urbanity is a recent phenomenon, a clear sign of the lifestyle changes occurring in the "New South." Part of this change, from the harsh realism of actual rural living to the lush romanticized idealism of "nature," can be explained by encroachment, as the affluent seek an idyllic, pastoral woodland experience by displacing the local working population. In this transition, they bring their accouterments of comfort with them, further modifying the landscape and the essential charm that drew them to the region in the first place.

The Shrimp

The dual nature of the highway is reciprocated in the shrimp industry, where a corporate model of distribution contradicts the prevailing mentality of a business dominated by lone operators and family-owned fleets. Profit margins, anonymous food sourcing and use of farmed products have decimated a once thriving, fiercely individualistic lifestyle. Diners that appreciate and in the past demanded—even expected without question—wild local shrimp, balk at paying the prices necessary to sustain this tradition. With all the stress and hoopla placed on foodie culture, product sourcing and authenticity, diners that actually know the difference between imported or local, farmed or wild, or even care, is diminishing.

Restaurants famous for serving wild south Atlantic shrimp no longer feel obligated to continue that tradition. They have forsaken their reputations, victims of revenue expectations, expenses, and the exigencies of supply and demand.

But wild local shrimp continue to be harvested along the U.S. 17 corridor. To get the best ones, you have to go to the source. They are most plentiful in seafood markets, where you can be assured they are actually fresh off the boat ... mainly because often the boat is moored in back of the market. These markets, with the boat out back, tend to be located well off the beaten path—that path being in this case U.S. 17. In southern Georgia, the highway runs directly through the supply network. Brunswick, Darien, Eulonia ... you don't have to pull very far off the highway to find shrimp on ice. The search becomes harder as you approach Savannah, as you need to run out to Lazaretto Creek just before Tybee Island. In South Carolina, it's necessary to abandon U.S. 17 altogether for a run into the Port Royal lowlands. Below Charleston, out toward Folly, Crosby's is legendary and worth the trip. Halfway to Georgetown, McClellanville supports one of the most impressive and productive fleets less than a mile directly off U.S. 17, and the small markets in Georgetown continue the tradition.

The hunt for fresh local shrimp changes as U.S. 17 rolls into North Carolina. The docks in Calabash and Sneads Ferry, both quick diversions just off the highway, supply shrimp right off the boats, but these ports mark a demarcation, after which U.S. 17 shifts to the inside strip of Pamlico Sound and basically never recovers. Morehead City is over 30 miles east. Oriental lies relatively close, but visiting Engelhard and Wanchese—along with Oriental, the most significant ports on the Pamlico—requires a special journey to the outer edge of the Croatan Sound, an hour's drive from U.S. 17. By Elizabeth City, the market is mixed, and locating dependable supplies of local shrimp depends less on where you're shopping than on "who you know."

As for restaurants, the number of establishments hawking authenticity and bragging that they serve only local shrimp while catering to tourists is a travesty. Volume belies the truth of their claims. There is simply not enough local product to go around. Rule of thumb: if you're looking for real local shrimp in a restaurant, go small. A chef that actually goes down to the market and buys what he needs for the night's entrées is rare. If there's a trawler out back, chances are the restaurant on the dock is serving shrimp off the boat. But you never know. And proof, as they say, is always in the pudding. Source the food.

The dilemma is self-evident. To stay in business, a restaurant has to turn tables. Lots of them. But the supply of fresh local shrimp is limited. Shrimping is seasonal. There are restrictions on how, when and where trawlers can drag. Mother nature is fickle. There are good seasons and bad. Good days and bad. Processing plants can handle only so many tons. Small suppliers don't have the capacity—or inclination—to properly grade, head and devein the catch. Prices fluctuate. Dependability is a luxury.

One tricky issue is that local shrimp are not always the "best." Shrimp caught in the "backyard" around Beaufort (SC) and Charleston can have a muddy aftertaste. Calabash shrimp are small and rubbery. Mayport shrimp might not be caught directly off Mayport, but they are harvested nearby, and they are among the best shrimp available on the coast. Firm, sweet, briny and, depending on the batter, crunchy and crisp. The shrimp are similar in Darien. Medium sized, either lightly dusted so the firm core holds its own crispness, or coated with a thick cornmeal that complements rather than detracts from the rich salty flavor of these strong shrimp. These shrimp—medium-sized Brown caught offshore—also turn up in Georgetown, distinctly *al dente* and salty sweet. But hands down, the best shrimp I tasted were called "channel" shrimp around Tybee, "creek" in Folly Beach, and "greentails" in Morehead City. They are late season Whites caught before they hit the open ocean. They are large, buttery and sweet, usually served with a medium thick coat of cornmeal, deep fried with the tails on (fantail style) and split (butterflied). They are delicate, not as firm or crisp as the Mayport variety, but not chewy either. The flavor resembles lobster, but not as sweet or pungent.

In the small communities, my shrimp sense, abetted with tips from certain locals, led me, I'm convinced, to restaurants that, if not the "best," were definitely indicative of what the area had to offer. Of course I regret the number of restaurants I didn't sample. The major cities are a wash. There's no way to eat your way through Jacksonville, Savannah, Charleston the Grand Strand from Murrells Inlet to Little River, Wilmington and on up the coast through the dying cities of the Inner Banks. There were places locals swear by, too numerous to mention. They range from small shacks that pop up and then disappear like mushrooms after a rainstorm to establishments that have graced U.S. 17 for generations. A lack of strategy became my strategy. Spontaneity my guiding research tactic.

One thing I learned, from both the local vendors selling whole shrimp on ice right off the boat, and from restaurants serving everything from fried shrimp baskets to Red Pistou Pasta with Shrimp and Crunchy Herbes de Provence Crumbs: shrimp is not just shrimp. This is an important lesson for anyone interested in discovering the secret transcendent essence of "real" shrimp. The various kinds of shrimp—Royal Reds, Key West Pinks, Whites and Browns—simply don't express the differences between the low Georgia Browns and the late season White greentails.

Night and day.

Another issue when it comes to finding the tastiest shrimp on the planet is that many seafood markets can be intimidating. On one hand, small operations are often located in remote, even isolated areas. Rockville, Varnamtown, Engelhard ... these are not easy places to get to. And once you find the place, you hesitate to step out of the car. Walking into a tiny shack with a hand-painted Fresh Shrimp sign at the end of a road in the middle of nowhere staffed by some old buzzard accepting "cash only" who scoops a mess of shrimp out of an ice bin and hands them over in a plastic bag while a woman and children watch silently from the stern of a 60 foot trawler can be an unsettling. The cumulative effect of all those Stars and Bars, those upside-down American flags, and those Never Mind the Dog Beware the Owner signs with images of guns pointed directly at you ... well, you're not alone if you feel a bit out of place. But the trawler is real, and those shrimp are as fresh and local as you're going to get.

On the other hand, large combines are equally daunting, if less personally threatening. McClellanville, Oriental, Wanchese ... some of these plants process tons of shrimp a season. These huge operations can seem impersonal to a casual consumer hoping to buy a few dozen shrimp for a Thanksgiving seafood casserole but who refuses to settle for the grocery store variety that combines the texture and flavor of a pencil eraser with a bit of frosty grey shell in a frozen food case. There is no intimate room with artificial wood paneling, no splotchy damp concrete floor with a drain sunk in the middle, no bins with whole fish on ice, no rattling cooler in the corner half-full of crabmeat and homemade fish dip. The parking lot is an expansive area surrounded by warehouses and crisscrossed by forklifts and cluttered with stacks of wooden pallets. Dozens of trawlers crowd the docks. Semis and refrigerator trucks line the lots. The smallest purchasable quantity available is a 50-pound bag. All the while, the noise of industry drowns out the meditative quietude that a reverent shopper often brings to the art of purchasing seafood.

"Fried" is yet another misunderstood concept. Just two miles apart, Mudcat Charlie's and Skipper's Fish Camp, in Darien, offer fried shrimp harvested right off the coast of Brunswick, but the technique, the coating, the oil and fryer temperature ... totally different. Mudcat's shrimp are lightly dusted, the batter flaking off a naked morsel. Skipper's batter is thick, a cocoon swaddling its treasure. Or take Calabash shrimp, and compare them to ones harvested from Pamlico Sound, served in Wanchese. Both from North Carolina—the former taken outside, the other inside, but both roughly the same count, fairly small, headed, peeled and deveined, served without tails. The Calabash shrimp are chewy, bland little nuggets lost in a heap of pancake batter. The Wanchese shrimp are lightly dusted with a crumbly meal and exude a strong briny flavor and crispy texture.

Night and day.

The People

You can often judge a book by what's left out, as much as by what's in it. One noticeable flaw in this journal is how limited the sources are. For every person I talked to, there were so many more I didn't. When it came to interviews, I intentionally came in cold. I didn't call ahead. Didn't make appointments. I just picked a place and dropped in. Works for spontaneity, but the aleatory nature of this strategy also meant I never knew what to expect, didn't know who might be working, what they might say. People were unavailable. Others did not want to talk. Many of the conversations occurred while people were working, so they had to fit me in as they plied their trade. Some people were dismissive. Some were skeptical. Some were suspicious. Others hostile.

The people I did talk to, for the most part, and those I managed to profile, are not composites, not invented. They are real. The conversations as verbatim as I can reconstruct from memory. Those that made themselves available were friendly, conversant, informative and fun to talk to. Those that didn't talk had their reasons.

Another criticism I anticipate is that I never went out on a trawler. Reasons as to why I didn't—some personal, some professional—should seem self-evident and obvious to a fair-minded reader. Working on a trawler is a serious business. It is definitely not an old man's game. (I remain in awe of Captain Royce Woodard and the few, very few elderly crewmen I met.) Just the process of getting invited out on a boat, or inviting myself, is not as easy as it might seem. Issues of trust, health, insurance—also, it was never my intention to write that kind of book. First hand accounts of life aboard a shrimp trawler are plentiful; they seem to be the subject of frequent "human interest" features or "A Day in the Life" stories gracing the ever-popular *Living* sections of a variety of local press along the coast.

Interviewing skippers was another dead end, for me at least. Working on a trawler is tedious, repetitive and similar from boat to boat. If you've heard one story you've heard them all, whether operating out of Mayport or Wanchese. Plus, the people involved—owners, crew, family—are hardcore. They know what they're doing, and that knowledge comes from years of experience. Life at sea requires skill not acquired from textbooks or how-to manuals. Shrimping is not a recreation. It can be dangerous. And even the people on the fringe, selling shrimp off the boat, or off the back of a pick up, or at a roadside stand, or a shack beside a creek … are a reticent bunch, to put it mildly, wary of outsiders and suspicious of inquisitive strangers. You want to buy shrimp, they can fill your cooler. You want information, they're busy.

So, many people didn't talk. The people that did talk, however, were friendly, approachable, and amenable to conversation … but these folks were rare and, sometimes aloof, often amused, as if the joke was always at my expense. For the most part, I relied on people in the service industry, rather than in the wholesale business. The service industry folks tend to be more comfortable talking to strangers—after all, it's part of their job. Also, because of the lifestyle of the trawler crews that go to sea, and their fluid, transient existence, the people in the service industry were, literally, much more grounded, inclined to discuss cooking, eating and serving shrimp, as well as recognizing (or denying, as my Shem Creek Viking did) the significance of how U.S. 17 informs and shapes their lives.

The "portraits" of people from my past—those that populate the dramatized Wooten's Drive-In sections, set off from the narrative in italicized text—are equally "real." They function as doppelgangers connecting my experiences with people currently living on U.S. 17 to types I identify from my past. The effect was to create historical continuity, to draw a straight line between the people I knew that shaped my life, and whose connection to U.S. 17 defined their character as much as it did mine, to the people I found today who continue this tradition.

Which brings me to the concept of the "17-er."

One discovery I made early in my research, and then worked into the design of the book, concerns the notion of this archetype. I define a "17-er" as a person who has spent a majority of his or her life on or near the highway, so that it becomes part of their daily routine, part of their makeup, infused into their personality, their ontology. Some are born in regions the highway serves, live near it, attend school there. Often, their parents lived the same way, a pattern that might have been replicated through generations. These residents of the highway might choose to stay and continue the custom of living in the community where they were born. They might move away, but in the case of a "17-er" they do not stray far from the highway, though they might move hundreds of miles from home. From Norfolk, VA, to Jacksonville, FL, the U.S. 17 corridor runs deep through the southeastern coastal range, offering plenty of opportunities for change within a familiar cultural framework.

Some "17-ers"—those that grow up near the highway but leave after high school—leave for good. They seek a new cultural identity in the mountains, the desert, the West Coast, the Northeast. U.S. 17 might have shaped their early life but they have reconstituted their consciousness within a different cultural context. They transform, as much as they can, but that U.S. 17 experience is in their blood; it's an ineluctable part of their Wonder Bread years. Others leave, incorporate a variety of experiential episodes into their psychic wiring, and then return to the highway, infusing diversity into the U.S. 17 zone, further enriching their return and enhancing, perhaps, the lives of those around them.

The "17-ers" that leave and come back are the most privileged: they have a choice. They might come back out of obligation, to family or friends, or they simply could not thrive outside their comfort zone. After all, life along U.S. 17 is rich. Familiar and foreign. Mundane and exotic. Local and strange. Among this group are the university educated that after the college experience and a taste of professional life return to the boutique charm of the contemporary Lowcountry style. Or the servicemen who finish their tours or careers and settle back into the familiar wilderness they cut their teeth on in their youth. Choice is the key, and it's a luxury.

But many "17-ers" have no choice. For them, the highway is just a road running by their window. It doesn't lead anywhere beyond work, school, a neighborhood, a place of worship. These are the hometown lifers that were simply too afraid to leave the comfort of the highway, or for various reasons can not muster the resources, the money, the opportunity, the imagination, the gumption. Of course, many choose to stay. But having that option separates those that live in freedom from those for whom choice is a chimera evaporating like rain sheen off a summer blacktop....

When I consider my own decision to move off the highway, I marvel at the chance encounters, the snap decisions, the sheer whimsicality of decisions that later seem so definitive and consequential in determining why and how I ended up where I did. And yet, no matter how far removed I am physically from the highway, it continues to connect me with my past, my youth, my family and friends, and mostly significantly with the coastal region that cannot be traversed without experiencing, somewhere along the line, U.S. 17.

Index

Numbers in **bold italics** indicate pages with illustrations